Praise for *Fields of Battle*

"*Fields of Battle* is a compelling true tale of how a Pacific wind blew the Rose Bowl from the West Coast to the East Coast and scattered its participants around the world to win history's largest war."

—James Bradley, author of *Flags of Our Fathers* and *The China Mirage*

"Brian Curtis's gripping story about the 'Greatest Generation' reminds us that the freedom we enjoy today came at a steep price. *Fields of Battle* vividly captures the uncertainty, fear, sacrifice, and heroism of a critical time in our history, and serves as a tribute to those who carried the scars of war with them—and to those who never came home."

—Senator John McCain, author of *Faith of My Fathers*

"In this remarkable book, Curtis masterfully connects two seemingly unrelated events: the 1942 Rose Bowl and World War II. . . . [*Fields of Battle*] has much in common with Laura Hillenbrand's bestselling *Unbroken* and should evoke similar strong emotions."

—*Booklist*

"With meticulous research and elegant writing, Brian Curtis has put together a page-turning narrative about a group of football players turned war heroes, men who entered gridiron lore and then did their part as members of the Greatest Generation. Football fans will enjoy reading about the unusual circumstances that enveloped the 1942 Rose Bowl, but all readers will appreciate the chance to learn about the times these men lived in and the sacrifices they made for all of us. This is a terrific piece of work."

—Seth Davis, CBS Sports analyst and author of *Wooden*

"College football aficionados know that the 1942 Rose Bowl was played in North Carolina, but the stories of the men who played that game and went on to fight in World War II were, until now, largely unknown. In *Fields of Battle,* Brian Curtis brings the WWII generation alive through the stories of these young men who moved so rapidly from the big game to the war to defeat the German, Japanese, and Italian fascists. Curtis gives us a vivid, invaluable portrait of life as it was lived in the face of so much uncertainty and danger, when nothing less than the fate of the free world hung in the balance."

—Jeremy Schaap, author of *Triumph: The Untold Story of Jesse Owens and Hitler's Olympics* and *Cinderella Man: James J. Braddock, Max Baer, and the Greatest Upset in Boxing History*

"In *Fields of Battle,* Brian Curtis takes you back to a time when honor and duty were more than mere video game taglines and athletes placed their patriotic duty above sport. Yes, it's a football story. But really, it's an American story."

—Jeff Pearlman, *New York Times* bestselling author of *Sweetness* and *Showtime*

"Where another, less-careful observer might have found coincidence in these events, Brian Curtis's keen eye found a confluence of historical circumstance. In *Fields of Battle,* Curtis chronicles, contextualizes, and makes meaning of the meeting of boys and men on both the ball field and the battlefield. . . . Where Curtis most profoundly succeeds is in never once allowing the reader to forget that what happens on the gridiron isn't war, and that what war has never been—and never will be—is a game. It's a timely message."

—Julie Checkoway, author of *The Three-Year Swim Club*

"*Fields of Battle* is a riveting account of the men who faced off against each other in the 1942 Rose Bowl, the only [one] to be played outside of Pasadena as a result of the Pearl Harbor attack. Tossing aside football rivalries, the men who played went on to fight alongside each other on WWII's battlefields. Football fans and military buffs will enjoy this powerful tale of courage, leadership, grit, and greatness."

—Bobby Bowden, former head coach of the Florida State University football team

"The Rose Bowl is woven into the fabric of America, and Brian Curtis's dramatic tale weaves together the essence of the game and the spirit of the country at a difficult period in history. Sports and history buffs will love *Fields of Battle*."

—Keith Jackson, Hall of Fame broadcaster

"*Fields of Battle* is not a sports book or a war book as much as it is a history book, telling the story of these men from the Greatest Generation who played in a historic football game, then represented their country—many of them on the battlefields—in World War II. . . . [Curtis paints] a vivid picture of what it was like for the teams of Duke and Oregon State, blending war on the gridiron with war on the battlefields, ably telling the characters' individual stories."

—*Portland Tribune*

"A fascinating and inspiring book that's about football, but also about a great deal more . . . Curtis brings to life, without glamorizing or sanitizing, the courage and determination of these young men. . . . This is a fine book. It's a riveting story—really, many stories—well told. It's also a revealing insight into our shared history and a reminder of how Americans can rise to meet daunting challenges."

—*News & Record* (Greensboro, NC)

"History, sports, Durham, World War II, Duke University—it's all here. . . . A story far beyond the field at Duke, and takes readers into war, too."

—*The Herald-Sun* (Durham, NC)

"For history buffs, *Fields of Battle* is worth a read."
—*The Florida Times-Union*

"A fine sports book with a stirring extra dimension." —*Kirkus Reviews*

"Following the players on the two best college football teams in 1941, veteran sportswriter Curtis charts a group biography of young athletes interrupted by war." —*The Boston Globe*

"*Fields of Battle* is a detailed intersection of sport and war in World War II that is gripping, occasionally tragic, but always rewarding, as heroes on the field become heroes in war."
—*The Daily Herald* (Everett, WA)

"A brilliantly told evocation of a time and a place . . . This is truly a needed book for our time, interweaving the war and the game and the young men who went off the field of play to battle for their country. It is all about courage and patriotism, timely and timeless."
—Harvey Frommer, Sports Bookshelf

FIELDS

OF

BATTLE

ALSO BY BRIAN CURTIS

A Team to Believe In: Our Journey to the Super Bowl Championship (with Tom Coughlin)

Every Week a Season: A Journey Inside Big-Time College Football

Go Long!: My Journey Beyond the Game and the Fame (with Jerry Rice)

How Good Do You Want to Be?: A Champion's Tips on How to Lead and Succeed at Work and in Life (with Nick Saban)

The Legacy Letters: Messages of Life and Hope from 9/11 Family Members (Editor)

The Men of March: A Season Inside the Lives of College Basketball Coaches

FIELDS

OF

BATTLE

Pearl Harbor, the Rose Bowl, and the Boys Who Went to War

BRIAN CURTIS

FLATIRON BOOKS
NEW YORK

To Tamara, Emily, and Daryn, the loves of my life

To those who sacrificed for our freedom

www.flatironbooks.com

Designed by Steven Seighman

The Library of Congress has cataloged the hardcover edition as follows:

Names: Curtis, Brian, 1971– author.
Title: Fields of battle : Pearl Harbor, the Rose Bowl, and the boys who went to war / Brian Curtis.
Description: First edition. | New York : Flatiron Books, 2016. | Includes bibliographical references and index.
Identifiers: LCCN 2016020829 | ISBN 9781250059581 (hardcover) | ISBN 9781250059604 (ebook)
Subjects: LCSH: World War, 1939–1945—United States—Biography. | World War, 1939–1945—Campaigns. | Soldiers—United States—Biography. | Football players—United States—Biography. | College athletes—United States—Biography. | Football coaches—United States—Biography. | Rose Bowl (Football game) (1942 : Durham, N.C.) | Rose Bowl (Football game)—History—20th century. | Pearl Harbor (Hawaii), Attack on, 1941—Influence. | BISAC: HISTORY / Military / World War II. | SPORTS & RECREATION / Football.
Classification: LCC D769.1.C87 2016 | DDC 940.54'8173—dc23
LC record available at https://lccn.loc.gov/2016020829

ISBN 978-1-250-05959-8 (trade paperback)

First Flatiron Books Paperback Edition: October 2017

10 9 8 7 6 5 4 3 2 1

CONTENTS

Part IV: WAR

Part V: HOME

AUTHOR'S NOTE

Almost every man who played or coached in the 1942 Rose Bowl is no longer with us, including the main subjects of this story, and I relied on family recollections, military files, newspaper articles, research papers, and published works to tell their stories as accurately as possible. In the event that there are no firsthand confirmations or documentation of actual dialogue or events, I have attempted to re-create a likely exchange of dialogue or scene based on the research of the subjects.

Much of the information on the players' military service was based on declassified United States military records from the National Archives and Records Administration in Saint Louis as part of the National Personnel Records Center. A devastating fire in 1973 destroyed many of the army personnel files up to that point, and where necessary, I have pieced together their service records through other sources. The military records include individual personnel and medical records, after-action reports for units, and unit histories.

The term "Negro" is used when verbatim in dialogue or documentation only, as it was commonly used in the era, despite its horrible connotations today.

Finally, so many of the men who played or coached in the 1942 Rose Bowl served their country valiantly. These are just some of their stories but I hope all of them will one day be told.

BC
March 2016

PROLOGUE

The bright colors of the flower centerpieces accentuated the remaining strands of gray hair on the heads of the guests seated around the tables. The silverware was polished to a reflection, the wineglasses filled with red or white. Conversations were loud, punctuated every few minutes by the roar of laughter. Many of the men wore blazers and ties—some mismatched—one wore his letterman's sweater that now could fit two; a few had their canes nearby. Every now and then during pauses in conversation, they looked around the room, still unsure of many of the unfamiliar faces, worn by war and life and the many moments that made them up. But if they looked hard enough, and if their minds could dig deep enough, it came back like a freight train.

It was Friday evening, October 18, 1991, and members of the 1942 Rose Bowl team from Oregon State had gathered in a banquet room in the Corvallis Country Club to mark the fiftieth anniversary of the historic season, joined by a handful of their opponents from Duke University. There were previous formal and informal team reunions in Corvallis dating back to 1961, but as the years went on, attendance dwindled. Teammates lost touch, others were too frail to travel, while still others had passed. But on this night, for the first time in fifty years, members of both teams gathered in the same room. It had been a half a century since this group of once-young men played out the greatest metaphor for American grit and determination that the country had ever seen—at a time when the country needed it most.

Sixteen Oregon State players were in attendance, including Rose Bowl captain Martin Chaves, Stanley Czech, and George Zellick, along with a handful of their teammates' widows, like Maxine Demoss Durdan, wife of the late Don Durdan, the 1942 Rose Bowl MVP. Lon Stiner, the son of the late Oregon State Rose Bowl coach, was popular at dinner. He was just seven years old when he boarded a train with his family and thirty players for a once-in-a-lifetime trip. As players swapped stories, there were laughs about the adventures aboard the *Beaver Express* and the practices held along the way in Chicago and Washington. But their journeys would take them well beyond America. Some would become heroes, some would never make it home, but all were forever changed by the experience.

The "Greatest Generation," as some have labeled them, did not all live happily ever after. Many veterans ended up as patients in Veterans Administration hospitals suffering from psychological issues from the war, at a time when PTSD was referred to simply as "battle fatigue." Many more vets became homeless or turned to alcohol to numb the memories of war—which were compounded by regrets they had carried with them to the battlefields. The divorce rate was high among veterans, and many married multiple times. Some contemplated suicide—others did more than contemplate.

These were ordinary men who would do extraordinary things when called upon in football, in war, and in life; who were willing to be great when good would have been enough; who not only earned championships and Silver Stars but had the audacity to believe that their achievements were nothing more than duty. They were first-generation college students, farmers, trash truck drivers, fishermen, and boxers, and their coaches were men whose own stories of rising from the depths were examples for their charges.

That night at the country club—if only for a night—the memories of a time *before* war changed everything ignited revelry and some historical embellishment.

Former Oregon State football coach and athletic director Dee Andros served as the master of ceremonies for the evening, and after dinner was concluded, he introduced Oregon State University president Dr. John Byrne and director of athletics Dutch Baughman, who welcomed perhaps the most famous team in Oregon State history and their visitors. The program included remarks from both Oregon State and Duke players and a taped phone conversation with former Duke quarterback and former Oregon State head coach Tommy Prothro, who remained in Memphis recovering from hip surgery. But the hum of conversations underneath the speakers ground to a halt when the names of deceased teammates were read solemnly one after another.

Charles Haynes Jr. felt his eyes moisten. He would have been on that list had it not been for the man who unknowingly compelled the seventy-year-old to make the nearly three-thousand-mile trip.

Haynes had been nervous for weeks in anticipation of this night, five decades in the making in his head. Haynes and his companion, Patsy Ashby, flew across the country from Durham, North Carolina, for the reunion, despite the fact that Duke would host a similar reception in a matter of weeks. Though the event in Durham would've required much less effort—a car trip of one mile—with so many of his living Duke compatriots unable to make it out to Corvallis for health reasons, he couldn't be sure the same would not be true for those on the Corvallis side, and he *had* to see them—him. Haynes had stayed in touch with some of his Duke teammates and was often the ringleader for informal gatherings at his restaurant, the Saddle & Fox, in Durham, but this would be the first time he would see any of his opponents in almost fifty years—including the man who had saved his life.

As the names of the deceased were read, Haynes glanced over at Frank Parker.

The last time Haynes had seen Parker before the reunion was in the Bremer Pass in the Alps in Austria in May 1945. The war was coming to an end, yet the men's jubilance over victory was tempered by the innocence lost in the days of war. Haynes would share the story of a day in 1944 that changed his life with friends, family, and members of the media over the years; Parker never spoke of it—not even to his family.

The Arno River in the Tuscany region of Italy runs for roughly 150 miles, originating in the Apennines and passing through Florence and Pisa on its way to the Tyrrhenian Sea. In 1944, the stunning Tuscan landscape was a smoky mural of grinding artillery and weary troops, many of whom had been on the front lines for weeks on end. Beyond the Arno in the north lay the North Apennines: rugged, hilly terrain. And it was on one of those hilltops that a bed was made for twenty-two-year-old Charles Haynes, who lay dying atop a ridge, blood streaming out of his chest—an orphaned soldier, dying in the chaos of battle.

Haynes was not your ordinary soldier. He embraced the challenges that war presented, and after his initial "kills," he paid little attention at the time to the emotions of killing other soldiers. It was kill or be killed on the battlefield. Never one to shy away from conflict, Haynes was often the first in his platoon to engage the enemy, and on October 4, 1944, Haynes led an assault on a German position with the 1st and 2nd Platoons of Easy Company of the 349th Infantry of the 88th Division, ironically known as the "Blue Devils," the same moniker as that of Duke University.

The Germans protected the hill like the thousands of others in Italy, with ferocity and timing, waiting for just the right moment to unleash their barrage. Just as Haynes reached the ridge of the hill with his platoon trailing behind, the German machine guns opened fire. The world suddenly went quiet as Haynes fell and lay there, almost motionless in the rain and cold, a hole in his chest the size of two fists. *This is it,* he thought. *This is how it all ends.*

In actuality, bullets continued to fly overhead—the blazing guns making it too difficult for his fellow soldiers to provide him aid, let alone rescue. So, for hours upon excruciating hours, Haynes lay helpless, his cherry-red blood staining the mud beside him. Seventeen hours passed, and so, it seemed, had his time on earth. Drifting in and out of consciousness, Haynes was resigned to death, when suddenly two brave soldiers appeared by his side. Haynes felt comforted by angels.

The pair grabbed Haynes's listless body, and he was lifted onto the shoulders of one of them. The men ran roughshod down the hill, what was left of Haynes's blood dripping onto the ground. They made it to a makeshift aid station, where medics immediately began to address the wounds. Haynes had a moment to recognize one of his saviors.

PART I

THE MEN

I know of nothing that is a better preparation for a young man who is going into the army than football. The greatest benefit that football gives to a young man is that it teaches him to be a competitor, to never give up, to get back up after you're knocked down. Success in both football and war depends on morale, loyalty, and sound fundamentals.

—Wallace Wade Sr., head football coach,
Duke University

1. THE MAKING OF A COACH

TRENTON, GIBSON COUNTY, TENNESSEE, lies in the western part of the state, maybe forty-five miles from the Mississippi River, and it has seen its share of history. It was a farming community until cotton mills took over in the late nineteenth century. In the last decades of that century and the first few of the twentieth, on a 2,500-acre farm in the confines of Trenton, Robert Bruce Wade and Sallie Ann Wade raised nine children, including William Wallace, born in 1892. (Robert Bruce and William Wallace were names taken from their descendants, the well-known Scottish freedom fighters of the late thirteenth century.) Robert rose in darkness before dawn and returned to the house well after sunset after overseeing the fields, with little time for his children. He was not especially close with his offspring, yet his actions spoke volumes to his sons, including young Wallace. *Keep your mouth shut, put your head down, and work hard.* Wallace and his siblings rarely stood up to their father, even when their own moral compass told them they should. Maybe they were afraid of the beatings, or maybe they simply understood it wasn't a child's role to challenge authority.

Robert impressed upon his sons the importance of education. Sons Mark and Isham would become successful businessmen who would one day own one of the country's largest apple orchards; Bruce would earn degrees at Vanderbilt and Johns Hopkins and would become a leading geologist.

Wallace was quite close with Mark, who was three years his senior, and followed him in school and in football, first suiting up at Peabody High School in 1909—just five years after the game of football reached Trenton—to play for coach Tuck Faucett. Wallace was a scrappy player, a fighter, who routinely pushed aside players who were bigger than he was. The 150-pounder never seemed to tire. He was the underdog who got more out of his talent simply through determination. After one season at Peabody, Wallace matriculated to Fitzgerald-Clarke School to learn the game under W. A. Bridges, who coached a more modern version of the game (though still nothing like what would come) and under whom Wallace played tackle and guard, just like Mark.

In two seasons at Fitzgerald-Clarke, Wallace lost just two football games. In 1912, Mark graduated from Morgan Park Academy in Chicago, and sure enough, young Wallace arrived that same year to play for the great Amos Alonzo Stagg, who would go on to fame at the University of Chicago. But Stagg replaced himself with John Anderson as head coach the season Wallace arrived, showing up only at the occasional practice, and only to mentor Anderson through the transition.

Feeling a bit let down by the experience—Wallace insisted in earnest that he sold a pig in Tennessee to pay for his travel to Chicago to play for Stagg—he played one season at Morgan Park, also playing baseball, before graduating and again following Mark, this time to Brown University in Providence, Rhode Island. He played on the freshman team in 1913 and earned a spot on the varsity team his sophomore year under coach Edward Robinson. Though out of his geographical element, Wallace Wade embraced Brown, the northeast, and the rigors of college work. He immersed himself—by choice—in classes on Latin, Greek, Spanish, and French and challenged himself with difficult mathematics courses. He was also working his way through school, running errands for wealthy families, assisting in a laundry service, and landscaping and shoveling snow when needed.

In 1915, Wade and his offensive line mates welcomed a new teammate, running back Fritz Pollard, one of two black students at the entire university and a phenomenal athlete who earned the job of starting back. When Robert Wade learned that his son would be playing alongside a Negro, he traveled to Providence and demanded that his son withdraw from Brown. But the young Wade was no longer simply the obedient young child fearful of standing up to his father. He was a man in every sense of the word who had moved away from home years ago, and when his father threatened to pull him out of Brown, the son stood his ground, chastised his father for his antiquated views, and remained at Brown as a teammate—and friend—of Pollard's.

Behind Pollard's record-setting on-field achievements his first year in a Bears uniform, Brown went 5–3–1, including wins over Yale and Carlisle. Despite the three losses, the Bears were selected as the eastern representative in the Tournament East-West Football Game, later known as the Rose Bowl.

The Valley Hunt Club in Pasadena in the late 1800s was the gathering place for the wealthy elite, who arrived in horse-pulled carriages and spent their time smoking cigars, drinking bourbon, hunting foxes, and talking politics. In the winter of 1889, club member Dr. Charles Holder, who had moved to the warmth of California from New York City, laughed at reports of the bitter cold and snow in the East and suggested that the Valley Hunt Club hold a festival. Fellow member Dr. Francis Rowland volunteered that his wife had visited the Bataille de Fleurs in Nice, France, and suggested the Battle of Roses for Pasadena.

The first Tournament of Roses was set for January 1, 1890, and close to five thousand participants enjoyed "tilting at the rings" (a medieval competition where riders on horseback try to insert lances into small rings) as well as burro and bicycle races. But the highlight was a parade of horse-drawn carriages covered with picture-perfect flowers grown in California and Mexico. The event became an annual rite in Pasadena, and each year, it attracted larger and larger crowds, which pleased the real estate men out West looking for sales. A marching band was added to the parade in 1891; a reviewing stand in 1894; and floats, a queen, and a marshal became staples in 1895. In 1902, twelve years after its founding, the Tournament added a football game, a matchup between powerful Michigan and Stanford. Of course, football was a much different game at the turn of the century, with no passing, a different scoring system, and two thirty-five-minute halves.

The inaugural game drew a crowd of 8,500, who shuffled in through one gate, some atop farm wagons. Michigan led 49–0 when Stanford mercifully suggested the game end. The Tournament would not be able to convince a West Coast team to participate in another football game again—fearful of a beatdown—until Washington State in 1916, so in lieu of football, the Tournament held chariot races.

Washington State's opponent in 1916 would be Wallace Wade's Brown team, selected over other candidates, including Michigan and Syracuse, to whom Brown had lost during the regular season. At the time, though traveling to California seemed exotic, the game itself was little more than another road game, with little national attention or meaning. It was an exhibition for a festival. Wade even considered staying behind in Providence over Christmas break to earn extra cash for the upcoming semester instead of playing in the game. Ultimately, he decided to go, making a little money along the way by writing a diary for the *Providence Journal* during the trip.

Brown used line plunges out of a double-wing formation against Washington State, a formation which had outscored Brown's opponents 167–32 during the regular season. With seven thousand fans in attendance, Brown was shut out 14–0, with Pollard limited to just forty-seven yards rushing. Perhaps more disappointed than Wade and his teammates were the Tournament's organizers and financial backers, who had to step in to cover costs left in the game's wake.

In the fall of 1916, Pollard, Wade, Ray Ward, and Josh Weeks returned to anchor the team and led Brown to an 8–0 record heading into the season finale against Colgate. A 28–0 loss took them out of national title discussions. Brown went 18–7–3 during Wade's three years on the team, with Wade even making All-Eastern teams in his final season. He earned his degree in 1917, married Frances Bell on July 1, and enlisted in the military.

On April 6, 1917, the United States formally entered World War I, and young men signed up from around the country. Wade first enlisted in the Tennessee National Guard back home but later shifted to the army cavalry—believing, as many military officers did prior to the war, that the cavalry would play a critical role in the upcoming conflict—and became a captain by August. Of course, the advent of tanks and machine guns mitigated the importance of cavalry during the war.

Wade was sent to Fort Sill in Oklahoma and then to Camp Sevier in South Carolina, Camp Shelby in Mississippi, and Camp Gordon in Georgia. But to his disappointment, he never saw a day of war. His regiment was en route to France when the armistice was signed, and he was discharged in 1919. In the meantime, in 1918 as Frances and Wade moved from military camp to military camp, Wade's son was born in Layton, Oklahoma, named William Wallace Wade Jr.

A college graduate, a veteran (officially), and an accomplished football player, Wade returned to Tennessee after his discharge to begin a career doing something. Anything. So committed was he to the war effort that he hadn't given any real thought to a life after his service. But when William Fitzgerald, the founder of Fitzgerald-Clarke—which Wade had briefly attended—and a mentor to Wade, offered him a chance to coach at the now military academy, Wade accepted.

In two seasons as the head football coach, Wade's teams went 16–3, going undefeated in 1920 and winning the Tennessee State prep championship, which led to an opportunity as a defensive coach at Vanderbilt under Dan McGugin, a winner of ten Southern Conference titles. In 1921, Vanderbilt demolished the University of Texas 20–0, stopping their twelve-game winning streak and proving that Wade's aggressive defensive approach was working. In seventeen games over two seasons, Wade's defense yielded just thirty-seven points, all of them allowed in just four of the games! Wade demanded excellence from his players but nothing he did not demand of himself. Like he had done as an undersized player himself, Wade coaxed every ounce of talent from the lads and got them to believe that they could always do more.

Now the father of two, with daughter Frances ("Sis") joining Junior in 1921, Wade was becoming known in national football circles at the same time as the University of Alabama was seeking a replacement for coach Xen C. Scott, who had stepped down while fighting cancer. Alabama first approached McGugin about taking over for the 1923 season, but he turned down the job and instead recommended his assistant, Wallace Wade. Alabama had not been playing football for very long and had just joined the Southern Conference in 1922. Prior to that season, it was an independent and despite some decent records was never regarded as an elite team.

At the same time, the University of Kentucky was also looking for a head coach, and Wade was close with a manager of athletics there. Following an interview with the Kentucky athletic council in Lexington, Wade sat irritated in a hallway as the council went behind closed doors to discuss the candidates and select a coach. As the minutes went by, Wade's impatience grew until he resolutely walked out of the building and soon publicly declared that he was going to Alabama. He leveled a shot at the men he claimed had kept him waiting, saying, "Kentucky will never win from a football team of mine."

At Alabama, Wade could not be compensated until the football season started in the fall of 1923, so he worked manual labor jobs in the heat of the Alabama summer, which may have set the tone for his first practice, on September 10. Alabama players were greeted with no benches and no water buckets on the field yet were put through a three-hour practice, a swirl of motion and commotion, focused on fundamentals and defense.

"Move it!"

"Get down! Lower!"

"Do it again!"

There was no mistaking who was in charge.

As he had done at Fitzgerald-Clarke and then at Vanderbilt, Wade wasted little time in showing early results at the University of Alabama, improving the team's record to 7–2–1 in 1923 from 6–3–1 the year before. To Wade's dismay, those losses included a twenty-three-point blowout to Syracuse and a heartbreaking loss to the University of Florida, which cost them a Southern Conference championship. In 1924, the Crimson Tide won the conference title, losing just once, on November 15, in what would turn out to be the last regular season loss for Wade's team until October of 1927.

Wade held coaching schools over the summers for college and prep coaches (which helped recruiting) and never wavered from promoting his core belief that anything less than the strongest work ethic was unacceptable. His players called him "Bear" behind his back, as his off-season and in-season workout sessions were legendary for their level of physical intensity. Wade believed that players would perform in a game as they did in practice, and that meant supreme year-round physical conditioning.

In his other incarnation as coach of Alabama's baseball team, Wade noticed how well the players were able to stabilize themselves and cut on the dirt and grass, even when wet, by wearing cleats, so Wade asked a shoe salesman to make a high-top football shoe with baseball cleats. His star player, halfback Johnny Mack Brown, was the first to lace them up and ran for a long touchdown, all the proof Wade needed of the cleats' effectiveness. By the end of the season, Wade had all the backs and receivers in football cleats, and eventually they would find their way onto the feet of every peewee and professional football player in the nation.

In 1925, for the second year in a row, Alabama won the Southern Conference, this time earning a berth in the Rose Bowl to take on the undefeated Washington Huskies. In 1922, the Tournament and city had constructed a fifty-seven-thousand-seat stadium for $272,198. The football game at the Tournament had been played continuously since the Washington State and Brown matchup in 1916, with service teams stepping in during World War I. The game was renamed the Rose Bowl when Harlan Hall, a local newspaper writer moonlighting for the Tournament of Roses, recognized the similarities between the newly constructed bowl stadium in Pasadena and Yale's famous Yale Bowl.

At the time, it was the only postseason bowl game, and, therefore, folks began to notice as newspapers covered the action. Despite the Tournament's hesitancy to select a Southern team like Alabama, Wade's team was picked to face the Huskies, led by All-American halfback George "Wildcat" Wilson. After trailing 12–0 at the half, Wade switched two of his guards to ends, and Bama turned its fortunes around, storming back to win 20–19 and securing its first national championship.

Shortly after the season, the University of Oregon, Washington State University, and his alma mater, Brown, expressed interest in prying Wade away from Alabama, but he and his family were content to be in Tuscaloosa, and he signed a five-year contract extension with the university. At first, he proved he was worth the investment when his 1926 team repeated as national champions after tying Stanford 7–7 on a late touchdown in the Rose Bowl. However, over the next three seasons, Wade's teams posted a mediocre overall record of 17–10–1, and, despite his past championships, which helped fund the brand-new Denny Stadium, which opened in 1929, Wade's critics had started to chirp that maybe he had lost his touch; that even though he was only in his late thirties, maybe the game had passed him by.

In mid-February 1930, Wade received a letter that would not just change his life but alter the histories of two universities. The typed letter was from Dean W. H. Wannamaker of Duke University in North Carolina, the chairman of the Faculty Committee on Athletics. Wannamaker had met Wade three times at Southern Conference meetings and was impressed by the coach, so much so that when Duke sought a new football coach, after deciding that James DeHart was no longer the answer, Wannamaker reached out to Wade for recommendations.

> *It is our earnest desire to build the very best possible physical plant and to provide for the coaching of our teams the best leaders we can secure . . . the man we bring in will have entire direction of the team and we will bring in the assistants he will want.*

It was not unusual for a university to reach out to Wade or to other prominent coaches to seek recommendations, and Wade responded with his in three days. On his list were Henry Crisp, line coach at Alabama; Lewis Hardage, backfield coach at Vanderbilt; Roy Morrison, head coach at Southern Methodist; and Clark Shaughnessy, head coach at Loyola University. But he added this:

> *If you decide to wait until the season of 1931, I should be glad to talk with you about the position for myself. If you care to discuss the matter further I expect to be in Atlanta March 2–4th for the conference basketball tournament.*

Wade shocked the college football world when he announced before the start of the 1930 season that he was indeed heading to Durham, North Carolina, to coach Duke—a school with little football tradition and a less-than-.500 record in the preceding four seasons. Yet he proved it was time for a new challenge when, as a lame duck, the Bear led Alabama to another national championship in 1930, his final year in Tuscaloosa, before being carried off the field by his players.

2. A NEW KINGDOM

In 1838, a small group of Methodists and Quakers reorganized Brown's Schoolhouse, a community school in Randolph County, North Carolina, renaming it Union Institute. Thirteen years later, the school became the first teacher-training institution in North Carolina and rebranded itself Normal College. Eight years after that, it affiliated with the North Carolina Conference of Methodist Episcopal Church South and had its third name in a matter of decades, Trinity College. Trinity began to establish a foothold in the North Carolina region, and in 1888, Julian S. Carr and Washington Duke—who had amassed enormous wealth in the tobacco industry—came together to change the fortunes of Trinity forever, donating money and land to move the campus to Durham. Duke also insisted that women be allowed to study on the new campus.

John Franklin Crowell, the president of Trinity in 1888, established a football team, having brought the game with him from Yale. Around that same time, the University of North Carolina and Wake Forest College also began to field teams, though they played a game more closely resembling rugby—including the use of a round ball—as opposed to the game being taught in Durham with a pigskin. Still, on Thanksgiving

Day 1888, Trinity defeated North Carolina in Raleigh 16–0, and the matchup created so much excitement that another game was scheduled for the spring of 1889, followed by a round-robin of games among Trinity, North Carolina, and Wake Forest later that fall.

The 1891 Trinity team went undefeated against its opponents, which included the round-robin mates, as well as the University of Virginia and Furman University. In fact, Trinity beat Furman 96–0, with every Trinity player scoring a touchdown, despite the fact that at the time, touchdowns were worth only four points, not six. Such was Trinity's dominance.

Four years later, football was gone from the Trinity College campus. As had happened at other football-playing schools, the Trinity faculty raised concerns of professionalism, injuries, and the adverse impact on academics, and the sport was banned from campus. Despite almost annual attempts to have it reinstated, it wasn't until 1920 that Trinity fielded another football team.

In 1924, Washington Duke's son, James, established a $40 million Duke endowment to fund higher education, medical care, child care, and Methodist churches, and, as part of that endowment, expanded and renamed Trinity College as Duke University, in honor of his father and family. From James B. Duke:

> *I have selected Duke University as one of the principal objects of this trust because I recognize that education, when conducted along sane and practical, as opposed to dogmatic and theoretical lines, is, next to religion, the greatest civilizing influence. I request that this institution secure for its officers, trustees, and faculty men of such outstanding character, ability and vision as will insure* [sic] *its attaining and maintaining a place of real leadership in the educational world, and that great care and discrimination be exercised in admitting as students only those whose previous record shows a character, determination, and application evincing a wholesome and real ambition for life.*

Building exploded on the new Durham campus with the gift, the number of faculty rose sharply, and additional construction in 1930 of thirty-one new buildings created the backbone of the campus.

Construction began on an English Gothic chapel at the heart of Duke's campus in 1930, and the work would take five years and cost more than $2.2 million. The exterior rock used was Duke bluestone from Hillsborough, North Carolina, and limestone from Indiana, while the inside was lined with Guastavino tile. The elaborate window displays depicted scenes from the Bible, and the oak pews held more than 1,500 worshipers. The hallmark of Duke University Chapel was a 210-foot tower with a carillon of fifty bells, which rang out every afternoon, on Sundays for worship services, and for special events.

As football became more popular across the nation, and as Duke experienced some success at it in the 1920s, President Robert Few began discussions about constructing a large football stadium and a new gymnasium and upgrading the athletic facilities. The athletic council accelerated the discussions by presenting actual plans in the late 1920s, with a goal of a fall 1929 opening. The land chosen was in a ravine adjacent to the current facilities, and designs were completed for a sunken stadium, with spectators entering at the top of the stadium at ground level. It would be a horseshoe structure to ensure strong sight lines with a capacity of fifty thousand. With the athletic council now running a surplus and with the anticipation that football and basketball revenues would only grow, the council began a fund-raising campaign to build the best stadium in the South.

They raised funds by selling stadium certificates for $100 and up to any alumni or friend of Duke. The investments would finance the construction of the stadium and provide up to a 6 percent annual return for investors. The purchase of a certificate also provided investors with the opportunity to buy the seats of their choice. The certificates could be paid for in as many as four installments, with some large investors buying $10,000 worth of certificates. As construction began and the concrete was poured in April 1929, it was clear that the funds would not allow for the construction of a fifty-thousand-seat stadium, and the decision was made to reduce the size to thirty-five thousand.

The stadium opened on October 5, 1929, when Duke welcomed the University of Pittsburgh.

By the time Wallace Wade arrived at Duke, né Trinity, in January of 1931, he was already considered among the premier college football coaches in the nation. Ironically, while Wade was winning the national title in his final season at Alabama in 1930, Duke rebounded under James Dehart and finished 8–1–2, aided by many of the directives of Wade's assistants he had added to the staff *before* he took over.

Even those closest to Wade have never truly understood why he made the move, but that never stopped speculation: that Wade was frustrated at the criticism directed at him from an ungrateful Alabama fan base; that he sought the private school environment he so admired at Vanderbilt, free of meddling school and government officials; that he could have total control of the program at Duke, something he felt he did not have at Alabama; and that Duke offered a large sum of money (thanks to James B. Duke), including a percentage of gate receipts, which, if true, would have been one of the more aggressive recruiting tactics to date, particularly considering the Depression.

Wade's official tenure as Duke head coach began on January 15, 1931, when he, Frances, Wallace Jr., and Sis were entertained at a dinner with players, staff, and outgoing Coach DeHart. In the coming days, he made it clear *he* was in charge and that he would not be subject to outside influences, including alumni, boosters, or school administrators—all of whom soon found that they could not buy their way into Wade's inner circle, as he declined almost every invitation to dinner parties, trips, and golf outings.

In addition to former Alabama players Herschel Caldwell and Ellis "Dumpy" Hagler, Wade hired Carl Voyles from the University of Illinois to coach ends and his former All-American running back at Alabama, Fred Sington. He also retained Duke assistant Eddie Cameron.

In the spring of 1931, Wade, who was also the director of athletics, an administrative job he took as seriously as his higher-profile coaching job, became a visible presence on campus, meeting with students—varsity athletes and students alike—to stress the importance of academics and athletics. True to the precedent he established at Alabama, his players, including starters, were not only allowed to miss practice for class, they were compelled to maintain close communication with their professors to negotiate their academic and athletic careers. In Wade's eyes, his players' football exploits were not an excuse to compromise their studies. Quite the opposite. They presented an opportunity to foster the right kind of relationships and actually improve their academic performance.

But to be clear, expectations—administrative and otherwise—for Wade's inaugural season were off the charts as Duke opened on the road against the University of South Carolina. His venerable defense allowed just one touchdown, but the offense was unable to score any of its own, and Duke lost 7–0. The following week, Wade's team posted its first win at home against the Virginia Military Institute (VMI), 13–0. The rest of the season included a 28–0 trouncing of Wake Forest in Durham, followed by a morally neutralizing 25–2 defeat against Robert Neyland's Tennessee team in Knoxville.

In the end, Duke posted a 5–3–2 record—respectable for its modest history but a drop-off from its 1930 season under DeHart and a serious disappointment to Wade. In the off-season, Wade established a year-round training program for his players and won a petition for a physical education requirement for every student at Duke.

Behind his back, his boys called Wade "the Old Man." The term in those days implied begrudging respect for an elder, but, more obviously, the stubbornness that comes with age and the demands of being a football coach.

The Blue Devils improved to 7–3 in 1932 and, in 1933, scored one of the greatest upsets in college football history, defeating Neyland's Tennessee team 10–2 in Durham and stopping the Orange and White's twenty-six-game winning streak. It set Duke up for a shot at a national title after winning every game on their schedule entering the finale against Georgia Tech in Atlanta.

A victory would put them in the Rose Bowl, as they had already been conditionally invited if they won. By this time, the Rose Bowl was so much more than the bicycle games and tilting rings of the 1890s. The game had grown in magnitude and stature, aided by national newspaper coverage and, beginning in 1927, national radio broadcasts by NBC and announcer Graham McNamee on fifteen stations around the country. The parade and festivities surrounding the game only added to the allure, as did the nearby movie studios and beaches of California, which made players, coaches, and fans of prospective participants eager to get an invite.

During halftime of the Georgia Tech game, Wade read a telegram to his team from the Rose Bowl committee inviting them to Pasadena, assuming they beat Georgia Tech. But his motivational tactic did not work, as Duke lost 6–0, one of Wade's biggest disappointments in his coaching career.

Yet the winning seasons kept coming: 7–2 in 1934, 8–2 in 1935, 9–1 in 1936, and 7–2–1 in 1937. They won two Southern Conference championships along the way.

The 1938 season was one for the ages. Through the first six games, Wade's team was not only undefeated but had yet to allow a *single point*. Yet the story lines heading into the seventh game against a tough Syracuse team weren't about the unbeaten Blue Devils and their impossible streak; they were about Syracuse's quarterback, Wilmeth Sidat-Singh.

Sidat-Singh was black, and for years there had been a "gentlemen's agreement" between Northern and Southern schools that when they played one another, blacks would not compete. The Northern schools needed big games for the revenue and were willing to oblige the Southern demands, what with the exponential growth of Southern college football. The pact was broken in 1936 when North Carolina agreed to play at New York University, which refused to play without star African American running back Ed Williams.

"So far, the University of North Carolina is still standing and none of the young men representing it on the gridiron appears to be any worse off for having spent an afternoon competing against a Negro player," wrote columnist Roy Wilkins. "It is a fairly safe prediction that no white North Carolinian's daughter will marry a Negro as a result of Saturday's play, much to the chagrin of the peddlers of the bugaboo of social equality."

But the precedent apparently set by the NYU-UNC game did not stop Duke alums and supporters from voicing their opposition to Wallace Wade's decision to allow Syracuse to play whomever they wanted when the teams met on November 12. One "supporter" wrote to President William P. Few, demanding that Duke not play "against that n———," with demands that Wade be fired if they did. Wade's moral view of the world persisted, and, remembering the battle he waged with his father over his old friend and teammate Fritz Pollard, who would go on to become the first black head coach in the NFL, he staunchly led the entire Duke team and entourage onto a train bound for the frigidly winter cold reaches of upstate New York. Wade wanted to beat Syracuse at its best, and that's just what they did, shutting down Sidat-Singh and the Syracuse offense, winning 21–0.

Wade's team went on to win the remainder of its games, and there was rampant speculation that Duke would get invited to the Rose Bowl.

From 1916 until 1923, the Tournament of Roses Association had selected both participants for the Rose Bowl, ideally one from the West and one from the East. In 1923, the association selected only the West Coast team and allowed that team to choose its opponent from the East. Then, in 1935, the association entered into an agreement with the Pacific Coast Conference (PCC) that its champion would automatically earn a Rose Bowl berth and then choose its opponent. (The association still played a pivotal behind-the-scenes role in the process, working back channels to ensure the East Coast opponent was attractive enough to fill seats.)

By 1938, the Rose Bowl had been joined by the Orange Bowl (originally called "Orange Blossom") in 1935 as well as by the Sugar Bowl, and in 1936 by the Sun Bowl and in 1937 by the Cotton Bowl. Still, these postseason games paled in comparison to the glamour of the Rose Bowl.

When the news came that Duke would take on the mighty Trojans of USC in Pasadena, there were celebrations throughout the Durham campus. West Coast critics of Duke's selection loudly voiced their dismay, insisting that Duke was not worthy, considering their "weak" competition in the Southern Conference, as Southern football was still regarded as inferior. Wade, meanwhile, would be making his fourth trip to the Rose Bowl.

Hundreds of Durham residents and students crowded Union Station to see off the team, which wore small Duke lapel pins on their jackets and attached blue-and-white stickers along with small red rose stickers to their luggage. Before stepping onto the train, Wade was even handed an unprecedented good-luck letter from bitter rival North Carolina's student body.

On January 2, 1939, in front of more than eighty thousand fans at the Rose Bowl, one of the greatest college football games—and finishes—took place. The Duke defense not surprisingly held up for much of the game, and a Blue Devils field goal put them up 3–0 late in the fourth quarter. Duke fumbled in its own territory, but once again, the defense stepped up and got the ball back. But with forty seconds left, the Trojans had the ball, and USC's Doyle Nave, the fourth-string passer, went to work, throwing three straight completions to reserve end Al Krueger on a march downfield.

With seconds left on Duke's sixteen-yard line, the previously unknown Nave dropped back, hesitated for a moment, and then launched a fourth consecutive pass to Krueger.

Wade couldn't see the conclusion of the play, seated in his customary position on the bench, with his players bunched together anxiously on the sideline, obstructing his view.

"Did he catch it?" the normally composed Wade pleaded, urgently trying to get a glimpse over the shoulders of star running back George McAfee. "Did he catch it?"

"Yes, Coach," the bewildered future college and NFL Hall of Famer mustered. "He caught it."

The game ended a few plays later with McAfee tackled at USC's forty-yard line. One play after one impossible drive, and the undefeated, unbeaten, unscored-upon season was over.

After the game, Wade made his way over to the USC locker room to congratulate Coach Howard Jones. After shaking his hand, Wade began to exit the locker room when he was asked by a reporter if he would go over and shake Doyle Nave's hand. In an incident that would shadow Wade for the rest of his career, the coach dejectedly replied, "I've had enough of *him* for one day."

It was a simple, cheeky response to an innocent question, but the West Coast writers pounced on Wade for exhibiting poor sportsmanship. The war of words grew nastier in the days that followed, with Wade claiming Duke's practices had been spied on and vowing never to return to the Rose Bowl with another team.

The bitter taste of defeat in Pasadena followed Wade throughout the off-season and into the 1939 season. A 14–13 heartbreaking loss to Pittsburgh on the road was their only loss that year, a game in which Duke's offense got confused on a lateral and fumbled the ball away in the closing minutes, killing their chance at a bowl game. But the non-bowl season in 1939 did nothing to dampen Wallace Wade's popularity. Come 1940, Wade was in demand as a sought-after speaker and clinician at schools around the country. The media took inventory of the remaining and incoming talent headed into the 1940 season, with the Associated Press giving the Blue Devils a number one preseason ranking. Wade's team finished 7–2 and second in the Southern Conference.

The sunburned brown grass resting under Wallace Wade's feet was well-worn before fall practice had even started. The field was hallowed ground for Wade. It was his comfort, his laboratory, and his respite from the nonsense beyond football. It was here, on Duke's practice field, adjacent to Duke Stadium, where he prepared his gladiators for battle. And make no mistake, Wade the tactician, the teacher, the authority figure, approached every game like a battle.

The forty-nine players out for the first day of fall practice on September 1, 1941, came in all shapes and sizes and from a variety of socioeconomic backgrounds, but all shared at least one thing: a sometimes-paralyzing fear of their coach, whose icy eyes could turn a lion into a kitten. The turnout on September 1 was the smallest in years at Duke. Of course, the new military uniform played a part. The Selective Training and Service Act of 1940 signed into law in September 1940 required all men between the ages of twenty-one and thirty-five to register for potential service for no longer than twelve months. In August 1941, with war looming, President Roosevelt pushed for, and Congress approved, extending the twelve-month period, much to the dismay of the young men. More and more students were voluntarily entering the service as fall camp opened, and Wade was missing six players, with the potential loss of more.

The players arrived early for the start of drills: as in Wade's world, early *was* on time. They dressed in sweats, mask-less helmets snugly on their heads. There would be no pre-practice rah-rah speech from Wade, no theatrical prose about the importance of fall camp or the upcoming season. Just a simple direction.

"Work hard today, boys!"

And work hard they would, suffocating on the sunken field surrounded by trees.

Practices under Wade often ran more than two hours and comprised fifteen-minute preplanned periods, punctuated by a student manager's whistle. There were no water breaks. In fact, there was no water. Or breaks. Even if there were breaks, there were no benches. Wade had a history of making his players run a play or drill over and over and over until he was satisfied enough to move on. Many of his diagrammed plays on offense and defense would not appear in a game for weeks or even months—until he believed his players had perfected them. The coach immersed himself in a particular position or drill, roaming the field, searching for deficiencies. The insistence on perfection that characterized the legend of Wade also prevented close relationships with his players. But while there was little personal relationship built between the coach and the players, there was a mutual respect.

The obvious challenges before Wade in 1941 were just too many to tackle after the "disappointing" 7–2 season in 1940, so Wade focused on the two big concerns: the strength and skill of the line and the ability of the inexperienced sophomores to make an immediate contribution. Accordingly, Assistant Coach Dumpy Hagler, a six-foot-tall, 240-pound guard who had played for Wade at Alabama, was tasked with rebuilding the line under Wade's direction. Hagler was a detailed and calculating scout of opponents, and he honed his football Zen by coaching the Duke golf team with equal enthusiasm, but he never lost sight of his passion for the pigskin.

In the off-season, Wade had borrowed new line formations and techniques from his good friend George Munger, the head coach at the University of Pennsylvania, and in return, Wade shared many of his defensive principles with Munger, who implemented them during his fall camp. Wade changed players' positions to better strengthen the line play and to take advantage of their size, including Mike Karmazin's. Bob Barnett returned to handle the center duties and was elected captain by his teammates at the start of the year. Steve Lach, a working-class kid from Altoona, Pennsylvania, the offensive star, was also stellar on the defensive side, and, in fact, opponents ran only for one first down to Lach's side in *all* of 1940.

Jim Smith was born to be a Buckeye, not a Blue Devil. Born and raised in Hamilton, Ohio, just one hundred miles from Columbus, his father had played football for Ohio State and was fraternity brothers with the Ohio State president and had played football with the head coach. His older brother by eight years, Jack, was an All-American football player for the Buckeyes and a javelin thrower. And for good measure, his uncle was a star baseball player in Columbus. Smith was a high school sports star in Hamilton, a working-class town of paper mills mixed races.

When it came time for Smith to select a college, everyone believed there wasn't even a decision to be made. He spent a great deal of time around the Ohio State team, knew the players and the coaches, and was familiar with the fight song. But Smith took a trip to visit Duke in Durham and came away believing that his home was there. He was impressed with Wallace Wade, a serious and focused man, like Smith. When Smith informed his family, they were supportive but disappointed. Off he went to Durham, and by the fall of 1941, Smith was a starter at end for Wade.

The sophomore class showed promise. Bob Gantt, son of a Duke legend, was big and talented, and Bob Nanni—who as a freshman not only struggled in the classroom but more than hinted at frightening temper issues—showed flashes of the ability to channel his anger into extraordinary performance. Sophomore Leo Long and senior Winston Siegfried were potential replacements in the backfield to join Tommy Prothro, who was returning as signal caller and blocker at quarterback.

The game of football in 1941 was a vastly different game from the one that would emerge in the ensuing decades. First off, there was very little specialization, with most players playing both offense and defense. Second, coaches routinely focused more on field position than on scoring, so punting was used not just on fourth down but at times on third, second, and even first down, if it meant putting the opponent in a difficult situation. Third, the equipment was still basic. There were plastic helmets—an upgrade from the old leather hats—but there were no face masks or face guards. Players would wear one only to protect a broken nose or jaw, and even then, they could be used by opponents to throw players down. Face-mask penalties were a thing of the future.

But other things about the on-field culture were changing in 1941, including the fact that it would be the first season of unlimited substitutions in college football. Prior to the 1941 season, coaches could sub players in and out, but once a player came out of the game, he could not return until the next period of play; that kept star players on the field, even those with serious injuries. The new rule of unlimited substitutions was opposed by Wade, who believed that "when a football player steps on a field, he should do it all. I realize a great running back doesn't like to play defense, but life isn't based on what you like. If everyone did what he liked to do, we'd be in real trouble." Despite Wade's protest, the rule passed, and there was a lot of work to do in fall camp.

One of the emerging sophomores in camp was Charles Haynes Jr., who grew up on the fields of Duke, living just blocks away from campus with his parents in a two-story house on Arnette Avenue. Born in 1921, with oak-brown hair and deep-brown eyes, Haynes was a descendant of the Confederate General Stonewall Jackson on his mother's side, reflected in a large portrait hanging in the downstairs foyer of his home. His thick Southern drawl would stay with him throughout his life. His father, Charles Sr., worked for the American Tobacco Company after serving in the U.S. Army during World War I, where he played trombone in the army band. He was strict with Charles and his older sister, Hazel, but nevertheless, the young boy looked up to his dad.

"Sonny," as those closest to him affectionately called Charles Jr., was particularly fond of his mother, Alice. She was larger-than-life and well-known in Durham, running the Durham Livery Stables and the Hillandale Stables. Not surprisingly, Haynes learned to ride horses and to care for them, winning blue ribbons in riding meets as a youngster in addition to becoming Durham's youngest Eagle Scout and a Sea Scout, learning water-rescue techniques as a teenager. He had a unique compassion for others, perhaps cultivated by caring for his horses, as well as an unbridled gratefulness for life.

In high school, he joined the football team and devoted much of his time to his gridiron pursuits, but he never gave up riding, often going for a gallop by himself after school or in the evenings with friends. He grappled on the wrestling mat, becoming one of the top wrestlers in the state. Haynes was an ordinary kid in so many ways, but what distinguished him from his peers was his maturity, as reflected in a diary he kept his last year in high school. His New Year's resolutions for 1939 were:

> *No Smoking, No Cursing. Try not to talk about anybody's bad points; really put out during coming football season and try for All-State team; to play football fair and square and be a good sport during games and practices; try not to string a girl a line. On my honor I will do my best to do my duty to God and my country, to obey the Scout law and to help other people at all times. To keep myself physically strong, mentally awake and morally straight.*

A few days after the entry, he was named his football team's MVP for the 1938 season and would go on to a fabulous senior year.

The Hope Valley resident was destined to be a Duke student, like his father before him, who'd attended Trinity. Once he was on campus,

Haynes and his mother donated the use of some horses and equipment to the Department of Physical Education, and Haynes taught coeds how to ride, which also helped him with the ladies. He increased his athletic purview by joining the wrestling team, keeping him in football shape in the off-season. Haynes stood five-foot-eight and weighed just 157 pounds and had poor eyesight, but Wade liked something about his tenacity and confidence to take on all comers, even those much bigger than he was.

On the first day of fall camp in 1941, despite starting with gusto, Haynes was unsure if he would even see the playing field during the season. The Eagle Scout saw service and leadership as privileges, and if that meant standing on a sideline in a clean uniform cheering on his teammates, then he accepted his role. It didn't mean he was not competitive, and the grueling next few weeks in camp for him and his teammates revealed that fire, with Haynes routinely taking on the biggest teammate and hardest hitters as Duke worked toward the home opener against Wake Forest. Wade started Haynes off at guard but would eventually move him to blocking back. The coach saw a lot of himself in his player.

On September 27, the Union in the middle of Duke's campus was buzzing. The building was home to most student organizations and activities, and the basement, dubbed "Main Street," was the center of the action. The Dope Shop sold everything from Coca-Cola to cigars, oranges to candy, and most things in between. It's where students and faculty would grab a ham-and-cheese sandwich and a milkshake or where young men could be seen trying to impress coeds on an early evening. The Haberdashery provided the latest in men's fashion, and the university bookstore was the hub for textbooks and supplies. A barbershop, bank, post office, and laundry service were also in the Union, near the offices of the student yearbook, newspaper, and government.

The Union was crowded but not cramped in the hours leading up to the opening football game against Wake Forest. The pep rally held the night before was the largest in years—perhaps ever—as Wallace Wade spoke briefly, and when captain Bob Barnett—a Golden Glove boxer from Albany, Georgia, who began his Duke football career in 1938 as a fourth stringer and was now a star—led the team onto the stage, the walls shook.

Yet despite the students' enthusiasm, fewer than fifteen thousand spectators filled the thirty-thousand-plus-seat stadium for the opener, which didn't seem to bother Charles Haynes, who had witnessed crowds smaller and larger through the years in Durham. The Duke cheerleaders, coed for the first time since 1936 by adding women, led the crowd in an impressive variety of new cheers and multiple renditions of the Duke fight song.

Among the crowd were a few thousand military men from nearby bases. A supporter of the military back to his army days in World War I, Wade offered football tickets for just fifty cents to any enlisted man, and the coach would often host soldiers at Duke practices. On game days, students enthusiastically welcomed soldiers and provided campus tours before and after games, including a private showing of the new eight-thousand-seat indoor basketball stadium, built with the money Duke received from participating in the 1939 Rose Bowl.

Before kickoff against Wake Forest, Wade made last-minute changes to the starting eleven, electing to go with sophomore Leo Long over Winston Siegfried, and sophomore Tom Davis over Moffett Storer in the backfield. His divine inspiration paid off just two minutes into the game when, from Wake's seven-yard line, Davis was handed the ball, took two steps to the left, cut back through a hole on the right side of the line, and scored Duke's first touchdown of the season. Two minutes later, after Duke had recovered a fumble, Storer took the ball to the right and, with Tommy Prothro laying devastating blocks, scored standing up. Long scored a touchdown, Davis threw a TD pass to Bob Gantt, and George Bokinsky added yet another score.

The final was 43–14, with Wade managing to get an incredible forty-three players onto the field of play, including Haynes at guard. Wade agreed with Wake Forest coach D. C. Walker to reduce the standard fifteen-minute quarters to twelve after halftime because of the 34–0 rout at the time. Most notable were the flashes of brilliance from Wade's sophomores, including Long, Davis, and Gantt, whom he would need going into the annual rivalry versus Robert Neyland's Tennessee Volunteers.

High above the field, watching Wake Forest closely, was a volunteer assistant coach for Duke. He rarely came to practices but was there for most games, always spying on the opponent's formations and tendencies and calling them down to the Duke sideline via telephone. His name was Wallace Wade Jr.

When the late bloomer's classmates had reached puberty and kept growing in middle school, Wade Jr. feared that he had inherited the genes of his mother, whose barely five-foot stature was dwarfed by his father's imposing physique. Metaphorically, he was in the shadow of a growing legend, which came with a reluctant sort of notoriety that only picked up throughout his schooling in Durham. In high school, he maxed out at an unimpressive five-foot-seven, 130 pounds. He was a well-behaved, quiet kid with rimmed glasses who did his homework, always had the answer when called upon by his teachers, and brought home high marks—making the elder Wade proud. The son, however, did not have the answers on the athletic field, as he was not as gifted an athlete as one might expect from the son of a coach. Though he worked hard—and his father pushed him—sometimes wanting something badly enough is not enough.

Despite his son's apparent complex, Wade Sr.—emotionally distant but enthusiastic about his son's potential—encouraged him to embrace his innate gifts and nurture his brain, and, after graduating from high school, the younger Wade matriculated at Duke, studying business and economics and pledging Phi Delta Theta, the home of several of his father's players.

Wade Jr. was high in the sky again during game two against bitter rival Tennessee, featuring a crowd of forty-eight thousand in Durham, including governors Prentice Cooper from Tennessee and Jim Broughton from North Carolina. Temporary bleachers were brought in to accommodate the capacity crowd that watched Wade's defense, led by tackle Mike Karmazin, dominate the vaunted Tennessee running attack by limiting Tennessee star Johnny Butler to minus five yards rushing in a 19–0 win. Tennessee coach Robert Neyland was in attendance but, having given up his coaching duties to reenlist in the army, watched the game in his uniform from the stands.

Duke was undefeated, yet their coach was still not impressed. Wade was never satisfied with his players, lamenting their mistakes and eager to get back on the practice field to fix them. He knew they were capable of more than they believed.

3. COUNTRY BOYS

On a fall afternoon, twenty-five years after Oregon Agricultural College's official founding in 1868, a band of Albany College football players hopped into carriages and made the ten-mile trek southwest to OAC's home in Corvallis, ninety miles south of Portland in the Willamette Valley. Not taking the game terribly seriously, the visitors patiently made their way through a full and satisfying meal in Cauthorn Hall before strolling to the parade grounds, where the Agrics of OAC—coached by quarterback (and son of the college's president) Will Bloss—were waiting to play them in the campus' first-ever football game. Supporters used carriages as seats and stood around the field as OAC demolished their food-comatose opponents 62–0.

The following year, OAC defeated state powerhouse the University of Oregon 16–0, but the succeeding six seasons were full of irregular games, unconventional rosters, and general apathy toward the game. There was a wave of concern among faculty over injuries, costs, and the impact on academics, similar to the concerns at Trinity College, and with scant financial resources, the regents of the school—established as part of the federal Land-Grant College Act of 1862, which included legislation demanding the building of more institutions of higher learning dedicated to benefiting local communities—shut down the football program in 1900 and 1901.

In 1902, OAC joined the Northwest Intercollegiate Association. Football was revived on campus, and the team enjoyed a competitive run over the next thirty years. The 1907 OAC team even went 6–0 while not conceding a single point. The 1914 squad went 7–0–2, giving up just twelve points and, the following year, won the Pacific Coast Conference in its first year as a formal league. In 1915, OAC went on the road and defeated Michigan State 20–0, which is commonly viewed as a turning point in fans' perspective of West Coast football. In 1924, Paul Schissler, "the Little Fire Eater," was hired as coach and produced dominant teams in Corvallis for the next nine seasons. His team's 1928 victory over New York University, then a big East Coast contender, cemented the view that teams from out West should be considered legitimate threats to nationally recognized programs. But it wasn't until Alonzo "Lon" Stiner Jr. took over as head coach that the soon-to-be dubbed Oregon State College became a major player in college football.

Stiner had always been determined, both as a student and as an athlete from Nebraska, shaking off nonbelievers, who thought his five-foot-nine frame was too small for a lineman. But Schissler, then the coach at tiny Lombard College in Illinois, was interested in Stiner and recruited him to play for his team. The young man earned playing time his first two seasons, but then Schissler left Lombard to become the new head coach in Corvallis after going 23–1–1. Stiner's stellar play at Lombard gave the University of Nebraska coaches reason to believe he could contribute to the team, and he transferred back home for his final two years of college, where he would become an All-American. After earning his degree, his first coaching job was at Colorado before Schissler offered him a spot on the OAC staff.

For five seasons, Stiner served as line coach for Schissler before his mentor's resignation after the 1932 season. Athletic director Carl Lodell went on a national search for his replacement but ended up hiring Stiner, partly because of who *wouldn't* come to Corvallis and partly because he could pay Stiner less than other candidates.

Stiner's first team in 1933 was considered by the media and by his rivals as one of the weakest in the Pacific Coast Conference, despite All-Americans Norm Franklin and Ade Schwammel. But as the season progressed, his team turned heads with their physical play. The coach spent most of every practice teaching his "rock 'em and block 'em gridiron tactics," his single wing with the option system, and the infamous Pyramid Play. The play became a spectacle, earning both praise and jeers from purists, as Stiner would have six-foot-two Schwammel and equally tall Harry Field hoist six-foot-six center Clyde Devine on their shoulders to attempt to block field goals and extra points.

Stiner's boys tied the top-ranked USC Trojans in 1933, ending their twenty-five-game winning streak, and defeated Fordham University at the Polo Grounds, en route to a 6–2–2 record, but they never reached the pinnacle of their conference in the succeeding years. And even eight years later, as spring practice opened in 1941, the expectation was that the mediocrity would continue.

Close to fifty players showed up in March 1941 for a team that many experts predicted would fight UCLA to stay out of last place in the Pacific Coast Conference. More than one-third of the 1940 team was gone. Stiner went to the chalkboard in his office and, like a mad professor, tried various combinations, working blisters into his palms. Traditionally on offense, Stiner used a single-wingback and short-punt formations for running plays, giving his multitalented backfield as many options as possible to gain yardage on the ground or in the air. Like many of his counterparts, Stiner used punting as an offensive weapon, even on early downs, to gain better field position, such great faith did he place in his defense. The quarterback for Stiner was the one who would make the on-field adjustments and who, on most plays, would be the key blocker for the backs. The left and right halfbacks would be signal callers and often the first to touch the ball, either running with it or passing it, and were also adept at punting it. The fullback had to be fast and elusive.

What if the left halfback was a righty and the right halfback a southpaw, and either was able to run the misdirection play and throw across the field? Stiner thought excitedly. It just so happened that the coach had the men to do just that in 1941.

Don Durdan, from Eureka, California, wasn't even destined to be a Beaver. The son of a banana farmer, Durdan was an all-American kid, involved with the local YMCA and Boy Scout troop, fishing with his father on the Mad River, and having an extraordinary talent for any sport he tried. He made Eureka High School varsity football as a one-hundred-pound eighth grader. His prodigious high school athletic career included setting a state high school pole jump record at twelve-feet-six inches using a bamboo stick. He lettered in track, tennis, football, basketball, and baseball; played running back, fullback, and quarterback on undefeated football teams; and served as the star of the 1937 Eureka squad, thought to be among the best prep teams in the nation. College coaches in all sports salivated over Durdan, and he settled on Stanford, even taking extra courses in the summer required by the university. But when Durdan visited Oregon State during his senior basketball season with his high school coach, an OSC alum, he was convinced to change his college destination, especially after meeting with OSC basketball coach Amory "Slats" Gill, who could be persuasive.

He came to OSC to play baseball and basketball; football was an afterthought. He was five-foot-nine and weighed 163 pounds when he came to Corvallis. Durdan struggled academically early on, his studies giving way to time spent on his sporting endeavors, Sigma Nu, and the Reserve Officers' Training Corps (ROTC), and he resolved to temporarily move from the fraternity house to a boardinghouse until his grades improved. He returned to the frat in January of 1939, but when it became clear that his academic issues were directly linked to the distractions of the frat house, he soon moved out again—at the urging of his parents and against the strenuous protests of fraternity leaders.

In the fall of 1939, as a sophomore, Durdan played varsity football and became a mainstay in the lineup. In fact, he went with the team to Hawaii for the Pineapple Bowl, giving up on playing varsity basketball that season, as missing crucial practices and games in December could not be overcome.

After an eye-opening 1940 season on the gridiron, Durdan received offers from multiple professional football teams to join their ranks. The Philadelphia Eagles went so far as to arrange for Durdan to take classes at nearby Temple University and the University of Pennsylvania so he could continue to work toward his degree while playing pro football for $350 a game. In the end, Durdan enjoyed college life too much, forging close relationships with his teammates, particularly Bob Dethman and Bob Saunders, with whom he went hunting and fishing, and the women, with whom he was, to put it mildly, quite popular.

Robert "Bob" Dethman stood five-foot-ten with a muscular 187-pound build, his brown hair and dark complexion in stark contrast to his mesmerizing, bright emerald-green eyes. Adding to his movie-star looks was God-given physical talent.

Dethman was a kid who just had *it* from an early age. Everybody in Hood River, Oregon, knew him, and everybody knew the Dethman family. In the days after high school games, he couldn't elude the endless line of congratulatory handshakes or the smothering hugs that awaited him as he made his way to Young's Bakery or the ice cream store next to JCPenney in downtown Hood River. Free muffins, ice cream, and admission to watch the latest film reels at the movie theater were among the perks of being a local hero. He skipped school on more than a few occasions, and when he did show up, he often appeared distracted or outright disinterested in most of his classes, though his Hood River

High School teachers conspicuously forgave him for his educational trespasses.

Dethman found his peace fishing on the Columbia River or in local streams, or shooting rabbits, deer, and pretty much anything else that moved in the hills along the gorge. Like many Hood River kids, he climbed the guard-less trails of Mount Hood with friends and drove to Lost Lake, twelve miles outside of town, to get into harmless teen mischief.

He was quite close to his large extended family and was a father figure to his younger brother, Wendell, eight years his junior, who had a fierceness that made him stand tall.

Up in the hill, about one mile from the banks of the Columbia River, beyond the small apple orchards of Hood River in the shadow of Mount Hood, almost in the town of Pine Grove, stood the Dethman homestead, where Bob and Wendell lived, a parcel of land claimed by their paternal grandfather, Christian. The homestead was actually split among three of Christian's sons, each residing with his family on a third of the land their father took hold of in the late 1800s.

One of his sons, Alfred, followed in Christian's footsteps, not only living in the house in which he was born but sowing the fruits of the fields to support his family—mainly apples and pears. He married Mattie in Hood River in 1913 and became a father to Leonard in 1914, to Bob in 1917, to Marjorie in 1920, and to Wendell in 1925. With four children and the orchards simply not bringing in enough income, Alfred drove the local school bus, making round-trips through Pine Grove and Hood River to the local junior high and high schools. "Uncle Pug," as he was known to his family and friends, enjoyed the outdoors, spending time in the woods with a rifle and in the water with a pole.

Bob was Alfred's star, shining for the Hood River Dragons in basketball and football, at a time when Hood River was one of the few teams to fully exploit the forward pass. In 1937, with Bob as their centerpiece, Hood River finished 7–1 under head coach Jim Carr, suffering their only loss to Jefferson High School in Portland, a defeat that cost them the state title.

As much success as Dethman had on the athletic fields, his struggles in the classroom—when he was in it—threatened to keep him in Hood River. Despite having the teachers and student body in his corner, excessive absences from class, poor motivation, and a "lack of purpose"—according to his principal—resulted in poor grades. Still, his marks in math and American history and civics were good enough for some colleges. And Oregon State was one of them.

On his standard application for the school, Dethman stated his interest in studying fish and game, a major he would change multiple times while enrolled in Corvallis. He graduated Hood River High School in December of 1937, one of eighty-eight seniors, and was a college student the first week of January 1938.

Within eight weeks of stepping onto campus, Dethman was already on academic probation with a GPA of 1.33. In August, the Oregon State registrar wrote a letter to his parents, warning them about the direness of the situation, yet despite seven Fs and one incomplete by the end of 1938, the academic probation was released after the first semester. His charms likely saved him from expulsion, but his poor performance in the classroom cost him his eligibility to compete on the Rooks, the freshman football team, and limited his participation to a practice squad. Helping the varsity team prepare for its games was as close as he would get to gridiron glory until he got his act together academically.

He spent his summers in Corvallis, saving lives as a lifeguard in Avery Park along the banks of the Mary River. He was the epitome of cool. When he picked up golf, playing regularly with Durdan, Saunders, and Warren Perryman, Dethman hit drives 250 to 300 yards off the tee and once carded a thirty-six on the front nine at Corvallis Country Club.

In April 1939, Dethman was a reserve on the Oregon State varsity team when they scrimmaged against a team of former OSC players. In the scrimmage, Dethman showed hints of brilliance and earned playing time on the varsity team in 1939, but it wasn't until 1940 that his ability to run and pass forced Stiner to keep him on the field, and he became a mainstay for Oregon State.

But while his prospects were good for a big season in 1941, Dethman had concerns beyond football. There were many broken hearts when, during his sophomore year, Dethman met Margaret Hancock from New Meadow, Idaho, and then married her on Alfred Dethman's homestead in Hood River in 1941. He now had a family to worry about and, as such, took on a more mature approach to life, committing himself to football and school. And it was a good thing, because Stiner needed every ounce of his star's ability.

Both Durdan and Dethman were exceptional athletes who could make split-second decisions simply by eyeing the defensive halfback. If a defensive back came up to the line to stop a run, Durdan or Dethman would throw it; if the defender stayed back behind the line, they would run it. Defenses could not favor one side of the line or the other, for Oregon State could strike on either side. The "Double Ds" could be a deadly combination.

There were other returning lettermen besides Durdan and Dethman who gave Stiner hope, including George Zellick, a very powerful left end from the hills of Montana; Bill "Ruck" Halverson at left guard; Quentin Greenough at center; and Martin Chaves, who barely played enough minutes to earn a letter in 1940 but who was a ferocious tackler, at right guard. Frank Parker, who had played quarterback, center, and guard during his time at OSC, would likely play a significant role in a variety of positions. Gene Gray could play halfback, and he split time at the position with Durdan in 1940.

Gray had always been underestimated. Perhaps it was his scrawny appearance, at five-foot-ten and just 150 pounds, which hid tremendous athletic ability and speed. His blue-gray eyes, auburn hair, and pale complexion didn't exactly invoke fear in opponents, either. Or maybe it was the fact that he grew up in the shadow of his older brother, Joe, whose accomplishments on the high school and Oregon State football fields were well chronicled, earning him the nickname "the Gray Ghost," as his quick moves made him disappear like a ghost. Surely there couldn't be another Gray sibling with sublime talent. But Gray was shifty and exceptionally fast, and though he was saddled behind Durdan and Dethman on the depth chart, Stiner believed he could be a secret weapon. When fall camp opened, Stiner didn't even know if Gray would be available until he received his deferment from the army in mid-September.

Also among the candidates for Stiner was an unknown slew of sophomores, including the agile and speedy Jack Yoshihara and left halfback Everett Smith. Smith was a good kid with the right approach and work ethic who was woefully unprepared for the rigors of college courses. He struggled academically, even in his core classes in agriculture, and the college required him to leave the agriculture program and transfer to another division; he ultimately chose mechanical drawing. He had football talent, which showed during his freshman year on the rookie team, and he had hope that he would play a lot in 1941.

During spring practice, Stiner tinkered with not only lineup combinations but also position placements. In past years, with players playing both ways on offense and defense at the time, he had the fullback and the right guard on offense back up the line on defense, with the center stepping out when a five-man line was called for. But in the spring, Stiner moved the fullback to the left halfback position on defense with the quarterback and right guard serving as linebackers, a new wrinkle for college defenses. Behind them would be the fullback with the right halfback and left halfbacks playing as safeties. The new defense gave Stiner the option of having a five-, six-, or seven-man defensive line with a variety of defensive formations, depending on the offense. Of course, it helped that Greenough, who spent his summers rolling oil barrels in the drastic heat of his native Southern California, was an outstanding defender and leader, whom Stiner trusted to call defensive signals by behind-the-back hand signals, making adjustments on the fly.

In Astoria, Oregon, a small fishing town on the northern coast, there was a sharp turn on a winding road just a stone's throw from the waters. Locals called it "Dead Man's Curve," and it had claimed many victims long before Charles Parker. It was Christmas Day in 1932. Before sharing the holiday with his wife, Bess, and their five children, Parker ran a Christmas bootleg whiskey run to help pay for the presents under the tree. There is no official account of what happened to Parker that day, but it is believed that Parker rounded Dead Man's Curve, lost control of his car, swerved off the road, and crashed, causing injuries that would later prove fatal.

In the hospital, before succumbing to his injuries, his final request to his brother Eben was that he take care of Bess and the children. Taking the plea to heart—and perhaps too far—Eben soon married his brother's widow and took Bess and the five children into a cramped house built on stilts, across the road from Young's Bay in Astoria. Eben and Bess would later add a daughter to the family.

One of Charles and Bess's children was a rambunctious and preternaturally driven young man named Frank, who was just twelve when his uncle became his stepfather. At the age of fourteen, Frank joined his brothers and uncle hauling garbage, rocks, construction materials, and any load that commanded a rate, giving a good portion of his earnings to the family to buy goods. Parker did not shy away from hard work, and he did not complain—a theme that he would carry with him the rest of his life. But every Christmas Day, in the dark corner of the bedroom, he cried, thinking of his father.

Raised Catholic, Parker was a student at Saint Mary Star of the Sea in Astoria, a Catholic grade school. But though his school provided him with a familiar social environment and a religious structure that allowed a rough, working-class kid to thrive academically, as he grew older, bigger, and stronger, so did his interest in playing football competitively, and Saint Mary Star of the Sea did not have a program. So, with his parents' support, he left Saint Mary Star of the Sea to attend Astoria Junior High School.

At Astoria, he met Peggy Prouty, who stood just four-foot-eleven and weighed barely ninety pounds—her tiny fingers were engulfed in Parker's large hands. Peggy's father owned the Warrington Lumber Mill, giving Peggy and her eight siblings an upper-middle-class existence, while Parker continued to struggle to help his family meet its needs. But he insisted on paying for their dates, so he would find the most economical route possible, taking her on rides in the garbage trucks and using her petite stature and youthful look to pay for one adult and one kid's ticket at the local movie theater.

Parker had always been large for his age, and he grew to six feet by his senior year in high school, his height complemented by sparkling blue eyes and sandy-blond hair. He was a man among boys. His prowess on the football field earned him acclaim and, perhaps, a chance to make more out of his life—to make himself more worthy of Peggy—than he could as a manual laborer. He decided his ticket was a football scholarship offer from Oregon State.

Parker enrolled in January of 1939, and once there, he joined the Reserve Officers' Training Corps (ROTC) like most incoming freshman men and soon pledged Phi Delta Theta, along with several teammates. Parker supported himself by working odd jobs on and off campus. He withdrew from school briefly in December of 1940, struggling with his classes in agriculture, but he returned weeks later for the spring semester, now an education major, thinking that maybe a career as a coach and teacher was in the cards. He and Peggy, who by this time worked in the Bumble Bee tuna cannery in Astoria, remained in touch and visited on weekends or holidays. Parker played on the freshman football team and then contributed sparingly to the varsity squad as a sophomore in 1940. By 1941, he was poised for a breakout season, and Stiner planned to use him at quarterback, center, and guard.

The opening third of the 1941 Oregon State schedule was daunting, with a visit to USC and games against Washington and Stanford, prompting one columnist to write, "It would be a miracle if Oregon State wins even one of its first three games." Yet Stiner was quietly gaining confidence in his team's prospects at the end of fall camp, going so far as to declare that OSC would "not finish far out of the first division" in the Pacific Coast Conference.

Stiner saw raw talent in some, obvious talent in others, but, most important, a willingness of his players to be coached. If he could get the players to play better than they were capable of, he thought they could go toe-to-toe with the big boys on the schedule. They wouldn't necessarily be bigger, faster, or stronger than their opponents, but surely this group of ordinary boys could flush out some extraordinary effort on Saturdays.

USC had suffered an uncharacteristically down 1940 season but had won two Rose Bowls in three years. Howard Jones, the Trojans' legendary coach (and coach of Duke in 1924), had died after suffering a heart attack in late July, and Stiner and assistants Hal Moe and Jim Dixon had no success collecting reliable intelligence on the strategies of his replacement, Sam Barry, Jones's former assistant coach.

The crowd was overwhelming at the Los Angeles Memorial Coliseum for the September 27 opener, and some of the younger OSC players seemed a bit bewildered by the spectacle, few having seen crowds of more than thirty thousand. But Stiner's reliance on offensive stars Don Durdan and Bob Dethman proved efficient, leading Oregon State to twenty-one first downs while completing fourteen of twenty-one pass attempts. The defensive adjustments, which had reflected a near-complete overhaul from the previous season, were holding their own, with OSC limiting USC to just ten first downs and one touchdown.

The defense held—that is, until the last thirteen seconds of the fourth quarter, when USC scored on a touchdown pass to clinch the home win.

It was a tough loss, but Oregon State could take heart—and the West Coast writers took notice—in knowing that they could compete with the best. But neither Stiner nor his players could imagine where their season would take them.

PART II

THE WINDS OF WAR

This generation is to be tested as by fire. I earnestly hope that every one of you tested by fire may prove to be of true gold.

—William Few, Duke University president,
Convocation, October 6, 1940

4. A WARNING

Inside the Duke University Chapel walls, just two weeks before passing away on October 16, 1940, from a coronary thrombosis, Duke president William Few addressed more than one thousand students gathered for a convocation. Four months earlier, Duke University had pledged full cooperation with the federal government to support a potential war effort in any way. And a month before Few spoke, with ominous developments in World War II in Europe, the United States Congress had passed the Selective Training and Service Act of 1940. The threat of American intervention in the war was real.

War did not suddenly creep upon the Duke campus or, for that matter, America. In fact, it had been building for years. In Europe, World War I and the peace that followed had left many unresolved issues about power, economics, and liberty, and the worldwide Depression created instability in many nation-states, Germany among them.

In 1933, Adolf Hitler rose to power, and his Nazi Party went about abolishing democracy and promoting the master race. Hitler set out to reclaim lands Germany had lost as a result of the Treaty of Versailles at the Paris Peace Conference. Germany entered into an alliance with Benito Mussolini and Italy, and in March 1938, Germany took control of Austria. After Hitler set his sights on Czechoslovakia, in September the leaders of Great Britain, France, and Italy joined Hitler in signing the Munich Agreement, which ceded the border regions of Czechoslovakia to Germany in exchange for vague promises of peace. Six months later, Germany took the rest of Czechoslovakia by force. In August 1939, Hitler and Joseph Stalin signed a nonaggression pact. A week later, Germany invaded Poland, and shortly thereafter Stalin joined in the conflict to carve up Poland between the Soviet Union and Germany. For much of the next eight months, there was little action in the so-called Phony War, as the Allies instituted an economic and military blockade of Germany and the German army redeployed troops and prepared for "Case Yellow," an invasion of the low countries and France in the spring of 1940.

In April and May 1940, Germany seized Norway, Denmark, the Netherlands, Belgium, and Luxembourg and broke through into France, occupying Paris on June 14, 1940. In July, the Germans began the Battle of Britain, but were held off by the Hurricanes and Spitfires of the Royal Air Force. The Luftwaffe then turned to bombing cities, putting the British people through a trying time known as the Blitz.

Meanwhile, most Americans were indifferent to the battles waged on faraway shores. America had rejected the Treaty of Versailles and the Covenant of the League of Nations at the conclusion of World War I, and in the 1930s, with isolationists pushing their agenda, Congress passed the Neutrality Acts, forbidding trade with belligerent nations and keeping America far from war. But that didn't stop preparations.

Since the end of World War I, the army had experimented with tanks, the Signal Corps had developed new communication techniques, the Marines took the lead on amphibious landings, and war contingency plans had been drawn up. The 1920 National Defense Act permitted an army of up to 280,000 soldiers, but until 1939, Congress hadn't funded the army to support even half that number. Military commanders decided to focus on a homeland defense strategy, with the navy as the front line, believing all along that Americans would not support intervention in the growing conflicts in Europe and Asia.

As war raged in Europe in the late 1930s, President Franklin Roosevelt took limited—but needed—measures to protect American interests. General George Marshall, head of the U.S. Army, and FDR ordered new war plans to be created as well as a limited preparedness campaign to protect the Panama Canal and the U.S. mainland from aerial attacks. Thus, greater emphasis was placed on—and more money went toward—the U.S. Army Air Corps, the precursor to the U.S. Air Force.

In September of 1939, the president declared a limited national emergency and approved an increase in the size of the army and National Guard. For its part, Congress began to chip away at the provisions of the Neutrality Acts, allowing for the sale of munitions to France and Britain. As for the populace, 46 percent of Americans believed the United States would end up in the European war with the outbreak of hostilities, yet many, like Charles Lindbergh, were urging Americans to stay out of the war. Washington & Jefferson College in Pennsylvania began teaching a course on World War II to educate its students, who might one day fight in it.

American industry had already begun to feel the impact of looming war, with government and the private sector spending in the billions for everything from airplanes to tires. In the wake of the fall of France in June 1940, when munitions began to flow to Great Britain and to an expanding U.S. military, war production increased at a steady rate.

As the disturbing events in Europe sped up, so did America's preparations for war. The army held full-scale maneuvers in 1940, and in August, Congress approved inducting the National Guard into federal service and called up the reserves. By the summer of 1940, just one in fourteen Americans supported the United States entering the war immediately, but five in eight believed it would enter it eventually. Meanwhile, 42 percent believed that the Germans would invade America if they defeated the British, and 48 percent believed that there were "fifth columnists" already working secretly in America in September 1940.

That same month, when the Selective Training and Service Act of 1940 was passed, America transferred fifty World War I destroyers to Britain in exchange for air bases in the Atlantic and the Caribbean.

The world was becoming an increasingly dangerous place when President Few addressed the Duke student body that day in October 1940 with a warning to a community that, at the time, rested on hope and not reality, which was dismissive instead of vigilant, ambivalent rather than committed.

> *I profoundly sympathize with you young people of this generation. Under any probable, even possible, eventualities you are bound for a hard world. Nothing soft and weak will save you. Hard circumstances can save you if you have the root of the matter in you. Remember always that storms are the test of seamanship. Without severe testings true character can hardly be developed.*
>
> *This generation is to be tested as by fire. I earnestly hope that every one of you tested by fire may prove to be of true gold.*

In March 1941, the passage of the Lend-Lease Act gave the president authority to sell, transfer, or lease war goods to any country whose defense the president deemed vital to the United States. President Roosevelt declared that America would be the "arsenal of democracy," and while he didn't totally commit America to the growing global conflict, he was inching it closer.

American and British military strategists were already working together on war plans, pending the eventuality of the United States entering the war. By June, the army had twenty-seven infantry, five armored divisions, and two cavalry divisions along with thirty-five air groups in various stages of readiness, a far cry from a sustainable and effective force with which to go to war. In September the U.S. Navy began to convoy ships into the mid-Atlantic.

Just before the start of fall classes at Duke and Oregon State in 1941, Roosevelt, Winston Churchill, and a bevy of admirals and generals met on Placentia Bay in Newfoundland. The meeting had been eight months in the making, as Churchill had been pressing to meet with FDR to establish a relationship to further draw the United States into aiding Great Britain. The key outcome was the Atlantic Charter, whose principles were supported by twenty-six nations. It would be the first of many war councils for FDR and the prime minister.

In July and August, Japan invaded Indochina, and the United States and Britain ended trade with the empire. America had a small military presence in the Philippines under General Douglas MacArthur, eight hundred miles from Japanese territory, with just sixteen thousand soldiers enjoying peacetime duty, including multiple rounds of golf and trips to the beaches. And in Hawaii, Lieutenant General Walter Short was in command of forty-three thousand troops.

There had long been a growing threat from Japan. The empire needed natural resources like iron ore, rubber, tin, and petroleum for its industries, and China and Southeast Asia were potential sources. But further afield lay the lucrative islands of the Dutch East Indies. The 1931 Japanese invasion of Manchuria sparked tension between the empire and the West, with militarists fanning the flames of angst with expansionist policies and increasingly threatening actions in the following years. In 1933, Japan withdrew from the League of Nations, protesting the league's belated condemnation of the invasion of Manchuria, and in 1937 it provoked a full-scale war with China, pushing the United States to begin to curtail trade in an attempt to force the Japanese to back down. When Japan signed the Tripartite Pact with Germany and Italy in 1940, promising assistance if any of the countries was attacked by a fourth party not currently involved in the world war, the United States responded with greater support in money and materials to its allies, including the Chinese.

The United States closed the Panama Canal to Japanese ships and embargoed metal shipments to Japan, on which Japan relied. In October 1940, Admiral James Richardson, commander of the Pacific Fleet, requested from the secretary of the navy and the chief of naval operations that his ships in the Pacific should not remain at Pearl Harbor in Hawaii, as President Roosevelt had ordered as a show of strength to Japan. Richardson believed that the forword positioning of the fleet far from its main base in San Diego compromised its readiness. Richardson would end up being replaced for his protests.

Since early 1940, some in Japan believed that after it invaded Western colonies, the United States would engage Japan in war, and therefore, Japan ought to inflict damage on the Americans' capabilities before they could strike. In early 1941, multiple attack plans were in place for the Japanese empire, including one calling for simultaneous strikes against the Philippines, Guam, and Pearl Harbor. With the help of spies on the islands of Hawaii, the Japanese were confident that a strike on Pearl Harbor would be devastating for the Americans.

To try to avert more agitation, Japan and the United States entered into discussions in 1941, but relations did not improve. The United States froze Japanese assets in late July and, on August 1, embargoed oil and gasoline—a major tactic, as, at the time, Japan relied on the United States for more than 80 percent of its oil imports. By November, Secretary of State Cordell Hull and Japanese ambassador Kichisaburo Nomura were meeting regularly to negotiate terms, but still to no avail.

In September 1941, 110 young men opened the naval ROTC unit at Duke, a program that Josiah Bailey, a United States senator from North Carolina, had worked hard to launch for months. The old gymnasium at Duke housed the ROTC program, one of twenty-seven operating on campuses around the country. But the ROTC was not the only sign of local activism; in the summer of 1941, the Women of Durham organized a chapter of the American Women's Voluntary Services. Noncredit courses were offered in first aid, physical education, lifesaving, home nursing, and knitting to support the British war relief. Of course, Fort Bragg was just ninety miles from Durham, and some of the young men on campus had either volunteered for service or would soon be drafted. War was around them, but still, many students at the private school opposed any American intervention and believed they would never end up fighting, in contrast to the opinion of the American public.

In his commencement address at Duke in June 1941, Dr. Alexander Loudon, British minister to the United States, delivered a stern warning:

> *But now it has been forcefully impressed upon us; just as every Christian must redeem himself every day, so must every democrat redeem his liberty every day. Freedom was not given to our ancestors to be inherited by us intact and unimpaired. Only by eternal vigilance, by never diminishing battle against the forces that would destroy it can we be assured of our liberty.*

Oregon State was public in every way that Duke was private. Part of the mission of every academic department within the college was to serve the people of the state of Oregon and to work with local industry. Partnerships in forestry, food production, farming, and horticulture were the norm. Oregon State had forty-two campus buildings on two hundred acres, with another thirty thousand acres of owned and leased lands for agricultural or forestry research throughout the state. The majority of Oregon State students came from rural areas within the state, many from parents whose children would be the first to earn degrees. There was a transient nature to Oregon State in the first half of the twentieth century, with students enrolling and then withdrawing and then reenrolling based on financial needs and circumstances on their family farms.

A major difference between Oregon State and Duke at the time was the emphasis placed on the military. Defense activities were taking place on the Corvallis campus long before they were at most other institutions of higher learning, including a heavy emphasis on ROTC, as it was mandatory for every freshman and sophomore male student under the age of twenty-six to be enrolled in ROTC. Every federal land grant school was required to have some form of military training for able-bodied men—a policy stemming from the post–Civil War era—and many of those young men filled the lines of ROTC.

A wide variety of science and engineering classes, necessary for defense and military purposes, was offered, and in 1939, the Department of Mechanical Engineering offered a flight training program, building on its predecessor, the civilian pilot training course. When the draft began in 1940, Oregon State ROTC students drilled on old World War I equipment and machinery, and OSC alums returned to campus to train the new crop of recruits. The Army Air Corps, Navy, and Marines routinely put on displays of power and showmanship in Corvallis to attract recruits who otherwise faced being drafted into the army.

In October 1941, the Army Air Corps offered enlistment for applicants who had two or more years of college credit by January of 1942; applicants had to be between the ages of twenty and twenty-six, unmarried, and have excellent health and character and perfect vision. Only 5 percent of applicants were accepted.

In the fall, the Office of Production Management requested that men studying certain subjects—such as medicine, pharmacology, and science—receive deferments, and Oregon State announced the creation of a campus committee of professors and others to make recommendations on deferments to local draft boards based on student curriculum. Also in October, the Oregon State Extension Service was expanded and developed programs to increase food production for the state, as many laborers began to leave for the military.

But the incident that offered perhaps the best illustration of just how close war was to Corvallis took place on Halloween 1941. In a preplanned and well-publicized drill, the Army Air Corps scheduled a practice bombing raid on the West Coast, including fifty bombers, one hundred twenty-five pursuit planes, and a series of five "bombings" on cities and towns, including Corvallis. As part of the drill, the army oversaw the first citywide blackout, initiated by a warning system, a series of whistles, and fire department sirens. During the blackout, all lights on campus and in the city were required to be turned off, and, with police enforcement, all drivers had to pull off to the side of the road. The drill came on the same day that word reached the States that the destroyer USS *Reuben James* had been sunk by a German torpedo off Iceland.

While the world was on fire, the boys playing football at Oregon State and Duke focused on the here and now, which for both teams meant a daunting run of games. War was something for the newspapers. For now.

5. A TEAM OF DESTINY

WITH THE OPENING VICTORIES over Wake Forest and Tennessee, the excitement of Duke football in 1941 only grew. Wins over Maryland, Colgate, and Pittsburgh came next, and Duke was being mentioned as a potential Rose Bowl and Sugar Bowl participant. Actually, after just four games, and even before the Pittsburgh game, newspapers in multiple cities reported that Duke had already received an unconditional invitation to play in the January 1 Sugar Bowl in New Orleans. Though no sources were quoted, it is believed that Sugar Bowl officials had put out feelers to Duke on an invite. Wallace Wade was not happy.

"Despite all other stories to the contrary," responded Wade to the speculation, "Duke has received no official invitation from any postseason bowl. Duke is not seeking, and never has sought, a bowl bid."

And then his obvious anger at the reports took hold.

"This is a very inopportune time for anyone to be thinking or talking postseason contests with one of the hardest games on our schedule—that with Georgia Tech—coming up. I personally think it very doubtful that we will accept any bowl invitation, even if we were lucky enough to win our remaining four games."

Whether Wade was simply downplaying a potential bowl bid so his players would focus on Georgia Tech or whether he was serious in his assertion that he was "doubtful" Duke would play in a bowl game, his words did little to quell the buzz around his team. They defeated Georgia Tech and then Davidson and sat at 7–0, with a top-five ranking, and just two Triangle opponents remaining.

Duke could be a candidate for one, maybe two, bowls—and that was *if* they finished strong and wanted to play an additional game and the faculty and administration were supportive. For now, their sights were set on their rival in Chapel Hill, just eight miles from Duke's campus—the same UNC team that had delivered a crushing loss to the Blue Devils the prior season. To commemorate the upcoming event, Duke students built a thirty-foot bonfire and held an all-night vigil, with freshmen standing guard to protect landmarks from UNC pranks.

The Blue Devils easily defeated North Carolina 20–0, and then on November 22, with Winston Siegfried, Steve Lach, Mike Karmazin, Tommy Prothro, Bob Barnett, and Al Piasecky, among the seniors playing their last regular-season game in a Duke uniform, the Blue Devils trounced the North Carolina State Wolfpack 55–6, with a 26–6 advantage in first downs and amassing 524 yards of offense.

At the end of the game, Duke students rushed the field and carried the players off in grand college football tradition. Lach broke down in tears. Wallace Wade—who had posted another perfect regular season to go along with his 1920 campaign at Fitzgerald-Clarke; his 1925, 1926, and 1930 seasons at Alabama; and, of course, his unbeaten and untied Iron Dukes of 1938—showed as much emotion as players would see him muster, with a semi-smile.

But the prospect of a final, triumphant battle on a national scale could not be ignored, and the question still lingered as to whether Duke would be invited to a bowl game—and, if so, would it accept?

It is unlikely that many in the crowd of twenty-five thousand at Portland's Multnomah Field in October 1941 noticed the Oregon State substitute for Washington kicker Elmer Berg's extra point try. Berg's teammate Bob Erickson had just scored a touchdown to punch back after Don Durdan's electrifying eighty-yard TD run, and though Berg's extra-point attempt was routine, the five-foot-ten Oregon State end looking to block the kick was not. Jack Yoshihara was a Japanese American playing major college football. The mere fact that he was in uniform was a testament to his fortitude and determination to overcome the challenges of being in a select minority at a time when discrimination was rampant.

The Japanese influence on the Northwest began in 1834, when three Japanese fishermen washed ashore several miles south of Cape Flattery, on the coast of Washington. Over the next century, especially between 1885 and 1924, more Japanese would arrive, most looking for fortune in the promised land of the American West but ultimately settling as day laborers building a society for others. They were called Issei, mostly second-born sons who would not inherit their fathers' wealth in Japan and who looked for new opportunities across the Pacific Ocean.

The 1890 national census counted just twenty-five Issei living in Oregon, though certainly the number was much higher. With the explosion of railroad construction—and with it, jobs—the Japanese population in Oregon soared to more than two thousand five hundred in just ten years.

The SS *Hawaii Maru* arrived in Oregon on April 12, 1924, completing a long journey from Kobe, Japan. As it turned out, the *Maru* would be one of the last ships full of Japanese immigrants allowed to enter the United States until 1952, as American immigration restrictions took hold. On board was Natsuno Yoshihara, a twenty-seven-year-old mother of two. She was returning to America—having initially come over as a picture bride before the practice declined. She married, divorced, bore a daughter, and was pregnant with a son when she returned to Japan after the death of her mother. According to the teachings of Buddhism, the spirit of the head of a family remains in a house for three years after death, so Yoshihara and her two young children, including the baby boy, Chiaki, remained in Japan until the spring of 1924.

When they returned to the States on board the *Maru,* Chiaki was given the American name of "Jack," and his mother remarried and, with her new husband, opened a restaurant in southeast Portland, where Jack would spend his time when he wasn't in school or competing in sports. In the early 1900s, Portland had become the hub of Japanese life in Oregon, and Japantown stretched from Ankeny to Glisan Streets, on the northwest side of the city. The arrivals soon established schools, organized community boards, and sponsored youth sports teams. As much as possible, the Issei maintained their culture and traditions, like cooking *manju,* a sweet bun filled with beans.

This was the city that Yoshihara grew up in, with friends who talked and looked like him, acknowledging but not quite understanding as a child the two worlds he inhabited: the familiar one inside the Japanese American community and the society outside its borders. The young children attended public schools during the day but spent as much as two hours a day, including Saturdays, in Japanese language schools, as education was a central tenet of Japanese culture.

From a very young age, athletics played an immense role in Yoshihara's life. First, it was the traditional sports of judo and kendo and sumo. Then basketball. Ultimately, it was football that consumed his time, though he still traveled to Seattle and San Francisco and Los Angeles for sports tournaments for Japanese Americans. At five-foot-ten and 205 pounds, Yoshihara was big among his peers and, at the time, a decent size for a football player. He loved the physicality of the sport he played at Benson Polytechnic High School in Portland, but he also loved the art of the sport, and he spent his afternoons drop-kicking the football fifty yards until darkness took over.

His athletic abilities and good grades earned him a scholarship to Oregon State in 1940, where he would play with the freshman team as an end, showing remarkable quickness and toughness. He was an underdog not because of size or physicality but rather the rarity of Japanese Americans playing college football. When the 1941 season rolled around, Yoshihara was one of many sophomores just looking for a way onto the field, beyond playing on the scout team in practice. Against Washington, in the second game of the season, he got his chance.

On the snap of the ball on the Washington extra-point attempt that would have tied the game, Yoshihara exploded off the line of scrimmage. Perhaps his adrenaline carried him too far as he leaped a second before the kicker made contact and actually jumped over the airborne football. Fortunately enough, Berg's kick sailed wide. A late safety gave Oregon State a 9–6 win and a 1–1 record, with their biggest test just days away.

Stanford coach Clark Shaughnessy's men had not lost a game in two years behind the famed offensive "T formation," yet OSC held Stanford in check in a 10–0 victory. An inexplicable loss the following week to Washington State, however, left Lon Stiner's team at 2–2. But victories over Idaho, UCLA, and California put them in a tie for first place in the Pacific Coast Conference after Washington State upset Stanford with just two games remaining, against Montana and rival Oregon. Many pundits and members of the media were surprised by Oregon State's success, but not Stiner, who believed all along that his team could compete with the best. A victory over Montana set up a do-or-die game against their bitter rivals.

OSC was 5–2 in conference play, and a Rose Bowl berth would likely be decided on the last day of the regular season, with the conference champion headed to Pasadena. But with Pacific Coast Conference teams' fortunes changing seemingly week to week, there were several scenarios that could present themselves: there could be a five-way tie for first place, a tie between Stanford and OSC, or one of the teams could win the league outright and earn the conference's automatic berth in the Rose Bowl. In 1916, Oregon faced off against its rival with a Rose Bowl berth on the line. They won 27–0 in Corvallis. Could Lon Stiner's boys return the favor?

In November of 1894, OAC defeated Oregon 16–0 in the first clash between the rivals separated by forty-seven miles. It was a mild-mannered affair, with players, coaches, and spectators more curious than fiery. That was no longer the case in 1896, when members of both teams placed blame on the referee for awarding a score, which led to the official being punched in the face and postgame accusations that players had deliberately tried to hurt their opponents.

Ten years later, in 1906, Oregon coaches accused OAC coach Fred Norcross of ordering his players to water down the field in Corvallis to slow down the Webfeet, perhaps one reason why the men from OAC won the game. But it wasn't until the 1910 clash that things turned really ugly. After a 12–0 Oregon win at Bell Field, Oregon students stormed the field and clashed with Oregon State students. When former Oregon star Fred Moullen drove a car onto the field, OAC star right tackle Tom May confronted Moullen, and things escalated quickly, leaving one student in the hospital. The postgame riots of 1910 convinced both schools to cancel the game in 1911. It was reinstated at a neutral site in Albany for 1912 and 1913, when opposing student bodies had to enter through separate gates to prevent clashes.

The rivalry games eventually returned and soon earned the moniker "the Civil War" as the institutions faced one another every season. During a 1934 Oregon win, players from both teams got into a fistfight during the second quarter, and two years later, after an Oregon State win in Eugene, another postgame confrontation ensued, and some OSC students stole Oregon's mascot—a live duck. And it wasn't over. Two days later, a caravan of OSC students drove to Eugene to continue the celebration, leading to more fisticuffs. In 1937, after an Oregon State 14–0 win, two thousand OSC students not only celebrated the next evening in Corvallis but took the party down to Eugene the following day, leading to multiple fracases and reports of tomatoes and water balloons being thrown about. Oregon students captured a few OSC students, stripping them naked, dipping their behinds in yellow paint, and making them slide down the gigantic *O* plastered on a hillside.

The young men preparing to clash in 1941 knew full well about the history of the rivalry—and about each other. They were high school teammates and the sons of farmers from the same small Oregon towns. The animosity was certainly greater between the student bodies than between the players, but that didn't mean an extra chop block at the knees or hit out of bounds was out of the question.

Stiner's mind-set as he prepared his team for its game with Oregon was that a team should focus only on what it can control. A spirited rivalry game was taking place between Stanford and California in Palo Alto on the very same day. But both games *did* matter, and the entire town of Corvallis talked about little else in the days leading up to the game but the potential of a Rose Bowl bid. Players were bombarded by encouragement from faculty and students, Stiner patiently obliged countless local and national media requests for interviews, and Director of Athletics Percy Locey, understanding the economic significance of a Rose Bowl berth, quietly worked on potential Rose Bowl selection plans should the Beavers win.

The weather in the days leading up to the game was typical of November in Oregon—cold, windy, and wet. Though Don Durdan had recovered from a bout of influenza, his teammates were feeling the wrath of the virus, with Boyd Clement and Glenn Byington fighting the same strand (likely by sipping water out of the same metal ladle during practices and games) and George Peters struggling to get back on the field after three days in the infirmary. At Friday's practice, as he ran the varsity against the freshman scouts, mimicking Oregon offensive plays, Stiner was still not sure who would suit up the next day.

This would be a game that could put Oregon State on the national map and garner attention from a national audience in the Rose Bowl.

At least on the surface, OSC was full of bravado.

"There is no rule in the book about how hard we should tackle the other guy," Bob Dethman was quoted as saying in a Friday paper before the climactic game, "but by the time we get through with Oregon they will wish there was such a rule."

Friday night, a car rally at 7:30 P.M. was followed by a traditional cheer rally, and at 10:30 A.M. on Saturday, November 29, OSC players, students, and the band boarded a train in Corvallis for the trip to Eugene. They arrived shortly after noon and marched to Hayward Field for the showdown. The visitors dressed in a cramped locker room underneath the Hayward Field stands. Twenty thousand tickets had been sold, and hotel rooms in Eugene were at a premium.

"This one is frosting on the cake," Stiner reminded his players before kickoff. "If you win, you got it all." He was interrupted by a knock at the door.

"Two minutes, Mr. Stiner," a voice beckoned from outside the door.

Stiner attempted to open the door to lead his team out, but it appeared to be locked from the outside. He jiggled the doorknob in frustration before backing up and sizing up the door.

"They aren't going to keep us in here!" Stiner exclaimed, suggesting that this was an unsportsmanlike ploy by home team Oregon. He took four steps back and, with the loud, enthusiastic encouragement of his players, burst through the locked doors, knocking them off their hinges. (The locked-door incident would be much talked and written about in the days and years after the game, with wide speculation that Stiner had orchestrated the stunt to fire up his players.)

The University of Oregon was led by halfback Curtis Mecham, who was a force on both sides of the ball. To counter a strong rushing attack and a line that outweighed his own by twelve pounds per man, Stiner moved Martin Chaves back to the secondary on defense. The crowd in the stands was loud, the student bodies doing their best to out-cheer the other as Norm Peters's opening kick sailed out of bounds at the Oregon thirty-five.

Oregon suffered a blow when Tommy Roblin was knocked out with a shoulder injury on the third play of the game, just another devastating injury for Coach Tex Oliver's team, which came in short on players. Mecham took over signal-calling duties as the teams exchanged punts throughout much of the first period. Late in the first period, Don Durdan connected with Dethman on a twenty-eight-yard pass play down to the Oregon thirty-four as the period came to an end. But OSC failed to score. The teams exchanged fumbles and interceptions in the remaining minutes and went into halftime scoreless.

"Well, we can win this one!" Stiner bellowed as he walked into a quiet Oregon State locker room. He went up to the chalkboard and—like a mad scientist—began to scribble as he designed a play before his players' own eyes. The play was intended to get the ball to back Joe Day. Stiner was so convinced it would work that his players left the locker room fired up and confident they would win this game.

The scoreboard finally changed midway through the third period when, after a fifteen-yard unnecessary roughness penalty gave OSC a first and goal from the three, Choc Shelton rumbled through the center of the line in a hole he would later describe as "Pasadena Avenue." Warren Simas's extra-point attempt sailed wide in the wind. Oregon State: 6; Oregon: 0.

Though his team was in the lead, Durdan was having a game to forget, fumbling in the first half and, more crucially, at a moment late in the third period, coughing up the ball on a reverse, giving Oregon the ball on OSC's thirteen. But a sack, a fumble, and two dropped passes bailed him out and kept OSC in the lead.

The final period got under way with Oregon lined up at their own forty-seven. OSC was fifteen minutes from a miracle Rose Bowl when Mecham took off with the ball. The Beavers missed tackles, as Oregon's Duke Iverson, Tony Crish, and Jimmy Newquist delivered crushing blocks. Mecham outran Durdan for a fifty-three-yard touchdown run. The extra point by Newquist was good, and Oregon took a 7–6 lead.

It began to look like the Civil War might be won by the home team.

Durdan passed to George Zellick and then to George Peters to pick up valuable yardage on Oregon State's next possession. Day gained a first down just inside Oregon territory. Dethman ran around the right end for nine yards for an OSC first down at Oregon's twenty-eight-yard line. Day took the snap, dove forward behind the right side of the line, and appeared to be stopped but suddenly exploded from the pile, jumping to the right, eluding tacklers, and rambling in for a touchdown before a crowd that included his parents, who had just arrived after their car broke down on the side of the highway en route to the game. Simas's unreliable foot was true to form as he missed the extra point, but at 12–7, OSC had the lead with nine minutes remaining.

The teams exchanged drives and punts, and Oregon had one last chance to tie or win the game in the remaining minutes. Coach Oliver went for broke, calling for trick plays and misdirections. His unconventional approach seemed to work initially, but Oliver's luck ran out when Oregon lateraled four times on one play before fumbling, with OSC recovering.

The Beavers stalled for the remaining seconds when referee Jack Friel blew the final whistle. It was over. The OSC players jumped on each other's backs, and their fans stood and cheered. News filtered into the press box that Stanford had lost to Cal 16–0, which confirmed that OSC had won its first Pacific Coast Conference championship and only its second conference title in its history. The Rose Bowl was a reality.

Rallies broke out on the OSC campus as students listened to the game on the radio and quickly spread to downtown Corvallis. The celebration lasted right up until players, college band members, and the OSC entourage disembarked the train as it pulled in to Corvallis Station. The train trip had tempered some players' general moods, as fatigue from a tough game and the subsequent adrenaline rush left Stiner's players exhausted and just looking to crash out on their beds. But the hundreds of spirited local supporters awaiting them would have none of it. A long motorcade, led by a car with a PA system attached to its roof, drove by, and spontaneous celebrations continued into the night.

They had done it. Stiner had convinced his players that they could do more throughout the season, and time and time again, they had. This effort sent them on the road to Pasadena.

By the time the coach walked in the front door of his Corvallis home on Saturday night, the incessant congratulatory phone calls and telegrams were already pouring in from family, friends, and members of the media, all looking for Rose Bowl tickets. The plan for the evening had already been mapped out by Percy Locey and Oregon State professor C. V. Ruzek, who, at the time, happened to be the chair of the Pacific Coast Conference and who would ultimately announce the official conference participant in the Rose Bowl. Though the PCC agreement with the Tournament of Roses had the conference champion earning the Rose Bowl slot, it would not be official until Ruzek received the formal votes from conference members anointing Oregon State as champion. Within three hours of the conclusion of the Oregon State victory over Oregon, the secret ballots via telegram with the code name "Used Automobiles" had been tallied, and the decision was unanimous.

That night, just hours after the conclusion of the Oregon State victory, the NBC radio network hosted by local radio host Bill Mock broadcast the announcement of Oregon State as a Rose Bowl participant. Thirty minutes before going live on air, Mock huddled with Ruzek, who would announce the selection and explain the voting process; Locey, who would discuss the selection of an opponent; and Stiner and Bob Dethman, who would provide enthusiastic answers to scripted, not terribly controversial questions, including "How does it feel to be the captain of the team on the day you win the game that places you in the Rose Bowl?," "Were you nervous when you first came on the field?," and "What did your wife have to say after the game?"

The broadcast went as planned, and the world now knew that a tiny agricultural school in the Northwest would be playing in the Rose Bowl.

Attention then turned to selecting an opponent, a task left to Locey, Stiner, Ruzek, and acting president F. A. Gilfillan. Discussions began around 10:00 P.M. and continued until 2:00 A.M. as anxious members of the media and students waited for an announcement. As the Pacific Coast champion, Oregon State could select its opponent, which was traditionally an East Coast or Midwest school with a national following that would help fill the Rose Bowl.

Top-ranked Minnesota, with Heisman Trophy winner Bruce Smith, was a member of the Big Ten Conference (soon to be the Big Nine, after the University of Chicago deemphasized sports), which did not allow its teams to participate in postseason games so as not to impact their academic studies, so they were out. Fordham was a logical choice and a popular selection among Oregon State players. But they were also in line for a Sugar Bowl bid with season-ending wins, and though the Rose Bowl was more prestigious in 1941, the Sugar Bowl also had a good-sized payout. Missouri was nationally ranked and Stiner's preferred choice, although it was well-known that they had also already been offered a spot in the Sugar Bowl. Texas was a strong candidate, but they had already played on the West Coast in 1941. Texas A&M and Mississippi State were potentials but didn't boast sexy enough résumés or fan bases, and Navy and Notre Dame did not play in bowl games.

The working group placed a call to Fordham officials late Saturday night (early morning in New York) but, not unexpectedly, did not reach them. Under pressure, their attention turned toward Missouri and then Duke. The Blue Devils had played a decent schedule, were ranked number two in offense and nationally, boasted good attendance numbers per game, and had drawn big crowds to prior Rose Bowls. And Wallace Wade was a national name, though still not a popular one in Southern California because of the cheeky response he'd given to the media about whether or not he would shake the hand of 1939 Rose Bowl hero Doyle Nave, on top of his pronouncement that he would never bring a team back to Pasadena.

Knowing both of their potential participants were in consideration for the Rose Bowl, Sugar Bowl officials made a $70,000 take-it-or-leave-it offer to Missouri and Fordham with a firm deadline of 10:00 A.M. on Sunday. Unsure of what the Rose Bowl was going to do and afraid to lose the Sugar Bowl invite, Missouri coach Don Faurot accepted the offer from New Orleans. According to Faurot, fifteen minutes after accepting the bid, the Rose Bowl officials called. On Sunday, Missouri and Fordham were announced as Sugar Bowl opponents.

Years after the fact, Locey continued to insist that Duke was the only team to receive an invitation.

Meanwhile, still unsure of a landing spot and hoping for a Rose Bowl invite based on rampant speculation, on Sunday Duke students and players huddled around teletypes at the Durham offices of the *Durham Morning Herald* newspaper waiting for word. When the official invite finally came from the West Coast, cars began to stream down Main Street, horns honking, coeds hanging out of windows. Word spread to campus, and the cheers from impromptu celebrations could be heard throughout Durham.

The reception in Southern California wasn't quite so enthusiastic.

When the Duke selection was announced from the press box during the Loyola-Nevada football game in Los Angeles, there was a thunderous round of boos. West Coast scribes who harbored strong feelings against Wade took to the papers to lambaste Oregon State for the selection, saying Duke was unworthy, their schedule was weak, and their coach, in the words of one writer, "has no con-man in him at all, no diplomatic savvy, no 'side' as the Anglicans say. And he's much too immersed in himself and the simple pattern of his life to think of his effect upon others."

With his season complete a week earlier, Wade had traveled first to Philadelphia to attend the annual Army-Navy game and then was a guest of his good friend George Munger at the Philadelphia Eagles–Chicago Bears game on Sunday. Munger's car was stolen from the Shibe

Park parking lot with Wade's luggage bag in it, but he still hopped a train to New York City for the *New York World-Telegram* Coach of the Year banquet honoring Frank Leahy at Leone's in Manhattan. Upon entering the restaurant, he encountered Fordham University coach Jim Crowley, who congratulated Wade not on the season, as the Duke coach initially believed, but on the berth in the Rose Bowl. That is how the coach learned of the invite.

After Duke administrators and Wade spoke, Duke officially accepted the invitation on the morning of December 1.

Oregon State administrators had held lengthy discussions even before the intrastate game about canceling classes for the Monday after the game, expecting a student celebration to interfere with teaching. But school officials had already granted students days off on select Fridays and Saturdays during the year, and as state officials were preparing to vote on reinstating a School of Commerce at Oregon State, the administration wanted to take no risks leading up to the vote—especially since the reason for the student holiday would be to celebrate a football game.

Still, students began to stream out of their classes midmorning. The chant of "Poor Duke!" resonated throughout the quad, and a student serpentine was formed, a half-mile human chain of excitement and school spirit. The line wrapped around buildings on campus, and soon students were either in the serpentine or in a car rally. A crowd of more than two thousand gathered in front of the Memorial Union, and students carried Stiner on their shoulders to the front steps to address the crowd as his players led their classmates in OSC fight songs.

The rally broke up around 11:00 A.M. for a convocation and dance. At the convocation inside the Memorial Union, members of the Rose Bowl team sat on a platform and listened as Bob Dethman thanked the crowd and encouraged them to make the trip to Pasadena. His buddy Bob Saunders commented afterward, "I haven't seen this much excitement since our sow back on the farm had sixteen pigs."

Meanwhile, in the athletic offices, the phones were ringing off the hook with ticket orders. As the host team, Oregon State was responsible for ticket sales and revenue distribution. It was decided that alumni would get first choice of tickets, followed by residents of the state of Oregon, in keeping with the mission of the land grant institution.

The standard Rose Bowl game contract had been amended since Duke last participated, in 1939, allowing for further distribution of Rose Bowl receipts to member schools of the host Pacific Coast Conference. Locey wrote to Wade detailing the changes and providing numbers from the 1941 game between Stanford and Nebraska, which resulted in a gate gross of more than $333,000. With expenses and additional revenue accounted for, there was roughly $320,000 for distribution, a far cry from the deficits of the early Tournament of Roses games. The Tournament received $71,000 in 1941, the PCC office received $25,000, Nebraska received approximately $100,000, Stanford received $50,000, and the PCC schools split the rest. Locey suggested to Wade that Duke could expect to receive a share similar to Nebraska's.

Hal Reynolds, the chairman of the football committee of the Tournament, immediately wrote to Wade welcoming him back to the Rose Bowl and requesting that Duke make it out to Pasadena by Christmas to help ensure strong ticket sales, as "neither Duke nor Oregon State have any considerable alumni in this area." He also listed the various annual Rose Bowl events, from parades to luncheons, that Duke would be expected to attend. Every day after the announcement, Wade received an invitation to a Hollywood luncheon, a movie studio tour, or some other Southern California event.

Locey and Oregon State publicity man Bud Forrester left for Pasadena on December 3 to set up the ticket office in Los Angeles. A two-way private phone line was established between the Union in Corvallis and the Rose Bowl office in Los Angeles to coordinate ticket sales. It was expected that one-quarter of Oregon State's 4,500-member student body would make the trip to Pasadena, and train tickets were offered at $17.50, with sleeping berths for two students costing extra. Student tickets for the game were $4.50. As Duke travel plans came into focus, Duke students were offered a package of round-trip train, hotel, and game tickets for $181.81.

By December 4, just seventy-two hours after formally accepting the invitation, Wade announced the team's travel itinerary, which would take the Blue Devils through Birmingham, Memphis, Dallas, and the Grand Canyon, with a stop in Lubbock, Texas, for practice. Duke planned to arrive on December 20, and would be headquartered at the famed Huntington Hotel in Pasadena, with a traveling party of ninety-six, Wade having elected to bring every player who came out for football in September, along with faculty, friends, and family. It was by far the largest Duke traveling party for a Rose Bowl, thirty more people than had traveled to the 1939 game.

In the days following the Oregon victory, Oregon State did not practice, as exams were taking place, but that did not mean that the players' attention was solely on their books. There was a dinner and fête in their honor in Portland—hastily arranged by the alumni association—and many congratulatory calls, telegrams, and ticket requests. Japantown in Portland was thrilled that one of their own would be playing on the big stage, and thus Jack Yoshihara was flooded with ticket requests from his proud community.

Meanwhile, Duke had not practiced for more than a week, believing that their season had ended with the win over NC State. Monday was a light practice day to get back into a football routine, followed by a more strenuous workout on Tuesday.

By December 6, a staff of more than thirty-five was working around the clock in the ticket office in Los Angeles. Wade had asked North Carolina State publicity man Dick Herbert to travel to Pasadena to represent Duke, as he had been to the 1939 game and was familiar enough with the Blue Devils to promote the team. The travel itineraries were set, the football planning was under way, and the most unexpected Rose Bowl matchup in history was just twenty-six days away.

6. INFAMY

On December 7, the typical beautiful early morning highlighted the sun-soaked beaches of Waikiki, in Hawaii, an oasis for tourists and businessmen and, on this particular morning, the football teams from Willamette University and San Jose State University. The teams had traveled together from the States to play the University of Hawaii and each other, but though Willamette had lost to the hosts 20–6 just the afternoon before, the young men from Willamette, a small college just forty miles from Oregon State coached by OSC alum Roy "Spec" Keene, were there for more than football—they were there for paradise.

On the lanai at the Moana Hotel, which first lured visitors to its beaches in 1901, Oregon state senator Douglas McKay, a big supporter of the local Willamette team, sat at a breakfast table with his daughter, Shirley, as planes suddenly began to fly at a low altitude over the harbor. "Just practice flights," the senator assured his daughter. Many of the Willamette and San Jose State players had already finished breakfast and were in front of the hotel, ready to board buses for a tour of the island—which included Pearl Harbor—when large explosions were heard in the distance.

"Just bombing drills."

San Jose State's co-captain Robert Hammill noticed large, periodic spouts of water coming from Pearl Harbor, about twelve miles to the east. "Just navy maneuvers," he shared with those around him.

The air outside the Moana began to fill with hazy black smoke and the stench of oil. The tour bus never arrived.

"Attention! This is no exercise. The Japanese are attacking Pearl Harbor. All army, navy, and Marine personnel to report to duty!"

At 8:08 A.M., the words came blaring over the radio by KGMB host Webley Edwards, who, ironically, had attended Oregon State before moving to Hawaii in the late 1920s. The boys from Willamette and San Jose State now knew that what they were seeing, hearing, and smelling was not a drill.

Back in mid-November, the American ambassador to Japan, Joseph Grew, had warned Washington that a surprise attack on the United States was possible. Operation Z, as it was code-named by the Japanese, was launched on November 26, when Vice Admiral Chūichi Nagumo commanded six aircraft carriers with 359 airplanes headed to Pearl Harbor. The shallow harbor was a perfect target for the Japanese: they could strike dozens of key military installations and naval ships in a short period of time, and if all went as planned, they could trap any escaping ships in the tiny harbor. Destroying the fleet would allow the Japanese to advance almost unchecked for months through the Dutch East Indies in search of oil, into Malaya for tin and rubber, and on to the Philippines, giving them a strategic base from which to launch attacks and protect the homeland. On November 30, after a call with Secretary of State Cordell Hull and his aides, President Roosevelt decided to cut short his vacation on Pine Mountain in Georgia and head back to the nation's capital.

In the late hours of December 6, Nagumo's command of thirty-three ships sailed two hundred miles west of Oahu in radio silence. A few minutes after midnight, five Japanese submarines prowled fewer than ten miles from shore, the lights of Waikiki—and the Moana Hotel—clearly visible. At 6:20 A.M., the first planes headed south and turned toward Oahu, and by 7:40 A.M., they had reached the shore, guided by transmissions from Honolulu radio stations. They broke into attack formations, one group flying inland to Wheeler Field, the other focused on Pearl Harbor.

The sailors and members of the Pacific Fleet were baby-faced young boys who had the choice assignment in the navy, their days filled with drills and maneuvers under impossibly blue skies, their nights spent under the stars with women and booze. The only real threat, the small country of Japan, was thousands of miles away—or so they'd thought.

Hickam Field and the naval air base at Ford Island were the first targets. The low-flying planes dropped their bombs one after another, the explosions waking the unsuspecting sailors, many of whom believed—like the college football players twelve miles away—that it was merely a readiness drill. While land installations were being attacked, Japanese torpedo planes took dead aim at the ships, skimming the surface above the waters of Pearl Harbor before releasing their deadly weapons. The USS *Oklahoma* was hit by multiple torpedoes and began to capsize, with sailors, many still in their underwear, jumping into the water to avoid the fires and the ultimate fate of the ship. The USS *Utah* was struck, and it sank in eight minutes. When the USS *Arizona* was hit at 8:10 A.M., more than one thousand crewmen were killed, many of them belowdecks. The explosion sparked enormous fires in the ammunition store, resulting in heat intense enough to literally burn the skin off many of the sailors. Soon there was enough thick black smoke in the harbor that even the Japanese pilots could not see their targets. As the American sailors realized one by one what was happening, they tried desperately to fire off their guns on board the ships and on land.

By 10:00 A.M., it was over. Eighteen American ships had been sunk, 170 planes destroyed, 2,403 Americans killed, and 1,178 more wounded. It would be more than two months before many of the surviving sailors could get word home to their loved ones that they were alive. The Japanese were modestly successful in their attack on Pearl Harbor in part due to a lack of American alertness and an inept use of intelligence information about Japan's intentions.

Within hours of the attacks, members of the Willamette and San Jose State football teams had been informally inducted into the army and the Hawaiian police force. They patrolled the streets with World War I–issue rifles and lined the beaches with barbed wire until they were able to leave the island on a ship bringing wounded men back to the States. Seven San Jose State players would remain in Hawaii and sign on as full-time Honolulu police officers.

Football meant nothing now.

Four thousand and seven hundred miles from the devastation in Pearl Harbor, Wallace Wade, after a morning at church and a couple of hours of casual reading, was in his old black Packard—thick exhaust smoke trailing his car as always—headed to his office at the old gymnasium on campus to attend to Rose Bowl preparations. Wade heard the news bulletin on the radio and called his wife from his office.

As word trickled across the Durham campus, Duke students huddled around the teletype once again in the *Durham Morning Herald* offices, just as they had a week prior, waiting for news on the Rose Bowl invitation. A late-afternoon special edition of *The Durham Sun* with a splashing headline informed the rest of the Duke community.

Most people hadn't even heard of Pearl Harbor before the attacks, but as the significance of the assault became clear, the Duke University campus was a mix of resignation about the fact that war had finally come and consternation about what it all meant for the futures of the men on campus—men like Durham native Charles Haynes. The loyal Eagle Scout knew that military service would one day beckon him, as it had his father and ancestors. He was not afraid, perhaps because, like so many boys his age, he believed that war was an extension of a game like football.

Most Duke professors postponed tests and lectures on Monday the eighth, choosing instead to discuss the geopolitical and military concerns of the students and allow them to share their fears. A student editorial in the Duke *Chronicle* on December 9 echoed some of the precarious and dark sentiments on campus.

> *The grim dance of death has begun in earnest. . . . One by one we shall realize that a heavy black curtain has been drawn across the future. . . . The whole American way of life will be distorted by our gigantic war effort, and Death will stalk freely up and down the land . . .*

Within days of the attacks, A. S. Brower, the campus director of the selective service, indicated that student deferments were likely to end, causing further panic from young men who'd believed that a Duke education might keep them out of uniform. Dean of Men Herbert J. Herring provided what reassurance he could at a Sunday chapel service.

Across the country, the news of the attacks on Pearl Harbor had a vastly different effect. Lon Stiner was on a recruiting-promotional trip with Hal Moe and Jim Dixon and basketball coach "Slats" Gill, driving to small towns around Oregon seeking the next Don Durdan. They called it the "green bean circuit," as they stopped at Kiwanis Clubs and high schools to spread the Oregon State gospel. They drove back to Corvallis on Sunday afternoon. The next morning, Stiner was up early as usual, dressed in a white shirt and a suit and headed to Palm Springs for PCC meetings, despite the attacks.

Overnight and into the morning, OSC players huddled around radios to receive the latest news from Hawaii. With so many of the players enrolled in ROTC already, and with a greater willingness to fight than many of their peers, they were confident they were going to war. As one student quoted in the student paper *The Barometer* remarked: "Glad that we are finally in war as long as there seemed to be no alternative."

Some of the students were so confident of their pending service, in fact, that they packed small duffel bags and headed to their hometowns, via train or automobile—some even hitchhiking—to be sure they got in as much time with their families as they could before their inevitable dispatch.

Frank Parker did not hesitate. He packed a small sack and hitchhiked back to Astoria to say good-bye to Peggy and his family. There was no hesitation on his part, perhaps because Parker always did what he had to do. Within hours, Stiner got word to every player involved in the exodus—including Parker—to return to campus immediately, for a failure to attend class or attend exams would make them ineligible for the Rose Bowl game. They listened to their coach, some incredulous that life would go on, including a return to practice.

Daily life for all citizens in Corvallis would change. The Western Defense Command and Fourth Army took control of the West Coast states, implementing a form of martial law. Radio stations in Oregon and Washington were ordered off the air, and guards were placed on all utilities and vital infrastructure locations. Airplane spotters were organized, and instructions on how to protect oneself against a gas attack were delivered through pamphlets—though gas masks were not.

Still, despite months of anticipation, many on the West Coast were not prepared for wartime. The practice blackouts and mock bombing raids in the fall of 1941 proved to have been ineffective, as San Francisco, Los Angeles, and Seattle struggled to get their citizens to follow blackout procedures.

Donald Hout, the chairman of the Civilian Defense of Benton County, announced that blackouts would continue every evening from 11:00 P.M. until 7:00 A.M., urging all citizens—including OSC students—to cooperate by staying inside, preventing light from being seen in homes and offices, and staying off the roads during those hours. With Oregon State still in the middle of exams, Hout requested that students studying past 12:30 A.M. place dark cardboard or blankets over their windows. Law enforcement had full authority to enforce the curfew.

On the evening of December 8, Americans gathered around the radio to listen to President Roosevelt's address to Congress.

> *Yesterday, December 7, 1941—a date which will live in infamy—the United States of America was suddenly and deliberately attacked by naval and air forces of the empire of Japan.*
>
> *The United States was at peace with that nation and at the solicitation of Japan, was still in conversation with its government and its emperor looking toward the maintenance of peace in the Pacific.*
>
> *Indeed, one hour after the Japanese air squadrons had commenced bombing in Oahu, the Japanese ambassador to the United States and his colleague delivered to our Secretary of State a formal reply to a recent American message. While the reply stated that it seemed useless to continue the existing diplomatic negotiations, it contained no threat or hint of war or armed attack.*
>
> *It will be recorded that the distance of Hawaii from Japan makes it obvious that the attack was deliberately planned many days or even weeks ago. During the intervening time, the Japanese government has deliberately sought to deceive the United States by false statements and expressions of hope for continued peace. . . .*
>
> *As Commander in Chief of the Army and Navy I have directed that all measures be taken for our defense. But always will our whole nation remember the character of the onslaught against us.*
>
> *No matter how long it may take us to overcome this premeditated invasion, the American people, in their righteous might, will win through to absolute victory. . . .*
>
> *With confidence in our armed forces—with the unbounding determination of our people—we will gain the inevitable triumph—so help us God.*

After the shock of the attacks on Pearl Harbor had begun to wane and reality had set in on the Oregon State and Duke campuses, the question of whether to play the Rose Bowl game while the country was at war quickly rose to the forefront of discussion. Hal Reynolds, chairman of the Tournament Football Committee, came out publicly the day after the attacks:

"We believe we will be expected to carry on with our entire New Year's Day program. This is based on our experience in the last war."

During World War I, the Rose Bowl had indeed carried on, though it matched service teams in the game, inspiring national fervor, and the West Coast was not under threat. The War Department allowed Major League Baseball to continue to play during the First World War, even after Secretary of War Newton Baker issued a "work or fight" edict. During World War II, the 1940 Olympics in Helsinki had been canceled, though Britain carried on with all athletic events during the Blitz.

The editorial pages across America weighed in. *The Charlotte Observer,* located just two hours from Durham, proposed canceling the game. "In the light of this historic and unprecedented crisis, the nation needs to turn itself to more practical pursuits than those of a program or pleasure." *The New York Times* disagreed.

> *No doubt the Rose Bowl at Pasadena is a good deal nearer to the Japanese planes than is New York, but it would be a fine and heartening gesture to go ahead with our annual blue-ribbon football game on the Coast and let the Mikado's war planes do their worst.*

On one side of the issue were those who believed that playing the Rose Bowl and carrying on with tradition and daily life as much as possible would show America at its finest. Arguing that Japan might have struck a naval base but not the American spirit, they believed that canceling the game would be seen as cowardice. They also argued that even during wartime, citizens needed a distraction, and playing the game would be good for morale and could help sell war bonds and assist in military recruitment.

War bonds removed money from circulation and reduced inflation and provided much-needed financial support for the war effort. The bonds yielded only 2.9 percent after a ten-year maturity, but the interest was not why Americans bought them. Buying bonds was the patriotic thing to do, and the advertising blitz that pushed the bond sales needed high-profile events—like the Rose Bowl—to spread its message.

On the flip side were those who proposed that playing the game was the last thing America needed to be doing as the war ramped up. Young men were headed overseas to fight—and die—and the energies of its citizenry should be focused on preparing for battle. The police, fire, and supply resources needed to stage the game in Pasadena would take away vital resources needed for the protection of the West Coast.

On Tuesday, December 9, Wade received a telegram advising him that because of the war, the team's visit to a movie studio while in California was canceled. But as the game was officially still on in Pasadena, bureaucratic preparations continued, including the sale of train passes for Duke supporters and students, which continued at a rate that belied any threat of a West Coast incursion. As for the team, Wade put his men through a rigorous eighty-minute workout on the ninth, and on Wednesday the tenth, he had members of his freshman team do their best Don Durdan–Bob Dethman impersonations against the first-string defense, having already gathered scouting information from coaches around the country.

The Men's Gym on campus would typically be filled with physical education classes at 1:00 P.M. on a Friday, but on December 12, it was teeming with young men unsure of their futures. Students who had previously registered for selective service were ordered to gather in the gym before the local draft board to verify their current addresses, provide any information on deferment requests, and ask any last questions of authorities. It was a striking acknowledgment of just how close war was.

After practice, Wade told his boys to take a knee. Motivational speeches weren't his thing—Knute Rockne he was certainly not—and

Duke head coach Wallace Wade Sr. *(Courtesy of Duke University Archives)*

Some of Duke's returning regulars pose before the 1941 season. *(Courtesy of Duke University Archives)*

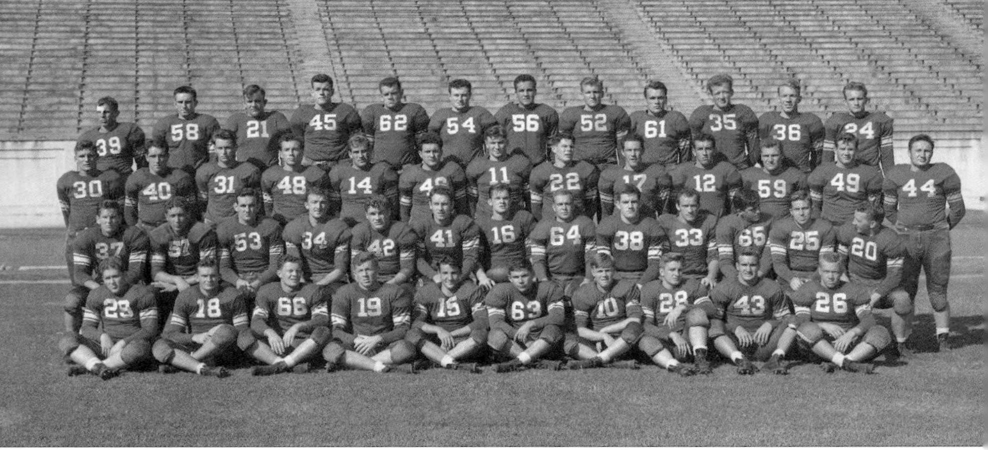

1941 Duke University Team. *(Courtesy of Duke University Archives)*

Oregon State head coach Lon Stiner. *(Courtesy of Harriet's Photograph Collection, OSU Libraries Special Collections and Archives Research Center)*

1941 Oregon State team. *(Courtesy of Harriet's Photograph Collection, OSU Libraries Special Collections and Archives Research Center)*

Oregon State's Bob Dethman, 1941. *(Courtesy of the Football Photograph Collection, OSU Libraries Special Collections and Archives Research Center)*

Oregon State head coach Lon Stiner with assistants Jim Dixon, Hal Moe, and Bill McKalip. *(Courtesy of Harriet's Photograph Collection, OSU Libraries Special Collections and Archives Research Center)*

Duke University's Charles Haynes. *(Courtesy of Duke University Archives)*

Duke students celebrate the announcement of the Rose Bowl invitation. *(Courtesy of the 1942 Duke University Yearbook)*

Oregon State's Jack Yoshihara. *(Courtesy of the 1942 Beaver Yearbook, OSU Libraries Special Collections and Archives Research Center)*

Jack Yoshihara's student photograph c. 1941. *(Courtesy of Harriet's Photograph Collection, OSU Libraries Special Collections and Archives Research Center)*

Minidoka Relocation Center. *(Courtesy of Oregon Nikkei Endowment, ONLC 90)*

Duke ticket office in Rose Bowl crush. *(Courtesy of Duke University Archives)*

Oregon State players boarding the bus to the rail station for the Rose Bowl trip. *(Courtesy of Harriet's Photograph Collection, OSU Libraries Special Collections and Archives Research Center)*

Oregon State players and Lon Stiner on train trip to Durham. *(Courtesy of Harriet's Photograph Collection, OSU Libraries Special Collections and Archives Research Center)*

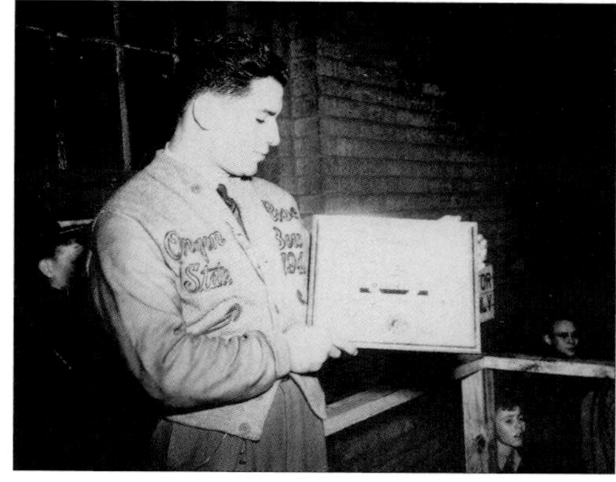

Oregon State captain Martin Chaves received key to Durham upon arrival. *(Courtesy of Duke University Archives)*

Aerial view of Duke Stadium during Rose Bowl. *(Courtesy of Duke University Archives)*

A packed Rose Bowl crowd huddles together for warmth. *(Courtesy of Duke University Archives)*

The teams battle in the mud. *(Courtesy of Duke University Archives)*

his eyes darted back and forth along the ground in front of him as he struggled to find the words to capture this sudden burst of inspiration.

"Boys," he started awkwardly, "war is much like football. You have to . . . prepare for your enemy and . . . study him. You must always go . . . full speed. You must . . . *hit hard.*"

The boys stared intently at their coach, not sure what to make of his uncharacteristically emotional display. They fidgeted with discomfort, struggling right along with their coach. For Charles Haynes, however, the mere mention of war sent his mind wandering once again as he tried to reconcile the panicked headline from Durham's *Herald-Sun* Extra Edition from December 7—HITLER'S WAR EXPLODES IN WORLD CONFLICT AS JAPANESE ATTACK U.S.—with images of Gary Cooper as celebrated WWI hero Sergeant Alvin York in the year's blockbuster *Sergeant York*. The thrill and terror of his murky vision blended with the anxious anticipation of the Rose Bowl in such a way that he could hardly contain himself.

"Boys, many of you will be called to serve," Wade concluded, "but serve you must."

Oregon State, meanwhile, had resumed workouts on Monday under the direction of Jim Dixon and Hal Moe, as Stiner was traveling home from PCC meetings in Palm Springs and promotional activities in Pasadena. Yet as Frank Parker and his teammates gathered together on the practice field, there was a greater sense of urgency. With most of the players serving in ROTC or already enlisted in a branch of the military, war was not only physically closer to them than to their counterparts in Durham, it was more of a reality. Within a matter of weeks if not days, the roster would be decimated by enlistments and draftees. They were rattled, and it showed in practice, which featured clumsiness rarely seen during the season.

Both Wade and Stiner were dealing with harsh, cold weather, with the addition of windy rain creating sticky mud for their players to push through in practice. Stiner was concerned about the collective mind-set of his boys, worried that their thoughts would be on war and believing that the off-week celebrating the Rose Bowl invite had affected their conditioning and desire. His concerns were warranted.

It seemed to happen lightning fast, though it had been building methodically for six days. Despite the columnists and op-ed pages and the participants weighing in, the only voice that mattered belonged to Lieutenant General John Lesesne DeWitt, commander of the Fourth Army and the man responsible for the protection of the West Coast. DeWitt's entire life had been spent attached to the military, from his birth at Fort Sidney, in Nebraska, in 1880, to his distinguished battlefield service in World War I, to his current charge of protecting the West Coast from the Japanese. Headquartered on the Presidio on the banks of San Francisco Bay, DeWitt had blasted the citizenry of the city after their blasé reaction to air-raid sirens on the night of December 8, when thirty-five Japanese planes allegedly flew overhead.

DeWitt was a no-nonsense, military-first, prepare-for-the-worst kind of general, and though he had made no comments on the Rose Bowl, he had decided that it was too tempting of a target for his enemy. On Saturday, December 13, DeWitt picked up the phone and called California governor Culbert L. Olson, requesting that he cancel the Rose Bowl game and parade. Olson, respectful of the wishes of the military, sent a telegram to the Tournament of Roses that afternoon:

> *General John L. DeWitt, commander general, Western Defense command, Presidio San Francisco, has requested that the Pasadena Tournament of Roses and Rose Bowl football game scheduled for New Years* [sic] *Day, be not held, and that arrangements therefore be abandoned for reasons of national defense and civilian protection.*
>
> *I join General DeWitt in this request which is supported by requests received by General DeWitt and myself from groups of the civilian population of the Pasadena and Southern California area.*

> *The congestion of the State highways over a large area, incident to this tournament and football game and its serious obstruction to their use in defense work, the concentration there of a large police force, now needed for defense services, the unusually large gathering of people known to the enemy, exposing them to the dangers now threatening, requires that plans for holding of this tournament and football game be abandoned.*

The decision to cancel the game was met with anger in Corvallis. After four decades of football, Oregon State finally had a ticket to the big stage—and the priceless publicity that comes with it. There were also huge financial implications for Percy Locey and his university, with more than sixty-five thousand tickets already sold. There was the excitement among the student body and the players. Of course, there was also the pride of the state of Oregon in the balance.

Fortunately for Locey, word came of the cancellation just hours before most of the tickets were to be mailed from Pasadena. First Trust and Savings Bank of Pasadena recommended that Oregon State not immediately offer refunds, as checks were being stopped by customers and a slew of refunds would wreak havoc on the bank balance.

"I wonder if General DeWitt intends to lock up all the department stores where people might gather, or restaurants, churches, and all the public meetings," said Bud Forrester, Oregon State's publicity man, who had been on the ground in Pasadena for almost a week. "We will do everything in our power to have the ban against the Rose Bowl lifted."

Everything in their power meant Locey and OSC officials driving to San Francisco to meet with DeWitt, Robert McCurdy, and other Rose Bowl officials on Sunday, December 14. The meeting lasted five minutes. There would be no Rose Bowl game. As if to prove the point, DeWitt ordered army engineers to bivouac in the Rose Bowl stadium. Locey called Governor Olson four times to plead but could not reach him.

Across the country, Wallace Wade, the master of preparation and of backup plans, huddled with Dean William Wannamaker, President Robert Flowers, and Vice President Henry Dwire. Before McCurdy and Locey even left San Francisco, an informal invitation by Duke to host the game was delivered. Frank Pierson, secretary of the Durham Chamber of Commerce, wired officials at the 4th Corps headquarters in Atlanta, and they provided no objections to Durham hosting the game. North Carolina governor Melville Broughton assured the War Department in Washington that the preparations and the Rose Bowl game itself would not interfere with the state's war mobilization.

There were alternatives to Durham. Offers to host the game came from all over the country. From Arch Ward, the editor of *The Chicago Sun-Times* and founder of the Major League Baseball All-Star Game, came an offer to host the game at Soldier Field in front of more than one hundred thousand fans; from Louisiana State University, to hold the game in Baton Rouge, just miles north of the Sugar Bowl, in New Orleans; from the American Legion base in Memphis, to play the game in Crump Stadium, with proceeds going to the Red Cross; from Washington, D.C., to play at Griffith Stadium, with proceeds going to infant paralysis, a charity dear to President Roosevelt.

But Duke could mobilize quickly, and, despite the disappointment of not playing in Southern California, the boys from Oregon State just wanted to play the game. Sure, the beaches and movie stars of California would have been nice, but the Beavers wanted their chance on the national stage, regardless of where it was played.

There was so much still to be worked out, after an informal agreement with McCurdy and Oregon State was reached. Duke Stadium could handle only fifty thousand spectators with temporary bleachers, not the eighty-thousand-plus Pasadena could accommodate, and the revenue split would be much smaller than in previous Rose Bowl games and would have to be negotiated. To be considered an official Rose Bowl game, the Durham game needed formal Rose Bowl sanction, which could not come until the Tournament voted, and the logistics of hosting such a spectacle with just eighteen days' advance notice were daunting, if not unachievable.

On December 15, Wade made the transplanted Rose Bowl official with an announcement over the local radio station: "This is Coach Wallace Wade. I've just received a call from California. They have decided to play the game in Durham with official Rose Bowl sanction." That meant the game would count as a Rose Bowl—with players receiving the customary trophies and blankets—and confirmed the idea that the Rose Bowl was more of a national institution than a location. That same morning, before the announcement, the *Durham Morning Herald* weighed in:

> *Now that military authorities have intervened with a motion to cancel the game we venture again in the field of the gentlemen of the sports pages to say that in time of war we are letting the military call the signals and it is verdict of the military that a [particular or all bowl games] be cancelled, we are for that verdict. And although there may be impressive arguments for and against the cancellation, we are so willing to agree that winning the war is so much more important than any sort of football game, anywhere at any time, that we lack the inclination to recite and weigh them . . . Naturally, we would like to see the game played, and we are not going to pretend that we would not like to see it played here.*

Despite the bureaucratic efforts on the parts of Duke, Oregon State, the Tournament of Roses, and the Durham community, the Duke *players* balked.

Shortly after the announcement was made of the cancellation, many Blue Devil players began to make plans to head home for Christmas break. If they couldn't play the game in Pasadena, they didn't want to play. A traditional Rose Bowl would have meant a trip across the country, parties with movie stars, tickets to sell for extra cash, and per diem meal money. A game played against a team many of the players had never heard of, on their home field, in cold weather, with an ongoing war, and missing out on Christmas at home were now the *only* factors so far as the Blue Devils were concerned, and the players voted 25–2 *against* playing the game in Durham.

Wade was shocked that his players would not want to be a part of a historic game. In fact, he felt it was their patriotic duty to participate. After Wade's best effort to put himself in his players' shoes, he made the following offer to his team: six days off for Christmas. It was very unlike the coach, but his offer swayed a revote, first to 17–10 against and then 15–12 in favor of playing the game. Not overwhelming by any means, but Wade had a team, the players had Christmas, and the most unusual yet meaningful Rose Bowl game was set.

A typical mid-December day in Corvallis meant cold, wind, rain, and a general malaise among OSC students. But for the OSC team, downpours day after day meant a veritable swamp for a field and players who came away from a rigorous Lon Stiner practice looking like mud monsters. Despite his player-friendly approach off the field, Stiner was demanding between the lines. In one practice, he ordered a player who'd had his jaw crushed—likely broken—to "go put a sponge in your mouth and get back on the practice field!"

Early on in practice, just days after the venue change, the team was broken up into position groups for skill work before gathering for team drills, when two men wearing dark suits, equally dismal-looking overcoats, and dour faces strode onto the field. They walked straight toward Stiner, oblivious of the mud spotting their slacks, and introduced themselves as they handed him a folder. He scrutinized its contents as the men paraphrased.

"This gentleman is wanted for questioning," started one.

As Stiner looked over the material, his look went from confusion to disgust.

"Jack!" Stiner called over to Jack Yoshihara, who had been working on blocking drills with the other ends in a far corner. "Come on over here!"

Yoshihara hustled over, hesitating when he saw the suits but trying to stay focused on his coach, whose distressed look he noticed right away.

"Yes, sir?"

"Son, these *men* from the FBI would like to have a word with you." Stiner attempted to sound kind and comforting, but he was unable to disguise his angst. Yoshihara's eyes darted between the men, each of whom grabbed an arm.

Yoshihara's teammates looked up to see him being escorted off the field like a criminal, sandwiched between the two men in a scene that felt all too much like something out of a Cagney flick.

"Hey, Jack, what's going on?" a teammate yelled out, ignoring the pleas of coaches to "get back to work!" Yoshihara could offer only a sad glance over his right shoulder as he continued walking.

The agents spent several minutes asking him questions about his background and allegiances and then told him that by immediate presidential order, he was an enemy of the state and restricted to tight boundaries—boundaries that did not include Durham, North Carolina.

Life had been different for the Japanese American since the attacks on Pearl Harbor just days earlier. But while Jack was able to cope with unwanted stares, dirty looks, and even whispers behind him in class about his heritage and "intention," that afternoon the Japanese American experience during this tense time became real for Jack.

At the time of Pearl Harbor, there were forty-two students of Japanese ancestry enrolled at Oregon State, all but two born in America. A handful of those students reported being spit on and pushed by fellow students in the days after the attack and evicted from boardinghouses by their landlords, despite pleas from college administrators to the landlords to not take action. The young men and women were, after all, Oregon State students.

The Barometer editorialized two days after the attacks: "There surely is no rankle in the hearts of the students, who are now so ready to fight the Japanese empire, against these American students of Japanese ancestry."

On December 11, thirty-six Japanese American students sent a letter to President Gilfillan pledging their loyalty.

Dear Dr. Gilfillan:

In view of the existence of a formal state of war between the United States and the Japanese Empire, we the undersigned American citizens of Japanese ancestry desire to express to you, our College President, our unswerving loyalty to our country, the United States of America, and to all her institutions.

We have found friends, peace of mind and inspiration here at Oregon State. It is our desire to continue our normal program subject to the new duties of citizenship imposed by war. Furthermore we shall endeavor to transmit to our parents a greater realization of the duties of citizenship through associations with them, some of whom share the joys of citizenship in our great country, only through us, their American born sons and daughters.

We will deeply appreciate any opportunity to prove our mettle and our devotion to the College and to our State and Nation. We hope that the trials of this supreme national test will prove a unifying and enlightening influence upon all Americans and their resident relatives from foreign lands.

When the letter was read aloud at a convocation, it was warmly received by students.

In letters of response sent a week later by President Gilfillan to the students, he wrote in part:

It is now unavoidable that you shall face difficult and embarrassing situations. In 1776 Americans of British birth and ancestry were called upon to renounce the mother country. Similarly, in 1917 Americans of German birth and ancestry had to decide whether they would be loyal to America or go over to the enemies of our country. Now in 1941 you have been faced with the same difficult decision and the College is pleased that you have declared your loyalty to the land of your birth.

The federal government had cracked down on "aliens" in the days after Pearl Harbor. There were roughly 127,000 Japanese Americans living in the continental United States, almost all in the West—93,000 in California and more than 19,800 in Oregon and Washington, half engaged in agriculture. Within hours of the attacks, Presidential Proclamation No. 2525 gave the attorney general sweeping powers to detain suspected threats. FBI agents arrested Buddhist priests and Christian ministers, businessmen, community leaders, teachers, and anyone thought to be a threat—real or not. Japanese bank branches were closed, and the U.S. Treasury froze accounts belonging to any Japanese-born resident. With the arrests of staff, Japanese schools were ordered closed, and many businesses owned and operated by those of Japanese ancestry were also shuttered. This was the new world that Jack Yoshihara lived in, and his coach resented it.

Later that night at home, after the FBI agents had removed his player from practice, Stiner could feel only anger. Yoshihara was a nice young man who worked hard and did everything a coach could ask. He stared at his dinner, unable to eat. Finally he stood up, walked out back, and poured himself a tall glass of bourbon.

By the next day, word had spread that Yoshihara was prohibited from traveling to the game, and behind student body president and teammate Andy Landforce, teammates and classmates drafted a letter and petition of protest to the college president. The documents were dropped off at President Gilfillan's office, and he hastily called over the ROTC campus commander to meet with him and Landforce. After sharing the letter and asking for an exception, the commander responded, "Gentlemen, the United States of America is at war, and the president's executive order will be carried out."

The man who perhaps should've been filled with resentment at his national government's actions, Yoshihara, was instead outraged at the foreign invaders whom he held responsible for his predicament, and he decided to do what many men of his age and courage would do—enlist in the armed services. But the twenty-one-year-old who had spent all but the first three years of his life in America was denied. He was, an enlisting officer repeated, an enemy of the state. Like many students of Japanese ancestry, he was also discouraged from returning to Oregon State, though not technically barred.

Oregon State would be going to Durham minus a teammate.

Despite having to travel to an opponent's home turf, it was still the Rose Bowl, and the Oregon State players looked forward to a trip east, where many of the boys had never been. Big cities like Chicago and Washington seemed a world away. Stiner created a travel itinerary for his team, departing Oregon on December 19, practicing in Chicago on the twenty-second and in Washington on the twenty-third, before arriving in Durham on Christmas Eve morning. The players received travel jackets for the trip, having been the only team in the Pacific Coast Conference without them, and spanking-new jerseys and pants for the big stage. Percy Locey was assisting with logistics and still dealing with the headache of answering angry calls from ticket buyers who wanted refunds. But that headache was nothing compared to the absolute chaos in the Duke ticket office.

Tickets went on sale—again—on Tuesday, December 16, and the ticket office was overwhelmed by crowded lines, jammed telephone wires, and telegram money orders. Duke had retained staff from the University of North Carolina athletic department to assist, but they barely made a dent. The local Western Union office was flooded with money orders, which had to be delivered to the ticket office for processing. They were twenty-four to thirty-six hours behind in delivering the telegram orders and actually hired a taxi driver to take a box of them to Duke. The driver had no idea where to drop them off, so he put the box in a corner of the old gymnasium. They were found three days before the game.

The more than fifty thousand tickets sold out in just forty-eight hours. Even the governor of North Carolina paid for his ticket, as Duke had instituted a "no pass" ticket rule, with complimentary access given only to members of the press. The restrictions on tickets weren't an issue just for the powerful but for the disenfranchised as well. DUKE ATHLETIC OFFICIALS BAR NEGROES FROM BOWL GAME BUT WILL ADMIT JAPS, the headline read in *The Carolina Times* on December 20, accompanied by a lengthy editorial by the paper's publisher. Blacks seeking tickets had been told that the game was "sold out," though after the publication of the editorial, fearful of criticism from the West and Northeast, Duke officials "found" one hundred and forty tickets.

Hasty preparations continued. Wade requested temporary bleachers from UNC, North Carolina State, and Wake Forest, as he had in the past for big games with larger-than-expected crowds. The temporary bleachers were erected within days, a new grass field was installed, and negotiations continued between Wade, Locey, and Robert McCurdy to determine a formal agreement on revenue splits. Nearby Davidson College offered the services of its marching band to Oregon State, who could not send its student band across the country due to costs. Duke officials were battling with their own student band about performing. The game would take place over Christmas break, and band members were demanding that Duke provide housing and meals for them, which the university decided against, prompting some members of the band to refuse to play at the prestigious game. Though this was the Rose Bowl, it was not the Rose Bowl parade, with its pageantry and sunshine.

The city of Durham and surrounding areas were also busy preparing for the invasion of visitors coming to town, with hotels booked beyond capacity and officials requesting that local residents open up their homes to accommodate an additional two thousand visitors shut out from hotels. The "Merry Christmas" signs on downtown light posts were replaced with "Welcome Oregon State." The Chamber of Commerce took the lead in arranging a full slate of welcoming events for the visitors from Oregon, intending to display true Southern hospitality and to give them a glimpse of Southern society, with a schedule that included a traditional barbecue, a polo match, a tour of a tobacco factory, and plenty of formal meals.

Of course, among the tasks for Wallace Wade was preparing his team to face an unknown opponent. Wade put the team through hard practices the week of December 15, knowing that on the twentieth, they would have the negotiated Christmas break layoff.

Wade took the term "scout team" to a whole new level. Duke alumnus and former football great George McAfee was supposed to be in Chicago, preparing with his Bears teammates for a January 4 game against a team of All-Stars in New York City. Instead, he was in Durham, scrimmaging against Wade's varsity team, joined by former Duke player and now assistant coach Jasper Davis—the brother of Blue Devil Tom Davis—on the scout team as well as by North Carolina State senior Dick Watts. It was a more than serviceable imitation of the offensive talent displayed by Oregon State with Don Durdan, Bob Dethman, and Joe Day. Duke looked impressive against the scout All-Stars, but the Old Man was nervous about the impending layoff and gave them a parting reminder:

"I hope you men will have a Merry Christmas and a Happy New Year. I doubt seriously if you can have both."

7. THE *BEAVER EXPRESS*

On December 19, Lon Stiner put his team through one last workout in the rain in Corvallis before boarding buses at 5:45 p.m. for the short drive to Albany. Southern Pacific No. 12 took them to Portland to connect with the *Portland Rose,* albeit after departing more than forty minutes late. Union Pacific superintendent P. T. McCarthy had delayed the train. He was not going to let the *Portland Rose* depart without the Beavers, telling the other waiting passengers, "We'll wait until midnight if we have to—can't let those boys down on a trip like this."

The official travel party included thirty-one members of the squad; Stiner; his wife, Caroline; his daughter, Betty; and young Lonnie; coaches, managers, trainers, and a couple of players' wives; and a few loyal supporters. As the travel party transferred trains in Portland, players received farewell hugs and kisses from family, friends, and girlfriends. Quentin Greenough was rolled on a stretcher from one train to the other, suffering from the flu. Stiner took a few minutes to answer questions from the media patiently waiting in the rain.

"I know little about the Duke formation," Stiner conceded, "other than that they use the single-wingback formation. I was in Honolulu when the Blue Devils played the Trojans in the Pasadena Rose Bowl so have not had a chance to see them perform. . . . From reading press accounts, the Duke team must be fast and is a stronger offensive club than the team which played against the Trojans." Despite these comments, Stiner of course knew Duke much better than he let on.

Frank Parker looked around wide-eyed as he boarded the *Portland Rose.* It was the fanciest train on the West Coast and billed itself as having an interior that "reflects the beauty of the 'City of Roses,' the great Pacific Northwest and the Columbia River." The *Beaver Express,* as it was dubbed, was not entirely for Oregon State—the team had just three state-of-the-art private Pullman cars, a parlor car, and, at times, a private dining car. But the entire train was air-conditioned, something most of the players and coaches, including Parker, had never experienced, and individual cars and even individual sleeping berths had climate control. Humidity was balanced throughout, with the windows sealed against noise, dust, dirt, and outside air. The beds had coil-spring mattresses with high headboards, the table linens were snow white, and there were new printed menus for every meal, which many players would send home as souvenirs. The parlor lounge included deep-seated armchairs, shaded lamps, writing desks, tables, buffets, drinks, and an assortment of magazines, newspapers, and a radio. Of course, no cross-country train would be complete without a barbershop (men's cut, fifty cents; women's bob, seventy-five cents), a valet to wash and press clothes, and an assortment of accessories for purchase.

Parker had never experienced such luxuries in his life. The small-town kid had just wanted to make something of himself, and now he would be eating off white linens with silver utensils. Though he felt slight trepidation at going far outside what he knew, Parker, as usual, revealed little besides confidence and calm.

The traveling party was all on board, the rush of adrenaline spurring shouts and loud conversations drowning out the steam whistle from the engine. As the cars slowly began to wheel forward, a few of the boys pressed their faces up against the windows to wave good-bye to the throng. Their faces switched from celebratory to ashen when they spotted Jack Yoshihara.

In a heroic but difficult gesture, Yoshihara had come down to the station to see his teammates off. He mustered a wave as a tear trickled down his cheek. It was harder than being yanked off the practice field a few days prior. His friends and teammates were headed toward potential glory as he was headed back to an uncertain future.

Players were assigned to berths, and a few went to bed, but most stayed up late, like children in a toy store, touching and feeling their new home for the next five days. As the train began to make its journey across Oregon, there were reunions at every stop. The Dethman clan and some high school buddies were waiting to greet Bob as the train pulled into Hood River, about sixty miles east of Portland. As the train came to a complete stop, Alfred Dethman jumped on board. In his hands were two boxes of fresh, recently picked Hood River apples from the family farm. He dropped the boxes and pulled his son in for a big hug. A few miles down the tracks at The Dalles, reserve Marvin Markman's family and friends likewise had hugs waiting—for everyone; in La Grande on Saturday, Choc Shelton, suffering from laryngitis, got up before dawn and hopped off the train for one minute to see his father, Bert; and in Baker, Martin Chaves's and George Bain's families joined in the reunions.

As all trains did in 1941, the *Portland Rose* made dozens of stops along its route to allow passengers to get on and off and to pick up supplies. The constant stops often delayed trains, and as the *Portland Rose* made its way through the hills of Idaho, it lost time at every stop, arriving two and a half hours late to Pocatello, Idaho. In Boise, Stiner had the players disembark and run up and down the train platform, to the delight of the Oregon State supporters on hand, many of whom attended OSC or had friends and relatives who had. In his remarks to a handful of reporters in Boise, the coach made a point of acknowledging that the full air-conditioning had helped improve Greenough's condition (as had the visits from the stewardess) and also prevented other players with colds from getting worse.

For some players on board the train, the novelty of their luxurious surroundings wore off quickly, and they caught up on sleep at every opportunity. Others spent time playing poker, bridge, and dice—though Stiner would pretend not to see the money on the table, distracting himself with the scenery outside the windows. The barren landscape passed by as the train crept closer to its destination. Parker kept to himself, taking long naps and gazing out the window at the unfamiliar land, his thoughts occasionally wandering to Peggy and war. But the Rose Bowl came first, and he had to do his job, just another assignment to complete.

Stiner, Hal Moe, and Jim Dixon made it a point to meet with the players each day on the train, sometimes going over details of the game plan they had in mind for Duke, punctuating the meetings by flashing one headline or another suggesting a Duke blowout, which, to Stiner's delight, fired up his players. At other times, the coaching staff engaged their players in more general leadership-development tasks like asking them to think about, write down, and openly share their personal strengths and weaknesses.

Dixon was the official photographer for the trip, armed with a seven-hundred-dollar camera, while Moe—"Mr. Money Bags"—who was in charge of the trip itinerary, controlled spending and issued player stipends, the average cash per player being five dollars. Two agents with the railroad, who had traveled with the Beavers on prior trips, joined them on their Rose Bowl journey and kept things running smoothly.

Late on Saturday evening, as the train sped past Glenns Ferry, Idaho, the eleven seniors on the team met in the private parlor car to elect their team captain for the Rose Bowl. In a unanimous selection, they picked Martin Chaves, an integral part of their Rose Bowl run and who was headed to the U.S. Army Air Corps immediately after New Year's

Day. Chaves's appeal to postpone his November reporting date to the army had been denied, so he had enlisted in the Army Air Corps. Chaves was well liked by his teammates and admired for his nonstop effort. Others would be going to war, of course, but the combination of his pending service and his leadership on the field earned him the honor.

Sunday morning, December 21, the players were up early, as Rawlins and Medicine Bow, Wyoming, passed by. Breakfast was chilled pineapple juice, hot and cold cereals, scrambled eggs, dry toast, orange marmalade, tea, coffee, and milk. The train pulled into Laramie around 8:00 A.M., and the players got off, stretched, jogged around the train, and jumped back on, before heading through the Sherman Pass and Cheyenne. Greenough was feeling much stronger by the day, but young Lonnie Stiner fell ill with abdominal pain and a fever that was thought to possibly be appendicitis, so the stewardesses, all trained nurses, packed his tiny seven-year-old body in ice to try to reduce his temperature as he read the funnies in the newspaper.

The train picked up time, reaching speeds of more than eighty-five miles an hour through a slice of Colorado and into Nebraska, Stiner's home state. His father greeted him at the rail depot in Grand Island, where Stiner guaranteed him a win. When the train pulled into Omaha, members of the University of Nebraska N Club, former varsity lettermen, met the train and congratulated their fellow N Club member, handing Stiner a horseshoe for good luck.

At 8:45 A.M. local time on Monday, December 22, the train arrived at the downtown train station in Chicago under a light drizzle and dark sky. Two Gray Line buses drove the team first to the Sherman Hotel, where Lonnie visited with doctors in a hotel room while his older sister, Betty, vomited in the bathroom, suffering from suspected food poisoning. The Stiners had their hands full, but thankfully, they learned that Junior did not have appendicitis but rather just a bad tummy ache.

The team boarded a bus at the hotel and headed to the University of

Chicago for practice. En route, George Zellick shouted to the driver to stop as he excitedly exited the bus and ran to the front steps of a building to greet his sister, who just happened to live blocks from the university.

When the buses pulled up next to Stagg Field, the team managers informed Stiner that equipment and practice gear had not yet arrived on a train traveling behind the *Portland Rose*. Nellie Metcalf, the University of Chicago athletics director, offered maroon warm-up suits and tennis shoes to the boys, and Stiner gladly accepted on their behalf. The players dressed, stretched, and tossed the ball around inside the field house. When the equipment and uniforms finally arrived, Stiner had them put on just the cleats—except for Chaves, Bob Dethman, Don Durdan, and Joe Day, of whom the gathered reporters wanted pictures in full uniforms.

Just steps away from where the boys from Oregon State were warming up, some of the world's top scientists would soon gather, preparing for another kind of battle.

Arthur Compton and Enrico Fermi sat under a tree in the main quad of the University of Chicago in early 1942, discussing details of a project too sensitive to risk being monitored by recording devices that might be hidden in their laboratory, just blocks from Stagg Field.

Compton was a brilliant scientist who had spent most of his adult life focused on the tiniest of tiny particles, the gamma-ray photon. In fact, the decrease in energy resulting from the interaction of a gamma-ray photon or X-ray and matter is called "Compton Scattering" or the "Compton Effect"—essentially, electromagnetic radiation—and was discovered by Compton while he was working as a professor at Washington University in Saint Louis. He continued his work on X-rays and electrons in the succeeding years and won the Nobel Prize in physics in 1927, soon becoming the dean of physics at the prestigious University of Chicago.

Fermi was born in Rome in 1901, and studied at the University of Pisa from 1918 to 1922 and at Leiden University and the University of Göttingen before becoming a professor at the Sapienza University of Rome. Eleven years later, Fermi would be awarded his own Nobel Prize for his "demonstrations of the existence of new radioactive elements produced by neutron irradiation, and for his related discovery of nuclear reactions brought about by slow neutrons." Fermi had laid the groundwork for the world's first nuclear chain reaction. After accepting the Nobel with his family in Sweden, Fermi immigrated to the United States, where he became a professor in physics at Columbia University in New York.

In April of 1941, Vannevar Bush, the head of the National Defense Research Committee, created a special committee to oversee the development of a potential uranium weapons program and asked Compton to chair it. One month later, Compton submitted a report to Bush confirming that one could develop a nuclear weapon using uranium.

Over the ensuing months, Compton worked with scientists from around the country—including Fermi—on uranium enrichment and the production of plutonium, and in October, he wrote about the practical uses of an atomic bomb. By November, Compton believed that an atomic bomb was feasible, and in December 1941, he was put in charge of the Metallurgical Laboratory at the University of Chicago. Scientists from Columbia, Berkeley, and Princeton joined the project, with the goal of creating an atomic reactor that would ultimately lead to an atomic bomb. Compton set a goal date of January 1943 for producing a chain reaction and of January 1945 for producing an atomic bomb.

In the coming months, Compton and Fermi would be joined in Chicago and at locations around the country by professors and deans from both Duke and Oregon State, all contributing to the Manhattan Project.

Some of the world's most brilliant minds would work on a project that would change the world, yet the boys warming up to practice football at the University of Chicago on a dreary day in December had no idea.

Prime Minister Winston Churchill arrived in Washington, D.C., that same day, relieved that America had finally entered World War II earlier in the month, though it had been an integral part of the war effort for many months. The United States had already been helping its allies with supplies, munitions, weapons, and financial assistance, and Churchill and Roosevelt had secret agreements on weaponry and financial support, communicating via a transatlantic undersea cable, by the time America formally entered the fray.

Churchill was joined in Washington by his minister of supply, the British ambassador to the United States, and a gaggle of advisers and technical staff. Their counterparts on the American side included Secretary of State Cordell Hull and Undersecretary of State Sumner Welles, as well as smaller delegations from twenty-four other countries.

"Arcadia" was the code name for the conference, which focused on deciding on an overall strategy for the war and reviewing the smaller details of joint operations. The discussions would last for more than three weeks, broken up by a four-day round-trip by Churchill via train to Canada to confab with Canadian prime minister Mackenzie King.

Later, on January 1, 1942, twenty-six nations committed to the Declaration by the United Nations, a pledge by all signers that there would be no separate peace with their enemies and that each would fight with the full resources of their nation. Over the course of the day and the following week of meetings, more initiatives would come out of Washington's first council: the decision to focus on defeating Germany before fully taking on the Japanese, as Germany was seen as a more perilous threat; the agreement by the United States to send bombers to bases in England; and the establishment of an organization, the combined chiefs of staff, to direct military strategy and operations of the key allies.

As one might expect, the Oregon State practice in Chicago was not crisp, with lethargic legs the likely culprit, and Lon Stiner did not even attempt blocking drills but rather focused on conditioning, passing, and punting. His players had been lumbered on a train for a weekend, and he merely wanted them to get a good workout in. After practice, the players bused back for lunch to the Sherman Hotel, where reporters were waiting to ask Stiner about the Pasadena cancellation:

> *Our student body celebrated for two days after we won the Coast championship. After all, we had never before played our way into the Rose Bowl. So naturally it was a terrible disappointment to our followers that the game was called off. The boys on the squad, however, take it more in stride. They want to play this game . . . and Durham is just as much all right with them as Pasadena would have been.*

The team boarded the buses and went on a short tour of the lakefront and Loop areas of Chicago before getting on the train again around 4:00 P.M., connecting with the Chicago B&O *Capital Limited* headed for the nation's capital. After passing through Gary, Indiana, and Akron, Youngstown, Pittsburgh, and Harpers Ferry, Oregon State arrived at 8:40 A.M. in Washington, D.C., and immediately transferred to another set of buses bound for the U.S. Capitol, Arlington National Cemetery, Alexandria, and Mount Vernon, George Washington's former home. But despite evidence to the contrary, Stiner dismissed any notion that his boys were on a sightseeing trip.

"We didn't come all this distance to see the sights and then lose. No, sir. We represent the Pacific Coast Conference."

As if to prove his point, the last stop on the bus was the Washington Redskins' and Senators' home of Griffith Field, where Billy Rinehart—a former University of Oregon basketball and baseball coach and an assistant coach in football, and now the athletic director at George Washington University—had made arrangements for the Beavers to practice. Stiner had planned for the team to hold a scrimmage over the baseball diamond, but after George Bain cut his toe in warm-ups on a shard of glass left over from fans in the bleachers, the coach didn't want to start a streak of bad luck, and he called it off, resorting to a vigorous, structured conditioning workout. The train departed around 10:40 P.M. for the final leg of their cross-country journey.

It had been an unprecedented seventeen days since Pearl Harbor; the core of the nation had been rattled. The team undertook a journey of more than 3,500 miles to an unfamiliar land, not knowing what they might expect to find in the South.

About six miles west of Durham, in a nondescript field near Hillsborough Road and Neal Road, stands a stone fireplace and a few small remnants of a farmhouse destroyed by a fire in 1921. It is where the Civil War truly came to an end. Even after Robert E. Lee surrendered at Appomattox Court House in Virginia on April 9, 1865, the Southern armies of the Confederacy were still at war. Led by General Joseph Johnston, based in Greensboro, and at the urging of Confederate president Jefferson Davis, hundreds of thousands of troops were still engaged in battle—or at least refusing to lay down their arms. But with Lee's surrender, Johnston saw no way out for the Confederacy and sent a courier with a request to meet with General William Sherman, then encamped near Morrisville, North Carolina, outside of Durham. Johnston, guarded by five dozen soldiers from the South Carolina regiment, made his way toward Sherman, as his nemesis, with more than two hundred soldiers, headed toward Johnston. They met at a farmhouse owned by James and Nancy Bennett, who had lost a son and son-in-law in the war.

At Bennett Place on April 17, the two sides entered into surrender negotiations, despite the telegram news that President Lincoln had been assassinated. The following day, April 18, they signed an initial surrender agreement, but it was soon rejected by President Andrew Johnson and Congress for being too lenient and favorable to the South. So the two sides met again, on April 26, at Bennett Place and agreed to new terms, including the surrender of more than ninety thousand Confederate troops.

Fifty-six years later, the historic farmhouse was gutted by fire, and in 1923, a handful of wealthy tobacco families in Durham thought enough of the historical site to erect the Unity Monument, a squared arch commemorating the site. Among the donors was the Duke family. The Unity Monument stood as a reminder that there were great divides in America that, in some ways, still existed. The South was still regarded as different by the rest of America, and the stigma of segregation entered into every conversation. The boys from Oregon knew about prejudice—and some, perhaps, even practiced it—but as they would soon learn, the South was indeed different.

The *Beaver Express* stopped in Greensboro, outside of Durham, at dawn on Christmas Eve and picked up a select group of passengers, including members of the Durham Chamber of Commerce, the city manager, Percy Locey (who had traveled ahead of Oregon State to Durham to help in the preparations), Duke officials, and a few reporters to cover the arrival. At 8:15 A.M., the train pulled into the Durham train depot, and the players stared out the window with amazement as an estimated crowd of two thousand awaited their arrival. The Durham High School band was on hand, blaring out the tunes of the Oregon State fight song, as Wallace Wade and city officials stood on a temporary platform. In a brief ceremony, Mayor W. F. Carr made Martin Chaves an honorary mayor of Durham, and the Beavers' captain thanked Durham for a warm welcome.

As the crowd dispersed, the travel party made its way to the nearby Washington Duke Inn for a breakfast sponsored by the Chamber of Commerce. Lon Stiner, who would quickly become a treasure trove of quips for reporters, remarked, "Honestly, everybody's been so nice to us that I just don't see how we can politely win the Rose Bowl game."

After breakfast, it was onto buses for the short ride to Chapel Hill and the Carolina Inn, the team's home base for the next week. In the grand lobby of the hotel, among the distinctive Southern charm of the decor, which fit in well with the gracious staff, hung portraits of Abe Lincoln, Daniel Webster, John Calhoun, General Robert Lee, and Henry Lee.

When the transplanted game was first announced, Oregon State had many offers from hotels and local colleges to host the team, but the University of North Carolina presented the best of both worlds, with a first-class hotel and a stadium field for practice. The university, opened in 1795, was Duke's rival and routinely hosted Duke's football opponents during the season, yet the North Carolina football staff went to great lengths not to share any scouting material on Duke with visiting teams.

UNC was passionate about football, and the ringing of the bell tower chimes to the tune of the alma mater, "Hark the Sound," after football victories was just one indication. During the rush to stage the Rose Bowl, UNC provided staff, equipment, and bleachers to Duke, in addition to opening up their well-known hotel and football stadium. The North Carolina student body even delivered a seven-foot-long sign wishing the Blue Devils luck in the game, signed by thousands of UNC students.

Despite the flurry of activity surrounding their arrival and it being Christmas Eve, Stiner scheduled a scrimmage for the afternoon in Carolina's Kenan Stadium. The coach allowed visitors and members of the press to attend in what would be a rare open practice during their time in North Carolina. The boys had yet to begin to get back into a routine after the modified practices in Chicago and Washington, but for the first time, they didn't have to worry about weather, glass on the field, or hopping back onto a train. A scrimmage with a no-open-field-tackling rule went well. Don Durdan sprained his wrist on Bob Saunders's stiff arm, but with game day eight days away, the training staff, Stiner, and Durdan weren't concerned.

The wives of the OSC coaches and trainers spent the afternoon setting up an impromptu Christmas tree at the Carolina Inn and, at Christmas Eve dinner that night, trainer Dell Allman dressed up as Santa Claus. During dinner, Stiner could barely make a dent in his meal, so frequently was he interrupted by friendly members of the Durham community.

"Mr. Stiner, I work at the bank here in town," one well-dressed man began. "If you want to cash any checks, I'm the man to see."

"The way the boys have been borrowing money from me on the trip east," Stiner quipped, "it looks like I'll be seeing a lot of you."

"Mr. Stiner," another man began, tapping the OSC coach on the shoulder, "if you want to use my car, I'll be glad to turn it over to you."

"Thanks, friend," replied the coach. "I've already been given the use of a brand-new car for the duration, but people have been so nice to me, I must be twins, so maybe I'll need two cars."

The kindness of the Carolinians continued on Christmas morning at breakfast before Stiner held a one-and-a-half-hour practice in the morning, under bright sunshine. The players did wind sprints—first fifty yards and then one hundred—with Gene Gray and Joe Day looking particularly impressive. Stiner put the offense through a passing scrimmage and worked with Frank Parker and the line on blocking. Durdan's wrist was already feeling better, and he and Bob Dethman shared most of the reps.

Duke University hosted a Christmas dinner at the University Union, complete with caroling, a visit from Santa Claus, and the singing of both schools' alma maters. The menu was replete with traditional Southern dishes, including Virginia baked ham and roast turkey with oyster dressing, and the Oregon State players indulged until their stomachs were about to burst. Duke vice president Henry Dwire served as host and master of ceremonies, and the OSC players were given an amazing array of Christmas presents, compliments of local businesses, including a walking stick, cartons of the big three brands of cigarettes, a one-pound tin of tobacco, a sack of Southern biscuit flour, ties, suspenders, shorts, a box of ladies' silk stockings (for their mothers or girlfriends), two pairs of silk socks for men, and pillowcases.

Stiner continued to be a hit with reporters—honest and self-deprecating—but when questions arose about the Beavers' record in 1941 and whether or not that justified participation in this holiest of college football events, he would get his back up. He stood up for Oregon State's strength of schedule and defended their style of play and their chances in the game.

"I don't know anything about Duke's team," he remarked, rather disingenuously—having studied as much intel as was made available to him in the weeks leading up to the game—"but I do know something about my boys. Nobody managed to score more than two touchdowns against us in 1941, and we don't intend to start the New Year on the wrong foot."

After six days off for Christmas break, the Duke players began to trickle back to campus on Christmas night in advance of the first practice the next morning, Friday the twenty-sixth. Wallace Wade was in full game mode and anxious to catch up on preparations with his players, so he had the gates to the stadium locked during practice, upsetting many curious visitors and the members of the press. It was a good thing, too, because the Blue Devils looked as though they had been enjoying themselves a little too much during the tenure of their break. On a wet and soft field, as Wade put them through an hour-long practice, his players were slow, winded, and lacked the killer focus they had displayed for most of the season and in bowl practices before the break. It didn't take much for the coach to recognize that his sacrifices for his players to *play* the game might actually *cost* them the game.

On Saturday, it was Oregon State's turn to walk away from a practice with some concern, as during a scrimmage in full pads, right end

Norm Peters went out with a back injury, and left guard Orville Zielaskowski was hit on the head and taken to the hospital for observation. But a rather disturbing event on the following day redirected their attention.

Stiner gave his boys the day off that Sunday and traveled with them to the famed Pinehurst Country Club, where they were greeted by Bob Harlow, a Portland native and former manager of the Professional Golf Association, who now worked in public affairs for Pinehurst. He was joined by the traveling pro at the club, who provided the visitors with an impromptu lesson, and by the manager of Pinehurst, who pointed out the irony of the seventy tons of *Oregon* rye grass seed planted each year for the club's three courses and the two hundred tons planted in the area every year.

The coach and the boys also got some pointers on the game of polo from the Pinehurst captain, who mentioned that his team was taking on a squad from Fort Bragg in an exhibition and invited the Beavers to stick around to watch—the first live polo match most of Oregon State's players had seen. During the game, Frank McCleur, a thirty-five-year-old lawyer from Aberdeen who was stepping in for a Fort Bragg player that day, sped along atop his horse toward the Pinehurst goalposts when suddenly his horse took off, running past the goalposts, headed for a string of pine trees. McCleur attempted to jump off before impact, but the horse threw McCleur against a pine tree, some one hundred yards from the playing field, killing him instantly and giving most of the OSC players their first personal experience of death. They were shaken as they returned to the Carolina Inn.

Surprisingly, with just seventy-two hours until kickoff, Oregon State, Duke, and the Tournament of Roses Association had yet to formally agree on a game contract, detailing everything from the kickoff time to the postgame revenue distribution. To Wade's credit, despite Duke serving as host and incurring much of the expense, he proposed that the revenue be split after the Tournament was reimbursed for its expenses. Wade and Locey signed a memorandum of agreement on the twenty-ninth, with a two o'clock kickoff set for Thursday "regardless of traffic, weather or other deterring conditions."

Oregon State practiced in Kenan Stadium for the last time on Tuesday, December 30, as visitors began to flood Durham and the surrounding areas. Meanwhile, Wade welcomed coaching colleagues from Pennsylvania, North Carolina State, Wake Forest, and Clemson to practice. Neither team went hard at practice. The game plans were set; the conditioning was over. It was all mental now.

The following day, NBC radio host Bill Stern emceed the kickoff luncheon sponsored by the Kiwanis Club, with many high-profile guests. Shortly thereafter, both teams dressed in full uniforms for a "workout" in Duke Stadium, primarily to provide photo opportunities for the press. Duke practiced at 2:00 P.M. in full pads, followed an hour later by Oregon State in uniforms but without pads, which provided a stark difference in size. The stadium was buzzing unlike at any other time in its fourteen-year history.

As night fell, Wade was concerned about his team's mental state, believing they were taking their opponents too lightly, and, forgetting his players' resistance to playing the game, he began to regret the extra time off for Christmas break.

Stiner's confidence, meanwhile, was at an all-time high. "We are going to win this game," he said matter-of-factly. "My boys are worked up for this as they were for any game on the coast this season."

By 9:30 P.M. on New Year's Eve, the lobby of the Carolina Inn was empty except for a few out-of-town visitors. After a week of overwhelming Southern hospitality, juxtaposed by uncertainty about their lives—let alone their futures—Oregon State players went to bed, the promise of history lulling them to sleep.

As The Sun goes to press today,
A little earlier than usual,

It is the Zero Hour,
For the Victory Rose Bowl Game.
It is a splendid circumstance,
That two great teams thus may meet.
Theirs is the exhilaration of aspiration realized.
East and West are enabled to know each other.
American's appreciation of American is heightened.
American nerves are soothed and morale is boosted.
Cowering and wailing in the chimney corner,
Is not the way to American victory.
—Durham Sun, *December 31, 1941*

PART III

A GAME LIKE NO OTHER

Regardless of who wins the ball game on New Year's Day, one thing is certain—America will triumph. Yes, the Japs and their cohorts caused the transfer of the game from Pasadena to Durham but they couldn't stop the Americans.

—*The Durham Sun* editorial, December 31, 1941

8. A ROSE IS STILL A ROSE

IN THE EARLY HOURS of the dawn of the new year, in Pasadena, Rose Bowl queen Dolores Brubach awoke, applied her makeup, and donned her royal regalia and her queen's crown. She met her court princesses a few hours later, and they gingerly climbed into five cars at the Valley Hunt Club.

It was unusually cold and overcast for Southern California, let alone for New Year's Day, but the Rose Bowl Parade went on. The caravan drove down Orange Grove and Colorado Boulevards at the standard parade speed of two miles per hour along the five-mile route. A series of trumpeters marched alongside the cars, the largest of which held a six-foot V for victory. Tournament president Robert McCurdy had declared this the "Victory Rose Bowl" as the Rose Court ("War Poster Girls") sold American ideals and war bonds in the game's lead-up. But this was far from a victory parade. There were no floats, no bands, and no spectators. The queen and her court waved to empty grandstands, 2,510 miles from Duke Stadium, as the occasional passerby gave nary a glance. Pasadena had had no choice in relinquishing the game, but it did its best to carry on with tradition, even in the face of war and bad weather. A few hours later, the parade made its way to the Huntington

Hotel for a small reception, as hotel guests "built" dozens of small floats to replicate the tradition.

Wallace Wade had made it clear early on in the relocation process that Duke and Durham would have to forgo the traditional Rose Bowl Parade and associated festivities, recognizing that they could not "match the Tournament of Roses spectacle—a show that has been in preparation for fifty years" in the two weeks Durham had to prepare. But the game went on.

Though the outcome certainly mattered to the men from Corvallis and Durham, the mere fact that the Rose Bowl game would go on was, indeed, a victory in and of itself for America. It was a distraction for some, a fund-raiser for others, a recruiting tool for the armed services. Of course, not everybody believed the Rose Bowl should be played in Durham—or anywhere, for that matter—with one North Carolina citizen penning a letter to Governor Broughton imploring him to cancel the game, as she was sure that the Germans would bomb Duke Stadium.

In addition to approximately 170 police officers on duty on game day, members of the Durham motorcycle club were sworn in as special officers to assist with traffic, along with twenty-five members of the State Guard and officers from the State Highway Patrol. Dozens of Boy Scouts stood in roads, parking lots, and by stadium gates to provide directions or simply a welcoming smile. Fifty special and regular deputies from the Durham County Sheriff's Office were on duty inside the stadium, keeping the peace and an eye out for gate-crashers or fence-hoppers. Despite the police presence, there were bound to be rule-breakers. Law enforcement warned visitors about strangers rubbing up against them in an attempt to pick their pockets. Officials also reminded patrons to remove all valuables from their cars and to lock all car doors.

Earlier in the week, ticket scalpers were receiving as much as $15 per ticket, well above the face value of $4.50. But by game time, the "get-in" price had dropped well below that number. The weather had something to do with it, as did the traffic, but so did the enforcement of a little-known Durham scalping law prohibiting the sale of tickets above face value. Police were instructed to arrest anyone violating the law, which greatly decreased the price, leading some to rid themselves of tickets at just ten cents apiece after kickoff. Perhaps the matchup of two-loss Oregon State College, little known even to the most ardent college football fans in Durham, with a Duke squad who would tell you privately that they had no interest in playing the game—and, in fact, had voted overwhelmingly against it—also played a role in the drop in prices.

Opportunists rimming the stadium were selling American flags and roses and anti-Hitler paraphernalia and umbrellas. This Rose Bowl was about America. Men young and old, including, incredibly, one Japanese man, hawked souvenir game programs at 25¢ each, with five cents of each sale going to the salesman. The traffic jams started around 9:00 A.M. and increased the cost of a taxi ride from midtown to the stadium to $2.50 after noon, as the traffic limited the amount of trips a driver could make. Many fans were in their stadium seats by 12:30 P.M., long before kickoff.

The Beavers boarded their buses at the Carolina Inn around 11:00 A.M., with a police escort waiting, but Stiner did not want his players to arrive too early for the game, so he had the buses sit idly in Chapel Hill. The bus driver took the opportunity to share his belief that Duke was going to smash his passengers in the game, a remark that ignited some passion in the young lads. All they had heard since the matchup was announced was how good Duke was and how badly they would pound OSC.

Once Stiner released the buses, they took many side streets to avoid traffic, but halfway to Duke, he had the buses stop, realizing they would still arrive too early. The coach stepped off and talked with the police escort. Suddenly, a shouting match erupted between Stiner and the policeman over something. His boys looked on from inside the bus as Stiner ripped into the officer. In true Stiner character, the confrontation was prearranged by the coach to fire his players up, orchestrated like busting through the "locked" doors before the Oregon game a month earlier had been.

It had rained overnight, but while the new grass planted especially for the game was soft, the field was not yet too muddy, as there was an elaborate drainage system with a stream built underneath the field that was holding its own. A steady drizzle began again around noon, making the forty-degree temperature feel much colder.

More than two hundred members of the media were on hand, crammed into the fifty-seat press box, in the president's box opposite the press box, and in every tiny corner of the stadium. Though only one reporter made the trip from Southern California, *The New York Times,* Associated Press, United Press, and others converged on Durham, including six newsreel companies. But the large contingent of reporters presented a unique challenge—the scarcity of copper wires. In normal circumstances, telegraph companies would simply add additional wiring in the press box to meet the demand. But America was now at war, which meant severe restrictions on copper wiring. So telegraph companies within fifty to seventy miles joined together to handle the usage expected from reporters on game day. Writers from the major East Coast cities would get the first opportunity to wire out stories, followed by those in Saint Louis and Chicago and, finally, those on the West Coast, including Oregon. The telegraph companies had motorcycle messengers on standby to drive the stories from the stadium to Raleigh and Charlotte for transmittal.

The members of the media sat poised, waiting for kickoff and the eventual outcome of their stories.

The fifty-six thousand fans crammed into the permanent and temporary bleachers in Duke Stadium were cold and wet. But the smell of southern barbecue, an occasional whiff of bourbon, and, of course, cigarettes, kept alive the senses of the throngs, some huddled under oilcloth table liners and a few warmed by contained fires in the stands.

The Duke players, led by captain Bob Barnett, jogged onto the wet field around 1:33 P.M., warmed up, and returned to the locker room. Charles Haynes had attended or played in dozens of Duke games in his lifetime, but he had never seen quite this kind of spectacle. The fact that he was dressed to play in the game seemed to slip his mind at times as he looked around in awe. Despite the bad weather and the lack of interest on the part of some of his teammates, Haynes's optimism would not be denied on this day.

Prior to kickoff, the OSC locker room was silent.

"This is the frosting on the cake, boys," Stiner blurted out.

Oregon State came out of the tunnel, led by captain Martin Chaves, warmed up, and remained on the field until kickoff.

Referee Lee Eisan called the captains to midfield for the coin toss. Traditionally, the referee flips a silver dollar and then gives the piece to the home captain. But Eisan had arrived only a few days before the game and could not find a silver dollar, as they were in low supply, so he used a fifty-cent piece—cheating Chaves out of fifty cents (as the champion of the Pacific Coast Conference, Oregon State was the home team despite playing at Duke). It wasn't entirely Eisan's fault. In the weeks prior to the new year, a battle over who would officiate the game had erupted between Percy Locey and Edwin Atherton, the commissioner of the Pacific Coast Conference, which resulted in Eisan officiating with little time to prepare. Duke won the toss and elected to receive.

Before Eisan whistled for the opening kick, the public-address announcer read the following message to warn the crowd of air traffic overhead: "At some point during the game, it is hoped to secure an air view of this great throng in the Duke Stadium, weather conditions permitting. Permission for this flight has been granted by aeronautical authorities in Washington." One can imagine the audience's terror if during the game, without warning, a plane screamed by overhead.

A moment of silence was held in honor of America's servicemen, including Lieutenant Foy Roberson Jr., a former basketball player at North Carolina and the first Durham man to be killed during the war, when his plane crashed over San Diego Bay during training.

Oregon State student body president Andy Landforce, whom Lon Stiner had added to the roster for the Montana game, was not in uniform at kickoff. Landforce never had a real expectation of ever seeing the field in Durham, believing Stiner brought him along to deliver speeches, to do media interviews, and to serve as a goodwill ambassador for Oregon State. Sure enough, just minutes before kickoff, Jim Dixon approached Landforce and told him he was going up into the press box to serve as a spotter for NBC announcer Bill Stern.

Oregon State's line outweighed Duke's by nine pounds, but Duke had bigger backs in their backfield. The offensive firepower of Duke, averaging 34.5 points per game, and having scored at least 50 points three times in 1941, was up against the stingiest OSC defense since 1926, having allowed just 33 points during the regular season. Duke allowed just 41 points and pitched five shutouts.

"Boys, listen up," Lon Stiner demanded of his players just seconds before kickoff. "We are going to hit first and hit hard. Right from the opening kick, I want you to absolutely destroy whoever catches that football."

Oregon State's Norman Peters skied the opening kickoff just after 2:00 P.M., but the trajectory of the ball was hard to follow, hidden by the dark gray skies and the sideways drizzle. But down it came, a brown dot collected neatly by Duke's Tom Davis at his own five-yard line. With a dash of clarity, Davis began his assault on the yardage markers, bodies flying, mud spouting everywhere. The gaps closed fast, the landscape shrank, and *boom*—a burst of thunder from the sky or the ground, or, most likely, from the Beavers' Lloyd Wicketts, who promptly forced Davis to disassociate himself from the ball at the twenty-nine-yard line. Oregon State's George Peters recovered. *Hit hard. Destroy.*

The first drive by Oregon State went as one might expect, based on their offense during the regular season. On first down, Bob Dethman took the snap and passed to his right to George Peters for a short pickup of three yards. On second down, Don Durdan took the snap, ran to his left, and let the ball fly, but the pass was broken up. On third down, Durdan broke tackles and gained six before Winston Siegfried brought him down. On fourth down, Dethman dumped the ball off to Peters again, this time for a first down on Duke's seventeen. Joe Day ran for two yards on the first down. On second down, Durdan was tackled for what seemed to be a nine-yard loss by Duke's Mike Karmazin, but officials ruled that Durdan had actually passed the ball, making it an incomplete pass rather than a sack or fumble. On third down, Durdan managed only a yard, and on fourth down, Duke's Tommy Prothro knocked down a pass in the end zone, giving Duke the ball.

The teams continued to exchange punts as the sloppy game played on.

Then Dethman, Day, and Durdan led a sustained drive, including a trick play, with Durdan in punt formation on third down but Day taking the direct snap and running for five yards. Durdan earned a first down with a one-yard run on fourth down. A few plays later, facing third down on Duke's fifteen-yard line, Durdan took the snap out of his right halfback position and dropped back to pass. With no receiver open and a wide hole to the right, the speedster slipped around the end and raced into the end zone for the first score of the game, with 1:40 remaining in the first period. Warren Simas converted the extra-point attempt and gave Oregon State a 7–0 lead on the heavily favored Blue Devils. The mainly pro-Duke crowd grew silent.

The drive fired up OSC's defense, and on the ensuing Duke possession, OSC's line frustrated the Duke offense with Quentin Greenough ultimately recovering an Al Piasecky fumble on Duke's thirty-nine-yard line to end the first period. Piasecky's concentration was off, as indicated by his remark to his teammates in the huddle that "there are a lot of pretty girls in the stands."

Four minutes into the second period, the Duke offense was showing its first signs of life as a nifty twenty-nine-yard run by Tom Davis got the Blue Devils into Beaver territory. A few plays later, Steve Lach scampered twenty-five yards on a reverse and was headed for a touchdown before Gene Gray pulled him down at Oregon State's nine. After short runs by Siegfried and Lach, Duke faced a third and goal. On the snap, a perplexed OSC line, believing Davis had taken the ball, chased him down, only to look over their shoulders to find that Lach was running a reverse again—this time for a score. Bob Gantt's extra point tied the game at seven.

Sloppy play continued with turnover after turnover until Duke's backup halfback Bobby Rute led the Blue Devils to a first down on OSC's five-yard line, threatening to take the lead. But Duke failed to get off another snap before Eisan blew the halftime whistle, and the players jogged off the field toward the locker rooms.

The score was 7–7.

Wallace Wade had gambled in the first half, using a slightly different, not-yet-perfected offensive scheme, with the running back serving as a pass receiver downfield. It was unusual for the coach to insert a new play or scheme unless it had been perfected in practice, but he thought he could surprise the opponent. The result was a misdirected offensive line in disarray, not entirely sure how to effectively apply blocks for its backfield. Wade didn't waste any time in the locker room, urgently directing the team to return to an offensive game plan in which his players—most important, his offensive line—had greater confidence.

Across the way in the visitors' locker room, Stiner stood before his team.

"Boys, we have this one. This is our game, and when—"

Just then, a man barged through the locker room door looking for a place to relieve himself. He was tipsy. The players burst out laughing.

On the field, local college bands, including some band members from

Duke and North Carolina as well as Durham High School, belted out songs sent to them by the Tournament of Roses, including marching formations, and, as it was New Year's Day, added "Auld Lang Syne" for good measure. NBC radio broadcast the halftime show live from the field in Pasadena, with the Rose Bowl queen and Hal Reynolds making an appearance. The scoreboard at halftime read 7–7, as hundreds of American soldiers camped out in the bowels of the Rose Bowl, sent there weeks prior by Lieutenant General DeWitt as a message that no game would be played there.

Oregon State took the second-half kickoff and went nowhere, with Durdan's punt rolling dead at Duke's thirty. Duke's first drive of the second half was a tale of extremes. A fake from punt formation took Lach downfield twenty-one yards, and a Davis pass to Gantt picked up another sixteen. But Jim Smith lost twelve yards on an attempted triple reverse, and Davis was sacked for a seven-yard loss. In the end, the drive resulted in yet another Lach punt.

Stiner's boys took over on their own sixteen-yard line and drove deep into Duke territory behind a big forty-one-yard run after a catch by Durdan. Simas missed a field goal attempt, and the score remained tied.

When Oregon State got the ball back, Day and Dethman worked the ball downfield, and with four minutes remaining in the third period, Dethman faded back, threw a bullet to George Zellick at the eight-yard line, and watched his teammate dodge tacklers en route to the end zone. Simas converted on the extra point, and it seemed the boys from Oregon were about to shock the world, leading 14–7.

On the first play from scrimmage after the kickoff, the All-American Lach fooled the Oregon State defense once again, went to his left, cut to the right, and broke into a small clearing before Day pulled him down after a thirty-nine-yard run. On first down from OSC's twenty-five, Siegfried was stopped. On second down, Lach cut inside on a reverse over the right tackle and picked up six yards. An unnecessary roughness penalty on Oregon State gave Duke a first down and a goal at the

OSC one-yard line. On the next play, Siegfried burst through the line for a touchdown with two minutes to go in the third period. Prothro converted the extra point to tie the score at fourteen.

On the sideline, Wade turned to one of his assistants and remarked, "It looks like 1926 all over again," a reference to the amazing second-half comeback by his Alabama team to defeat Washington in the Rose Bowl.

It was now well after three o'clock in the afternoon, and most fans had been in their seats since 12:30, with thousands having arrived at eleven, when the gates opened. The metallic-gray skies were unsuccessful in holding off the sunshine that had been visible for days but that had been in hiding since dawn. The rain had stopped midway through the first period, but by then, the grass had succumbed to the ten hours of rain, and the players' uniforms were indicative of just how muddy the field had gotten. The ball was slippery, the traction was poor, and players wiped the condensation from their brows.

The clock at the south end of the stadium showed the official game time of just under one minute remaining in the third period, with a 14–14 tie. Oregon State had the ball on its own thirty-two-yard line, and center Quentin Greenough stood over it.

Eisan blew the ready-to-play whistle, and Dethman quickly took the direct snap from center. Halfbacks as receivers are taught to go out in the flat and turn downfield only if the defensive back comes up, and substitute halfback Gene Gray did just that. Dethman cocked his arm, took one final glance at Duke's All-Southern Conference back Tom Davis playing close on the receiver, and launched a thirty-three-yard pass. Davis, convinced the interception was his, confidently stepped toward the ball in flight. But Gray extended his arms as far as they could reach on his five-foot-ten frame, reeled the ball in, and took off. Duke's Moffett Storer closed in to make a surefire tackle, but Gray broke toward the goal line, some thirty yards away, stopped dead in his tracks, and Storer flew right by him. After a half pirouette, Gray's eyes focused on the end zone ahead of him, with perhaps the fiercest opponent, Duke captain Bob Barnett, standing helplessly at the line of scrimmage some fifty yards behind the play. Duke was in pursuit but failed to bring him down, and Gray converted a sixty-eight-yard touchdown pass, then the longest in Rose Bowl history.

The enthusiasm of Oregon State was tempered by Simas's blocked extra-point attempt, but the scoreboard read 20–14 Oregon State, with seconds remaining in the third period.

After interceptions by both sides, Durdan dropped deep into his own end zone after a bad snap from the three-yard line. He attempted to escape, but Mike Karmazin, leading a team of Duke tacklers, sacked Durdan for a safety, bringing the score to 20–16. And Duke was getting the ball back. Amazingly, more turnovers and stingy defense kept the score at 20–16, with just two minutes remaining in the game, when Duke took over on their own thirty-three-yard line.

With Duke fans on their feet and in full voice—not quite believing what they were seeing, but far from ready to concede—Davis took the ball on first down, dropped back, spotted Lach thirty yards downfield, and lofted the ball . . . It hung in the air just long enough for Durdan to step into the passing lane and pick off the throw.

With the ball on his own forty, Day faked a spinner behind the line and was dropped for a loss of five yards.

On second down, Durdan gained back three yards on a run to the right.

On third down, Stiner had Durdan punt, with the ball going out of bounds near Duke's thirty-six. Duke had one more chance to win the game.

With under one minute remaining, Wade substituted Bob Nanni, Bob Gantt, Moffett Storer, and Bobby Rute into the game, and on first down, Rute found Jim Smith for a gain of seventeen yards to OSC's forty-six.

Tick, tick, tick.

The players hustled back to the line of scrimmage, and Rute took a quick snap, but his pass was knocked down by Day. On second down, Storer went deep for the potential winning score, but Rute overthrew him.

It would come down to one play. All the buildup, from preseason practice until the final whistle, was about this one play. To many Americans listening on the radio, the result was secondary. Victory had already been achieved simply by playing the game. But to the men on the field, it mattered. It mattered to Jack Yoshihara, who was listening on a small radio in his parents' house in Portland.

Wade called for a Lach reverse, which had proved so successful on the day. But on the field, signal caller Tommy Prothro changed the call to a pass play for Davis. Duke's offense had as much confidence in their ability to score as if they were in the lead. But Wade was helpless on the bench as he watched the snap go to Rute, not to Lach. As Davis slipped on the still-slick field and as Bob Dethman intercepted the pass, the underdogs from the West sealed their victory over the mighty Blue Devils on their home turf.

Charles Haynes, who had spent the game on the sideline, anxiously anticipating an unlikely call to substitute, stood stunned as the final whistle blew and the OSC sideline rushed the field to embrace their teammates. Wade, stoic, walked over and extended his hand to Stiner, whose gleeful expression hid the bitter pill in his throat.

"Nice work, Coach," he managed to choke out, trying to conceal the conflicted anger he felt at his players for apparently ignoring his pleas to take Oregon State seriously—as evidenced by their lackluster performance after the extended Christmas break—and at himself for his own off-the-field distractions, what with staging the Rose Bowl in just two weeks. Stiner was gracious in victory, thanking Wade for being such a welcoming host. This somehow aggravated Wade as he forced a smile and looked over to see his star center, Barnett, standing perfectly, almost eerily, still at midfield. His eyes were cast toward the muddy grass beneath his feet, concealing tears. This would be his last time in a Duke football uniform.

Meanwhile, Dethman—who ended his OSC days rushing for 42 yards and passing for 148 to go along with game MVP Durdan's 46 rushing yards and an average 44.6 yards per punt—was overwhelmingly greeted by his teammates as he entered the Oregon State locker room. Dethman could barely get the neck of his jersey up over his head before a teammate would bring him in for a congratulatory hug. In a moment of reprieve, he threw the jersey over his head and got into a snap position, jokingly glaring at his teammates, who returned the gesture before falling over laughing. He then caught the eye of half-dressed Durdan, who was likewise transforming from football star back to civilian. In a conspiratorial gesture of appreciation, Dethman shot him a nod and a subtler version of the characteristic Dethman grin, which Durdan returned with a two-fingered salute.

Frank Parker, who had played twenty-eight minutes at guard, allowed a smile or two to escape an otherwise earnest facade that betrayed more-pervasive thoughts of his girl, Peggy, and the military assignment no doubt awaiting him on his return home.

Parker sat down on the stool in front of his locker and laced up his single pair of Oxfords, which leather rationing had made a valuable commodity, and, not wishing to fall back into a reverie, quickly threw his MacGregor Goldsmith–issue shoulder pads and helmet into his travel bag and exited the locker room, the last of the OSC players to do so.

Across the way in the Duke locker room was collective shock. To a man, they could not accept that they had actually lost the Rose Bowl. They hadn't lost the entire season. This was a home game. Against Oregon State. Coach Wade's admonitions rang in their ears, reverberated in their skulls. Tommy Prothro sat on the floor of the locker room and hung his head between his knees. Jim Smith stared at no one in particular, apparently still confused, like the outcome was a joke and the real game was still to be played. Steve Lach got undressed and, despite his characteristically brilliant performance, berated himself for not doing more.

Fans headed to the parking lots, many noticing not only their wallets and keys missing as they reached into their pockets but that their cars had been broken into during the game, a ripe target for thieves.

The telegraph wires were overwhelmed by writers filing their stories on the great Rose Bowl upset and by congratulatory telegrams pouring in from around the country for Stiner and his players.

Following the game, after the players of both teams had showered and dressed, they met at President Flowers's house for food and drinks just before OSC's long journey home. The jubilation and the disappointment had already begun to wane. Just after midnight, the Oregon State travel party was sent off by hundreds of Duke and Durham supporters at the train station, completing the circle of hospitality that began on their arrival.

And America was buoyed, if only for a day, by a game on a wet field in Durham.

"I'm going in[to the service]," the victorious captain Martin Chaves said to reporters after the Rose Bowl game. "I can die happy now. That's what winning a Rose Bowl game means to a fellow."

The afterthought boys from Oregon State—the sons of banana farmers and fishermen, the dump truck driver, the college dropouts who returned to finish school—had pushed themselves beyond the possible, with the subtle and not-so-subtle psychological maneuvers of their coach, himself an underestimated soul.

9. A NEW OPPONENT

Somewhere on the tracks in the plains of Texas, George Zellick, Bill Halverson, and Jim Busch established an impromptu committee. The three Beaver players huddled and decided that the situation had become too dire, too critical to continue, as after another rousing and drunken singing session on board the train, there simply was not enough fuel to last them the more than one thousand miles that remained on their journey home.

New Orleans had been a hoot—Bourbon Street on January 3 had set the bar pretty high for the train ride home. After stops in Charlotte, Atlanta, Montgomery, and Mobile, the Crescent City was a welcome diversion. After attending the transplanted East-West Shrine Game, the players took in the sights, sounds, and beverages of New Orleans before heading through Lafayette and Houston.

Their head coach was no longer on board, having left the team with his family in New Orleans to ride to Nebraska to visit his parents, charging Hal Moe with the responsibility of maintaining social order. But Moe wasn't much of a physical presence on the return trip, let alone a disciplinarian.

So Zellick, Halverson, and Busch pooled the players' remaining money—most of which had been made scalping Rose Bowl tickets in the days leading up to the game—and created subcommittees for the tasks at hand, with self-explanatory titles like Bourbon, Scotch, Gin, Coke, and Cheese and Crackers.

The plan was simple. During a fifteen-minute stopover in El Paso, the players would spill onto the streets around the railroad depot and stock up on as much as they could carry—until the money ran out.

As the *Beaver Express* pulled into El Paso, Frank Parker and the boys were dangling out the doors, ready to sprint. Parker saw the stopover as a mission to be accomplished. He scaled a six-foot-high wall between the station and downtown El Paso and attacked the unsuspecting stores with a fury. All made it back on board before the train pulled out of the station, and the sojourn was successful. Extra food and beverages were stored in the unused barbershop, in piles rising as high as the top of the empty barber's chair. The resupply held out until the train entered the dry state of New Mexico and the alcohol ran out again. A stopover in Tucson further addressed the issue.

Yuma and Palm Springs and Los Angeles followed, the train stopping in LA for three hours—Oregon State finally did make it to Southern California and the Rose Bowl stadium. Everywhere the train stopped, word spread quickly that the victors had rolled in, and the boys received hearty congratulations and well wishes from countless locals, many of them not even football fans. They came out to see the Rose Bowl champions, the boys who were front-page news.

What curbed the players' enjoyment of this newfound celebrity was that as the train made its way across the nation, they noticed more and more men who looked their age in uniform at train depots, jumping on or off trains headed to military bases. The drinks kept pouring, but thoughts and discussions gravitated toward their own uncertain futures.

On January 7, Don Durdan and Warren Simas got off the train near their hometowns of Eureka and Arcata to visit family and to be honored at a banquet at the Hotel Vance on the tenth. The others made their way through Sacramento and arrived in Albany, Oregon, at 5:16 A.M. on January 8. The local businesses hosted a breakfast for the returning heroes, after which each player was driven in a separate car to Corvallis.

Four thousand strong staged a rally in front of city hall in Corvallis, with Mayor H. W. Hand presenting a key to the city to the players. Martin Chaves, Jim Dixon, Andy Landforce, and trainer Dell Allman spoke to the crowd, and bands from Albany High School and Oregon State played. The celebration spilled into downtown, where local businesses had agreed to close down for two and a half hours for the celebration. There was no planned campus celebration that day, as the school was mourning the loss of a popular professor, H. T. Vance, though a rally and convocation had been scheduled for the following week.

Local newspapers displayed full-page advertisements from businesses the following day celebrating the Beaver win. One ad from Portland Gas & Coke Company, complete with a full team picture, included these words:

> *And in this war emergency, more than ever, let the achievements of Oregon State's truly great team stand as a timely example of what all of us can do by shoulder to shoulder teamwork—by resolutely turning the bad breaks into redoubled effort—by cooperating without dissension throughout every second of the game!*

The Oregon State student paper, *The Oregon State Barometer*, covered the arrival with much fanfare, though the story's placement next to a story on officials encouraging pedestrians to wear white clothing at night to avoid pedestrian fatalities during blackouts put things into perspective.

The celebrations continued throughout the night, and Oregon State administrators had little choice but to cancel classes the next day, about which they had few misgivings since they had more than made up for the missed classes by curbing the holiday break and resuming classes right after Christmas Day (even holding them on New Year's Day) to accelerate graduation for the many students who were being called to duty.

When University of Nebraska head coach Biff Jones rejoined the army, Lon Stiner's alma mater was in the market for a new coach. While Stiner and his family loved living in the West, speculation ran rampant that the coach was shopping around to put pressure on Oregon State to step up financially. In addition to those from Nebraska, there were whispers about Illinois and Yale showing interest. OSC quickly recognized Stiner's value as the Board of Higher Education approved a raise to $7,000 per year with a $2,000 bonus spread over six months on a four-year contract, allowing him to move his family to Arnold Way, an upscale Corvallis street full of Oregon State professors and their families.

The proceeds from the Rose Bowl game helped alleviate any financial concerns about the retention of Stiner, and Director of Athletics Percy Locey began the arduous task of refunding some $120,000 in purchases for those who had scrambled to buy tickets for the Pasadena game. In the coming months, the final numbers would come in. After deducting expenses and the agreed-upon sum to the Tournament of Roses, both Oregon State and Duke received $81,267.22 for their share. But there were more pressing concerns than money.

In the first ninety days after Pearl Harbor, more than 1,000 Oregon State students enlisted in the services, including Martin Chaves. More of Chaves's classmates left school every day as the spring of 1942 approached. There were 1,683 students still on Oregon State's campus in some form of military training or service, with 110 students commissioned immediately when war was declared and sent off to train recruits around the country. Uniforms on campus became more common, and both civilian and enlisted students were often friends or roommates. In some ways, war had less impact on daily life at Oregon State than on most other campuses around the country.

In early January, Oregon State registrar E. B. Lemon met with hundreds of students for a Q&A on the draft and selective service. Among the notable points he delivered to the men in attendance: local draft boards make the ultimate decisions about deferments; the OSC selective services advisory committee could write letters on students' behalf only to request deferment; students could enlist in the navy as long as they had not already been inducted into the army; and those students in advanced ROTC could complete their schoolwork before being commissioned.

That same day, word reached the student body of the V-7 United States Naval Reserve Midshipmen's School program, which would allow current juniors and seniors to obtain commission in the U.S. Navy Reserve as deck and engineering officers after earning their degrees. The army, still in need of soldiers and leaders, canvassed West Coast schools for new officers.

Contributions to the war effort were not restricted to students, as dozens of faculty members gave their time or expertise. President Emeritus George Peavy was appointed defense coordinator for Benton County, KOAC radio station became a key part of the emergency warning system, and professors served as plane spotters or on state and national boards, such as the War Price and Rationing Board. The need for an abundance of wood during the war, both at home and on the fields of battle, stimulated OSC research in various departments, leading to the use of fir bark as a cork substitute; the School of Agriculture determined more efficient ways to increase production. The Chemistry Department researched antimalarial drugs, and Professor Joseph Schulein of the Chemical Engineering Department led research into the use of chromium in aircraft. The Bacteriology Department instructed sanitary engineers, while the Department of Foods and Nutrition was established to assist in nutrition for Americans during the national emergency.

This was a campus at war.

In January, days after the Rose Bowl loss, the Duke University trustees awarded unlimited power to a small executive committee to deal with war-related issues and the resulting impacts on Duke, including transforming its mission, if needed. Administrators formed a committee to review how Duke could accelerate graduation to allow a faster entry into the military for its students. The ultimate recommendations included increasing the semester course loads, reducing the number of hours required for graduation from 122 to 120, and eliminating the annual spring break. Incoming freshmen were permitted to begin classes in the summer, before their freshman year traditionally began. Students in the School of Law could complete their degrees in two years, as opposed to three, in an accelerated program. Even in the critical course of study for students in the School of Medicine, two classes of students per year would be admitted, and they would complete their studies in three years.

Duke assured students that those in good standing who left for enlistment or the draft could resume their studies at any time without having to reapply to the university and at no additional charge. No matter the acceleration plans, it was clear in the spring of 1942 that a large percentage of Duke men would not complete their degrees before putting on military uniforms.

Shortly after New Year's Day, the navy V-7 program was announced, and it was swamped with junior and senior applicants who sought to remain on campus through graduation before being commissioned. More than 130 students signed up for a midyear navy ROTC class, avoiding the possibility of being drafted into the army. The Civil Pilot Training Program (CPTP) course work included seventy-two hours of ground school and thirty-five hours of flight time and was limited to upperclassmen in the navy V-7 program. Under normal circumstances, both the Army Air Corps and the navy required two years of college work, but in wartime, the completion of the current college year was the minimum to move to active duty.

One of the more notable and noticeable changes at Duke was the controversial offering of courses. The College of Engineering, for example, created classes in technical drawing for those seeking drafting positions in war industries, practical astronomy and navigation for future flight navigators, communication engineering to prepare students to operate military communications, and meteorology and aviation. The Department of Mathematics offered plane trigonometry and mathematical and artillery fire. A heavy emphasis was placed on physics and chemistry majors, who could help manufacture bombs, and on engineering and math students, who could design wartime machines and planes. Duke appointed faculty and military advisers to assist students in selecting the right war-related courses.

Not all administrators, faculty, students, and alumni were supportive of the new course offerings. Some believed that Duke's mission was to provide a well-rounded liberal arts education for its students and that military course work and training should be left to other institutions. Duke would struggle during the war years to maintain its commitment to liberal arts education while indulging in the realism of the times, preparing students to defend that education. Despite the debate, summer school registration exploded, as many students attempted to finish their degrees before being drafted.

The impact of war, beyond the sight of men leaving campus or walking to classes in uniforms, was felt in the rationing of sugar and Coca-Cola products (and eventually coffee, oil, bicycles, typewriters, and more) and in a shortage of cafeteria workers, including waiters and staff who were now working on nearby military posts, slowing things down at chow time. Production of radios and phonographs stopped. Students were bombarded with advertisements and promotions for war bonds and stamps in the Dope Shop and elsewhere on campus. In fact, as a way to raise money for the war effort, the student-run Duke War Council proposed that men voluntarily purchase a twenty-five-cent defense stamp before taking off with their dates on East Campus.

Though Corvallis had been experiencing air-raid drills and blackouts since Halloween, Durham officials did not conduct their first drill until April 1942, when Durham County instituted an air-raid warning system, using the whistles of local tobacco factories and cotton mills to alert citizens, with phones in the boiler rooms of the plants on standby to connect with authorities. On April 24, the first Durham/Duke blackout was held between 9:00 P.M. and 11:00 P.M., which just happened to coincide with the Naval Relief Ball taking place in the new gymnasium on campus. Attendees were permitted to continue to enjoy the dance, but students on campus were required to obey the blackout prohibitions.

The more than one thousand air wardens in Durham organized and monitored the trial blackout, with cars stopped in their tracks, homes and businesses shut down, Duke coeds mandated to leave their dates within three minutes and return to their dorms—and their dates required to assemble in the science building. Any violations resulted in fines of fifty dollars. The drill was viewed as an inconvenience by some, an entertaining nighttime activity by others, and it showed Durham just how far it needed to go to be ready for an attack.

The changes in Corvallis and in Durham were mirrored in the early months of 1942 by significant organizational and operational changes in the United States military command as it fully prepared for a world war. The first troops were sent to Britain in January, but they were a long way from fighting, as the Allies had yet to decide where to attack first in Europe. The army reorganized its command structures and the Joint Chiefs of Staff was created to advise the president and to work with the British Imperial General Staff. At home, President Roosevelt extended daylight saving time to year-round, conserving precious electricity for production.

Winston Churchill was opposed to the full-scale invasion of France in 1943 advocated by the U.S. Joint Chiefs of Staff. Rather, the British prime minister suggested landings in North Africa to chip away at the Axis foothold and to enlist the French armies there in aiding in the larger battle against Germany. After a second Washington conclave in June and further discussions in London, Roosevelt sided with Churchill and planning began for an Allied assault in North Africa by the end of 1942.

"You know, Coach, before this war is over, they might call you up," Duke publicist Ted Mann joked to Wallace Wade Sr. shortly after Pearl Harbor.

"They might not have to call me, Ted," the forty-nine-year-old replied.

Even before America's entrance into World War II, as the country mobilized for war and as many of Wade's former players and coaches entered the service—either on their own or through the draft—Wade felt guilty. Guilty that he had not served in combat during World War I. Guilty that he was merely coaching a game of football while some of his current and former boys were preparing for battle. Guilty even that his mind was wandering from football, a disservice to his team. It was his duty to serve. In keeping with his very private nature, he shared his desire with no one outside of his family, but after December 7, Wade was resolute in his decision to join the military and fight, and, shortly after the Rose Bowl game in 1942, Wade reached out to the United States Army and volunteered.

"My boys were going in and I felt like we should stay together as a team," Wade was later quoted. "We were just participating in a different battle." Of course, Wade did not really have a close personal connection to his players, but as a collective, they were *his*. He wasn't going in to fight alongside Bob Barnett or Charles Haynes, per se, but he did want to do what his players were being asked to do.

Sixteen days after his father's Rose Bowl loss, Wallace Wade Jr. walked into a recruitment center in Durham and enlisted in the United States Army. Like his father, he had already decided to enter the army shortly after Pearl Harbor. Like most of his friends, Wade Jr. could not have understood just what lay ahead, but he stood firmly and proudly when he informed his parents he was leaving the comfort of their home for combat. He packed his bags with the intention of being away from home for a good long while, but he didn't have to travel far for basic training, as his assignment lay just ninety miles south, at Fort Bragg. Named after Braxton Bragg, a Confederate general, the permanent military base would be home to the 9th Infantry Division, 2nd Armored Division, and the 82nd Airborne Division, among many other army units in the coming years, and swelled from a population of 5,400 in 1940 to well over 70,000 by late 1941.

On March 16, Wade Sr. was notified of his appointment as a major in the army and ordered to report to Fort Bragg himself. Dean Wannamaker responded on behalf of the university:

> *Naturally, we regret to lose a man who has meant so much to our institution. But it has been the policy of Duke University to cooperate in every way possible with the government in the matter of releasing faculty members for the armed forces when they are needed.*
>
> *In a crisis such as confronts our country today, the needs of the government are of first importance.*

On campus his speech was met by a mixture of shock and sadness yet understanding, and to show their support, the day before he departed for Fort Bragg, Duke students gave Wade a ten-foot scroll with a U.S. coat of arms at the top and a clear message of appreciation.

Best of luck, Coach Wade. We, the students of Duke University, wish to take this opportunity to express our sincere admiration to a fine gentleman, a great coach, and a true soldier.

The students walked with Wade from the presentation spot in front of the Duke University Chapel to his home on campus, serenading him with Duke fight songs along the way. Two beautiful rose bushes stood alongside Wade as he bid adieu to the students in front of his home. The bushes were just two of the fifty prize rose bushes sent by the Tournament of Roses to Duke University in appreciation of all their efforts toward holding up the Rose Bowl tradition. Forty-six of the bushes were planted in two beds behind the north goal in the stadium and two on the grounds of Dean Wannamaker's home.

Later that afternoon, Wade Sr.'s longtime assistant, Eddie Cameron, took over as head football coach and director of athletics. In a diary entry that night, March 27, Wade Sr. expressed his sadness.

Put on uniform 3 PM and had pictures made with Eddie and staff. Turned the keys over to Eddie. Felt very queer to be no longer connected with Duke University after 11 ⅓ years.

Wade Jr. came home from Fort Bragg on the day of his father's departure and traveled back with him, leaving Frances by herself. Wade Sr. had always been protective of his wife, and it was a shot in the gut to leave her alone in Durham.

Left home at 7:45 PM with Wallace. Mother at home alone, Sissy in hospital. Was awfully hard to leave her. She seemed to be very brave about it. Hope she does not mind too much and does not get too lonely. Arrived at Camp at 10 PM.

On his way out of town, he stopped by a media relations staff member's house and requested that he check in on Frances in the coming days. He was afraid his absence would be long.

Major Wallace Wade Sr. reported for duty and was welcomed by Brigadier General E. P. Parker and other Fort Bragg notables—a reception reserved only for someone with high military accolades or commensurate national stature. Wade Sr. quickly recognized that much had changed since his military days more than twenty years prior, from the type of young men in uniform to the new forms of weaponry. In World War I, the Springfield bolt-action rifle was standard, but with the introduction of the M1 Garand in 1936, the Americans now had a superior weapon that allowed soldiers to fire off multiple rounds before reloading.

In addition to adapting to changes, Wade Sr. learned that his value to the army was not just as a soldier but as a promotional and motivational tool, as he and his son appeared on a Fort Bragg radio program together on his first full day. He began his assignment of supervising training and instruction with the 10th Battalion, 4th Regiment, Field Artillery Replacement Center, under the command of Lieutenant Colonel John C. Butner Jr., the battalion commander, who had been a teammate of Wade Sr.'s on the 1916 Brown University football team.

Wade Sr. served as assistant battalion executive for a few weeks and then spent time in the basic cannoneer course, studying for four weeks in the replacement center school, taking refresher courses alongside boys three decades younger than he was. But here, Wade Sr. saw an opportunity to inspire. The Old Man routinely ate lunch on the training field with his men, instructed them on proper firing technique on the range, and made himself available for miscellaneous military counsel. Military training was like football training, Wade Sr. believed, with specialization for each man but enough common knowledge of the other positions to work as a team.

In May, the coach returned to Duke for a war rally day, to honor those students and faculty currently serving in the armed services and those who would soon join them. He listened to the beating drums of the Duke marching band and the Fort Bragg drum and bugle corps.

"In the past, I have participated with you in many athletic pep rallies," Wade Sr. reminded a crowd of thousands, "and we thought them important. Today you are staging another kind of pep rally, one of the most important contests in the history of the human race. And that covers a lot of time and a lot of contests."

The fight was under way in the South Pacific when Wallace Wade shared those sentiments in may. The Pacific war would be fought with a different kind of soldier and strategy from those to be used in the European theater. First off, unlike Europe, the Pacific was largely a maritime war, meaning the navy would lead one of the major drives towards Japan with Marines and army forces conducting invasions in the Central Pacific, while General Douglas MacArthur led another drive in the Southwest Pacific towards the Philippines. Second, America would not only take the strong lead in the Pacific theater but would provide the vast majority of forces and be relatively free of the diplomatic requirements of the European theater. Third, the Japanese would be much different from the Germans, not only in their tactics but in their willingness to fight to the death. Finally, the war in the Pacific would feature intense fighting in the jungles and mountains of New Guinea and in the Philippines as well as a methodical island hopping over thousands of miles of remote islands in the South and Central Pacific.

As the calendar turned to 1942, Douglas MacArthur and his mixed bag of Filipino and American forces was no match for the better trained and equipped Japanese invaders, supported as they were by air and naval superiority and proximity to home bases. In January 1942, the general and his troops were on the island of Luzon when he made the decision to withdraw to the Bataan Peninsula, knowing that the Japanese were converging on Manila from many directions. MacArthur believed that the narrow peninsula would make it difficult for the Japanese to outflank his forces and could provide enough delay for American reinforcements to arrive.

The reinforcements would not be sent. The American military knew that after the attacks on Pearl Harbor had seriously depleted the American Pacific fleet, they simply were not ready to fight off a superior Japanese force halfway across the world.

Roosevelt ordered MacArthur to safely evacuate to Australia to ensure a continuity of command, but that meant leaving his troops with little food, even less ammunition, and suffering from widespread malaria and dysentery. The units held out until April 9 (though American forces on Corregidor, a small island in Manila Bay off the tip of Bataan, held out for another month).

Roughly seventy thousand Filipino and American soldiers were ordered to surrender and begin what would be chillingly commemorated as the Bataan Death March. The march was really several marches of groups of POWs over a period of weeks—including the sixty-mile trek leading to the train depot in San Fernando. They marched in the burning sun with no fresh water and no food. They marched through the day—and sometimes through the night—and were given only a few hours to sleep at irregular intervals in open fields. Any soldier who slowed down or got out of line was shot, stabbed by a bayonet, or beaten to death with clubs, his corpse left on the road for stray dogs to eat. Men urinated or defecated while they walked and were often subject to random acts of unspeakable violence by Japanese soldiers as they did so. If the POWs were "lucky" enough to survive, they were boarded onto trains to concentration and POW camps, where thousands more died from disease, starvation, or random execution.

The war in the Pacific was brutal, and the Americans were already losing.

10. *SHIKATA GA NAI*

Shikata ga nai. The Japanese phrase, passed on from generation to generation, means simply "It can't be helped" or "No control over events." Yet it is more than a phrase; it is a philosophical approach to many of life's hardships that the Japanese people have endured for centuries. But while the Western perception of the concept might be hopelessness, to the Japanese, it's a rather apathetic understanding of reality.

Jack Yoshihara had heard the phrase many times growing up in Portland but never fully understood its meaning. It became clear as he listened to the Rose Bowl victory on the radio.

Despite angst about returning to Oregon State after New Year's, all but six students of Japanese ancestry returned while four others actually enrolled for the first time. Life was not easy, with constant stares and racial slurs, and the general insecurity about being the "enemy" behind enemy lines took its toll. President Gilfillan did what he could to ensure not only their safety but the continuation of their education. However, in addition to the curfew and travel restrictions already imposed on them, the students were prohibited from attending night classes.

By early May 1942, just twenty-two Oregon State students of Japanese descent were still enrolled, according to the school, some transferring to colleges much farther inland, others simply moving home. Quakers and other religious groups paid tuition for Japanese American students from the West to enroll at acceptable schools far from the coast in the Midwest and East, and some OSC students took advantage. As a testament to their determination and resolve, five Japanese American students earned their Oregon State degrees in May of 1942. Yoshihara stuck out the semester and completed his sophomore year in good standing.

Lieutenant General John L. DeWitt would have been satisfied if every man or woman of Japanese ancestry were expelled from the United States. The next-best thing in his mind was to remove the "aliens" from the West Coast, where they were more likely to inflict harm upon the country through subterfuge and spying. But the decision to remove Japanese Americans from the West Coast and create "relocation centers" did not happen overnight and was the result of many months of politicking and public-relations fearmongering.

Though Japanese Americans already faced travel restrictions and prohibitions on cameras, radios, and weapons, DeWitt and the government took steps to minimize the potential—but unfounded—threat from the Japanese Americans, many of whom had known only America in their lives. After President Roosevelt ordered all "aliens" in the West to reregister with the government in mid-January, the process moved quickly. First came Attorney General Francis Biddle's issuance of orders declaring certain areas along the Pacific Coast as "strategic" and ordering the removal of any aliens from those locations. A few weeks later, DeWitt recommended to Secretary of War Henry Stimson that all "Japanese and other subversive persons" from the West Coast be removed. On February 19, Roosevelt signed Executive Order 9066, doing just that, and Stimson put DeWitt in charge of the removal.

His first move under his new authority was to declare portions of

California, Oregon, and Washington and one-third of Arizona as military zones requiring the removal of the Japanese. That was followed by the designation of additional areas in Idaho, Montana, Utah, and Nevada. All told, more than one thousand areas were off-limits to Japanese Americans. On March 18, just a month after signing Executive Order 9066, Roosevelt created the War Relocation Authority (WRA) to oversee the detention camps. Many Japanese communities were gutted in the late spring and summer, and residents were sent either directly to hastily built internment camps or to assembly areas near major cities.

The first forced evacuations began on March 30, when Japanese American residents on Bainbridge Island were forcibly removed from their homes. Residents of Oregon had just weeks or even days to sell their property and pack only what they could carry to move to a camp. There were other options, howerer. The military allowed a three-week window in which Japanese Americans could evacuate the exclusion zones to move to new towns and cities in the Midwest, which some took advantage of, though they often faced extreme prejudice in their new "homes."

By early August, more than 110,000 Japanese had been forced from their homes. The Yoshiharas were among them.

After Pearl Harbor, the family restaurant business in Portland dried up, and the family lost its lease on its space downtown. Jack Yoshihara began the process of selling the family's belongings in the spring, including his cherished 1941 Chevy, a sparkling, brand-new automobile that he sold for just twenty-five dollars after buying it for hundreds. Along with his entire family, Yoshihara arrived, as ordered, at the Portland Assembly Center, otherwise known as the Pacific International Livestock Exposition, the temporary home for almost four thousand Japanese Americans.

The Portland Assembly Center stunk like horse and cow manure for good reason. It was on a site where hundreds of animals slept, ate, and relieved themselves. Military authorities had placed simple wood planks over the ground for flooring, as if that would protect the new arrivals from the stench. When families arrived, they were registered, given ID tags, assigned a small cubicle, and given a mattress cover with instructions to fill it with hay to form a rudimentary mattress. Plywood separated the cubicles, there were no ceilings, and the doors were really just small holes in the plywood. The summer heat only exacerbated the smell.

Those held at the Portland Assembly Center attempted to create a daily routine, especially for the children and teens. The Japanese organized work squads of skilled laborers, who steadily improved conditions as much as possible and provided daily maintenance of common areas. There was a makeshift barbershop, a post office, a police and fire department. And unfortunately for the children, who, ignorant of the nefarious implications, saw their new quarters as a place to play for the summer, schools were established inside the assembly center. Yoshihara spent his days playing basketball or competing in judo and talking with friends about girls. One in particular.

Most of the young Japanese children in Japantown knew one another through neighborhoods, school, sports, and often through churches, the basis for organization in the community and the place where Yoshihara first became acquainted with Elsie Masuda. Elsie, the daughter of Ryonosuke and Fukiyo Masuda, was four years younger than Jack, but easy as it was to behold her young beauty, he was taken by her maturity and passion for athletics. They became more closely acquainted inside the walls of the Portland Assembly Center, and among the daily tension of uncertainty, love began to bloom.

In the third week of August, authorities announced that the Portland Assembly Center would be closed and that its inhabitants would be placed in one of ten permanent incarceration camps established by the WRA around the West Coast. Yoshihara, along with thousands of others—mostly young, strong men—were herded like cattle into 1920s-era train cars at Portland's Union Station, the blinds drawn tight, headed for an unknown destination. His family would join him later.

The train came to a stop about 560 miles east of Portland. Yoshihara stepped off the train, immediately overwhelmed by the heat and the dust and the wind that seemed as thick as Oregon fog as it filled his lungs. He was taken to the Minidoka War Relocation Center.

The camp was thirty-three thousand acres of sagebrush, basaltic lava flow and ash, rattlesnakes, and dust, fifteen miles north of Twin Falls, near the town of Hunt, in the Snake River Plain. Construction on the massive Minidoka camp had officially begun in June 1942, but as early as February, 151 Japanese Americans from Alaska were sent to Minidoka. Construction was still in progress when Yoshihara arrived with his fellow detainees. Six hundred buildings, five miles of barbed wire, eight watchtowers, and tens of thousands of unused acres. The tar-papered barracks were subdivided into four groups with thirty-six blocks, each housing twelve barracks, a mess hall, latrine, showers, and a laundry. Families shared one room with cots and one light.

Yoshihara was promptly assigned to help complete fire stations, but the complex construction project and planned infrastructure gave Yoshihara the frightening impression that this might be his final stop.

Once the general population arrived at Minidoka, Elsie Masuda and Yoshihara lived separately with their families but found time for private conversations in back areas of the laundry. The difficult circumstances drew them closer. Masuda and Yoshihara received special permission from camp administrators, and in April 1943, they went to the county seat to get married. No family and friends. Just a piece of paper.

They roomed together once married. Yoshihara worked for the camp's fire department while his wife worked in the kitchens and dining areas, earning eighteen dollars a month washing dishes and setting tables. Yoshihara also received permission to work on local farms and to drive a delivery truck, though he was prohibited from going west of Arlington, Oregon. He passed the time at the camp outside of work by using the technical skills he'd learned at Benson Polytechnic High

School in Portland to carve little toys and construct pieces of furniture from leftover wood pallets brought into the camp. He also helped construct raised walkways between the barracks and the mess hall and laundry so residents could avoid thick mud or sticky dust when walking between the buildings. He helped fathers dig small holes underneath the barracks where young children could rest in the shade in the stifling midday heat.

Like at the Portland Assembly Center, "residents" of the camp attempted to create normalcy, even within the confines of their predicament. There would eventually be recreational areas, general stores, barbershops, a watch repair store, a health clinic, a theater, a social hall, and elementary schools. The junior high and high schools and community offices were in Block 23, and later a gym was added as well as nine baseball diamonds. Yoshihara participated in recreational activities, including the Japanese baseball and basketball leagues, and the "Sagebrush World Series" between resident blocks. The internees cleared and cultivated 350 acres for a vegetable farm after building a small irrigation canal, and they increased the size of the farmland each year.

But despite the efforts to create a close-to-normal lifestyle, internees were constantly reminded of their plight by the barbed wire and sentry towers and guards with weapons. The barracks were cramped, and the temperature could dip well below zero in the winter and reach stiflingly hot levels in the summer. A cemetery was created in the northwest areas of the camp, as men and women, mostly elders, passed away. The population of Minidoka reached over nine thousand at its peak.

Of course, at times, with American prejudice and resentment running at a fever pitch outside the camps, some of the internees felt more comfortable within the camp fences. In locales like Hood River, the home of Oregon State star Bob Dethman, anti-Japanese sentiment ran high. In the hours after Pearl Harbor, federal agents had stormed Hood River in the middle of the night, arresting supposed leaders of the Japanese American contingent.

Anti-Japanese exclusionists initially refused to serve Japanese in restaurants or to sell them goods before they were relocated, and then, instead of caring for their neighbors' land as promised, Hood River residents often used the land for their own gain or simply let it go to waste. Well before the outbreak of war, the harassment of Japanese in Hood River was increasing. Leading Japanese community leaders protested the treatment and refuted a charge of "Japanese domination" in Hood River, pointing out that there were only seventy Japanese farmers controlling just 2 percent of the land. In early 1942, the Issei of Hood River signed a pledge reinforcing their love of America and pledging their "loyalty to the Stars and Stripes." Portland Japanese residents sent a telegram to President Roosevelt pledging their services to "destroy Japan and her Axis partner . . ." Yet in the winter of 1942, as the federal government enacted orders restricting Japanese Americans, the Hood River Apple Growers Association openly fought to take control of Japanese farms. The message was clear.

In January of 1943, Secretary of War Henry Stimson announced the formation of the 442nd Regimental Combat Team, a special military unit made up solely of Japanese men in America, including the territory of Hawaii, led by a group of Caucasian officers. Ironically, there were 3,188 Nisei—the children of Japanese immigrants born in the United States—in the U.S. military when Pearl Harbor was attacked, and not surprisingly, many of them immediately faced scorn. But by 1943, the government believed that Japanese Americans—with proper control—could be trusted to serve. In the process of forming the unit, authorities required an Application for Leave Clearance, commonly referred to as a "loyalty questionnaire," to be completed, which, in essence, was a loyalty test for all Japanese men over the age of seventeen. Among the questions:

> *28. Will you swear unqualified allegiance to the United States of America and faithfully defend the United States from any and all attack by foreign or domestic forces, and forswear any form of allegiance to the Japanese emperor or any other foreign government, power, or organization?*

Within the camps, a strong divide became readily apparent between those who declined to swear allegiance to the United States, a group dubbed the "No Boys," and those who pledged their loyalty to the country that had imprisoned them. Arguments and even fistfights erupted between family and friends as individuals struggled with the decision. The "No Boys" organized their own defiant groups and were eventually relocated to the Tule Lake Relocation Center in the uppermost parts of California, near the Oregon border, along with other Japanese Americans who refused to pledge their loyalty to the United States.

Yoshihara did not hesitate to pledge, having already attempted to enlist in the U.S. Army when war broke out, and he pledged his allegiance to the only country he had ever known.

Pledging allegiance to the United States is one thing; raising your hand for battle is another, and many men in the camps who had signed the pledge did not voluntarily join the 442nd. Many Japanese Americans in Hawaii did, following in the footsteps of the all-Hawaiian 100th Infantry Battalion, formed in 1942. With the exception of approximately three hundred people held in detention, the Japanese Americans in Hawaii were never interned in camps like their brethren on the mainland, and, in fact, many were already serving in uniform for the Hawaii National or State Guard. Eventually, the army held a special draft for Japanese Americans to fill the spots in the unit.

Over the summer of 1943, Yoshihara learned that Quakers were sponsoring Japanese Americans in the camps, allowing them to attend colleges throughout the country. Yoshihara had already been given the privilege of leaving the camp to work and wondered if he could finish his college degree somewhere else. Via letters, he reached out to the football coach at the University of Utah, who agreed to give him a spot on the roster if he attended the university.

In the fall of 1943, Yoshihara was released from Minidoka and enrolled at the University of Utah on a Quaker-funded scholarship, working as a busboy in Salt Lake City to support himself. He suited up for football and rarely came off the field during the 1943 season, playing quarterback and fullback despite suffering a knee injury. It was a far cry from the occasional game appearance for Yoshihara at Oregon State. Of course, he still noticed the stares and dirty looks in Salt Lake City, but at least he was in college and playing football again.

Ultimately, Yoshihara decided to leave school and return to Minidoka, preferring to be behind guard with his wife and newborn daughter, Lynn. Elsie had given birth in the camp's infirmary on October 20, with Japanese doctors and nurses assisting but with no narcotics or anesthesia. It was a happy day in an otherwise difficult year.

In June 1942, Wallace Wade Sr. received a letter from Major General Alexander Surles offering Wade an assignment to coach a team of Army All-Stars in exhibition football games against professional teams around the country to boost morale, aid in recruitment, and sell war bonds. Wade had not reenlisted in the army to coach football—he could have done that staying at home in Durham. He asked to be relieved of the assignment "in order to have a better chance of getting combat duty."

The conversation was put on the back burner, and on June 15, his fiftieth birthday, Wade took charge of the 5th Battalion at the Field Artillery Replacement Training Center, in addition to his duties assisting with the physical fitness training program at Fort Bragg. But on July 13, Wade was summoned to Washington, D.C., to meet with Major General Surles, who informed Wade and his old nemesis and friend, Robert Neyland, also in the army, that he was going to speak with General George C. Marshall about the two football legends coaching the Army All-Stars. Again, Wade requested to remain in the field artillery. A few hours later, Surles told the coaches that Marshall had selected them to coach the army team. In the commander's eyes, Wade was more valuable to the army as a coach than in training with troops. In a diary entry the night of July 13, he wrote: "I was terribly disappointed, about as low as any time in my life."

Wade returned to Fort Bragg and prepared to coach again. On July 15, an army plane at Pope Field took off at 6:00 A.M. with Wade on board, headed to Norfolk, Virginia, picked up Neyland, and flew to New York City for a press conference announcing the football exhibitions. By 10:30 P.M., Wade was back in his quarters at Fort Bragg.

Despite his disappointment, his personality dictated that he throw himself wholeheartedly into everything he did, and on July 20, Wade traveled to Washington to begin work on the football team. A week later, he and Neyland submitted a list of forty army soldiers to be ordered to Camp Cooke in California for training.

Wade himself arrived at Camp Cooke on August 2, with the first practice scheduled for the seventh, and the first game, against the Washington Redskins, on the thirtieth. On the twenty-third, Wade drove to San Diego and watched Washington play, and Redskins receiver Al Kruger made some sensational catches. This was the same Al Kruger who had caught the winning pass from USC's Doyle Nave in the 1939 Rose Bowl game to spoil Duke's unbeaten season.

On the twenty-fourth, when Wade's team of Army All-Stars held a practice at the Rose Bowl, the Tournament of Roses Association took the occasion to present Wade with a certificate of appreciation for all that he had done for the Rose Bowl. Wade was gracious but simmering with disappointment as he forced his lips to curl into a passable smile before the committee. Though he had saved a Rose Bowl and had been forgiven for his publicity faux pas in 1938, the machinations to stage the game in Durham had taken away meaningful hours from his game preparation. He was appreciative but understandably still raw about the loss.

On August 30, sixty thousand fans saw Washington easily defeat the Army All-Stars 26–7 in the Los Angeles Memorial Coliseum. Redskins great Sammy Baugh was spectacular, throwing two touchdowns and putting on a rushing display that showed off the athleticism for which he was known. Most important, despite the loss, the army team achieved its goals, promoting the armed services, spiking morale, and—with gate receipts of more than $80,000—contributing $45,000 to the Army Emergency Relief fund.

After Los Angeles, it was on to Denver, where Wade's team defeated the Chicago Cardinals 16–10 in front of twenty thousand spectators, with former Texas A&M star and now enlisted soldier John Kimbrough scoring twice. Over the next ten days, Army beat the Detroit Lions and lost to both the Green Bay Packers and the New York Giants, finishing the promotional series 2–3.

Wade returned to Durham on September 23, visited Frances and Sis, and watched Duke practice in the afternoon. The following day, when he returned to Fort Bragg, he felt out of place—guilty for letting down his men by having to travel the country as a football coach. He immediately went into the field with his men and reimmersed himself in the soldiering life, pausing only briefly on October 3 to see Sis marry Lieutenant Robert Clark in a ceremony in the Duke University Chapel followed by a reception at the Wades' house. He headed back to Fort Bragg on the fifth, but not before saying a sad good-bye to Frances.

> *Wallace and I left at 6:30 PM Left for Bragg. Seemed like old times. Also the same, sad feeling, leaving Frances at home all alone. She is little and needs somebody with her. This is undoubtedly the hardest part to me of being in the Army, leaving her at home alone.*

Wallace Wade Jr. had already completed basic training and transferred to Fort Sill in Oklahoma, the same place his father had trained in World War I, and spent two months in a special service school for signalmen over the summer. When he returned to Fort Bragg, his leave days were spent at home with his mother in Durham or on the sideline of Duke football games. In October 1942, Wade Jr. was assigned to the 60th Field Artillery of the 9th Infantry Division, with an expectation of going overseas in the coming weeks.

In the fall of 1942 Duke welcomed a whole new type of student, as the army had selected the university to host the Army Finance School. Duke had actually lobbied the army to host the school, as Duke administrators were worried about the financial impact of the drop in enrollment of traditional male students. Hundreds of soldiers descended on Duke for ten weeks at a time (more than 2,850 would eventually pass through). They rose at 5:30 A.M. for conditioning, took classes from 7:30 A.M. to 4:30 P.M., and then drilled on the fields. To accommodate the soldiers, four fraternity houses were cleared for lodging, and classes were held in the law school and in the president's house.

The traditional students and the soldiers did not always get along, with some students making fun of the men in uniform, prompting an editorial in *The Chronicle*.

> *Student jocular imitation of members of the armed forces now stationed here for the duration, although not malicious, is an insult to the uniform. We would not think of showing disrespect for the flag. The uniform is just as much an emblem of our national unity as the flag. And wearing that uniform are those who have shown themselves willing to sacrifice their lives for our nation. We owe them the utmost respect.*

Of course, men were not the only contributors to the war effort in America, as women enlisted in the United States Coast Guard to draw much-needed maps while others undertook traditional male jobs in factories and in business. Duke's engineering college would soon allow women to enroll in select classes, and coeds across campus helped the war effort by making more than sixteen thousand surgical dressings for Duke University Hospital and the military and by training in the Women's Army Auxiliary Corps (WAAC) and the navy's Women Accepted for Volunteer Emergency Service (WAVES) to learn how to march, salute, and drill. Women also supported Fort Bragg and Camp Butner and assisted with the United Service Organizations, the Red Cross, and at Duke Hospital, and more than six hundred female students took noncredit classes in first aid, child care, nutrition, and civilian protection, with some taking a leading role in establishing and supervising the air-warning system for campus.

Duke was very much a campus at war by late 1942, but loss and sacrifice had not been felt—yet.

PART IV

WAR

There are no great men, just great challenges which ordinary men, out of necessity, are forced by circumstance to meet.

—Admiral William Halsey Jr., United States Navy

11. THE FIRST

CHARLES HAYNES COULDN'T WAIT to fight, but his early attempts proved futile. Even before America's entry into the war, he tried to enlist in the Royal Canadian Air Force, which was already engaged in battle, but when Haynes couldn't read all the letters on the eye chart from a distance, he was denied. He vowed that he would never let those eyes fail him again. It was not a surprise to his mother—though she was against his decision—that Haynes left Duke in good standing in May 1942 to enlist in the army, memorizing the eye chart to ensure he passed. He initially volunteered for the cavalry, with his experience on horseback and with the false belief that the cavalry would play a vital role for the Americans, just as his father had left Trinity College during World War I to join the horse riders.

Haynes set off for basic training, assuming it would be like preseason football camp under Wallace Wade. As it had for many of his teammates, it took only a few months away from his parents and from Duke for the young man to grow up quickly. Still, his constant gratefulness and optimism remained strong. In a letter home from Texas in December 1942, Haynes wrote:

Hope I am not disappointing your first expectations. I owe you both more than I can ever repay, for being the best parents a soldier ever had. I could never begin to thank you enough for all the opportunities you've both given me. You've never disappointed me in anything I ever wanted or asked for and I'm not too spoiled, am I? . . . I hate to say it, but I didn't realize fully how fortunate I was at home and how much having an education really meant to me until I joined the Army . . . I won't let you down. Here's a kiss for you mother, and a salute to you, Lt. from Pvt. Jr.

Haynes trained at Fort Clark in Texas and, set on becoming an army officer, applied to Officer Candidate School. Like his colleagues, Haynes was ordered to ship all photography equipment home—the government was fearful that plans, equipment, and locations might be revealed—and undertook a round of drugs to prevent spinal meningitis. He spent his rest time writing letter after letter home to his parents, sending two to three a week. He moved to Fort Riley in Kansas, where he starred on the fort's polo and football teams and served as his company's athletic officer. He was offered the opportunity to transfer to Washington, D.C., to take care of President Roosevelt's horse stable, but Haynes declined, preferring battle to horse care. He was destined to lead, he believed, though nothing extraordinary about Haynes would hint at that belief. And, despite his reminiscences of home, he longed to be engaged in battle. He was a soldier's soldier, following orders to the tiniest of details and emerging as a leader among his training groups.

Back at Duke, new football coach Eddie Cameron had big shoes to fill, having been at Wallace Wade's side for more than a decade, and his task in 1942 was made tougher by the loss of twenty-four members of the Rose Bowl team to graduation or to military service, including every starter but three. Jim Smith returned and was elected captain by his teammates before spring practice. Bob Nanni, Tom Burns, Bob Gantt, and Al Hoover were among the other returning players, but the average age of the 1942 squad was more than one and a half years younger than in previous seasons.

Another challenge for Cameron was the ever-changing schedule, as schools, including scheduled opponent Texas A&M, dropped off, having to account for limits the war efforts placed on transportation, finances, and rosters, which had been decimated by military enlistments and the draft. Among the additions to the Blue Devil schedule were the navy's University of Georgia Pre-Flight School and Naval Air Station in Jacksonville. The Blue Devils finished with a record of 5–4–1, perhaps not unexpectedly with a roster in constant change.

In the summer of 1941, Bob Dethman had petitioned the local draft board in Hood River to defer his induction for fear of losing his athletic scholarship, which Oregon State verified with the board. Dethman was allowed to finish his degree and ROTC classes before entering active duty. With his football eligibility over but with more schooling to do, he served as a student assistant to Lon Stiner during spring practice of 1942 and was selected to participate in a college All-Star game against the Chicago Bears in August.

In May 1942, Dethman and his best friend, Joe Day, traveled to Portland to enlist in the Marine Corps, getting ahead of his eventual entry into the army. (As a married man, Dethman was ineligible for the Army Air Corps.) The strong letters of recommendation for his admittance into the corps came from, among others, the postmaster and superintendent of schools in Hood River and Stiner, all of whom noted his athletic abilities and stressed his Rose Bowl participation and success.

His teammate Frank Parker enlisted in the army in 1942 but would continue his schoolwork until after the spring semester of 1943. Parker would suit up for Stiner on the 1942 team on a squad that was almost unrecognizable, with most of the Rose Bowl participants gone. Parker started on the line, but OSC won just four games. Football was now an afterthought in Corvallis. Oregon State had moved beyond the euphoria of the Rose Bowl.

After the season, and knowing that active duty was just months away, Parker borrowed a tuxedo from good friend and teammate Jim Busch and married Peggy Prouty on December 16 in a hastily called ceremony in Astoria. He was wise enough to know that many young men were not returning from war.

Football was still played in Durham and Corvallis in 1942 but without much of the fanfare—and meaning. The dramatic events on and off the field in 1941 were replaced by the daily tasks of a country at war. On December 7, 1942, Duke held a one-year anniversary service in the chapel in commemoration of the Pearl Harbor attacks and the ten Duke students already lost to battle or in training, including one member of the 1942 Rose Bowl team.

Walter Griffith suited up for the Duke varsity team as a backup in 1941 and saw little action on the field, watching from the sideline with a clean uniform as his teammates allowed the winning score in the Rose Bowl game. Twenty days after the circus left Durham, Griffith dropped out of Duke and enlisted in the United States Marine Corps. Just 102 days after the Rose Bowl game, Griffith was aboard the USS *Kit Carson* in San Francisco, a member of M Company, 3rd Battalion, 8th Marines, 2nd Marine Division, bound for Pago Pago, on Tutuila Island, in American Samoa, headed to war.

The battalion remained in Tutuila through the summer and into the fall, serving as infantry defense for the island while training, when possible, for the expected fight in the Solomon Islands. Because of the nature of Tutuila, the Marines lived in small groups in enclaves around the island and became very familiar with life in the jungle—darkness, insects, strange sounds, and the heat—a familiarity that would be helpful in their next assignment. But the island did not lend itself to large-scale training and mock amphibious landings.

From the bombing of Pearl Harbor, in December 1941, until June 1942, with the Americans focused on building up their strength in the Pacific and strategizing on how best to take on the Germans in Europe, Japan advanced almost without check. But by mid-1942, Admiral Chester Nimitz and his carriers were able to repel further advancements in the Coral Sea and at Midway Island and kept the Japanese limited to gains already made. Finally, the Americans were ready to take the fight to the enemy.

The counterattacks began in late summer on the Solomon Islands, with Marines and army soldiers, and in counteroffensives in New Guinea, with U.S. Army and Australian forces. The initial target of the Marines was the island of Guadalcanal, on the southeast end of the Solomons, a chain of islands some six hundred miles long that received close to two hundred inches of rainfall per year, with high temperatures and an unforgiving jungle swamped with insects and disease.

The transport ship armada, including the USS *Hunter Liggett,* with Griffith aboard, sailed on October 25, initially ordered to sail to Wellington but changed en route to Guadalcanal by way of Efate, for a large-scale practice landing on its beaches. The Americans had landed on Guadalcanal in August, and the prolonged battle was being waged by novice soldiers with limited supplies. The Japanese continued to flood the tiny island with troops while the Americans countered with their own buildup in the fall. Griffith disembarked on November 4 and was sent out on his first patrol on the tenth, but like all the 2nd Marines, he had not been briefed on the tactics of the enemy that had been devastatingly learned by the 1st Marine Division since their arrival in August.

Any kind of movement at night was challenging, with intense darkness, thick terrain, muddy and narrow roads, and a constant threat of

Japanese snipers. Griffith camped under a pup tent or found some caves on hillsides or slept in a hammock. The heavy rains came every night, and the strong heat came during the day, with Marines dropping from heat exhaustion with too little water and too-heavy packs. Griffith's battalion took heavy mortar, sniper, and machine-gun fire on the morning of the eleventh and made just small advances. He was struggling to stay fit enough to prove useful.

The 8th Marines were assigned to defend the Matanikau River, with each battalion sending out three daily patrols consisting of one officer and fifteen enlisted men, probing the jungle for four to ten hours at a time. Griffith's 3rd Battalion had a difficult sector to protect and faced challenges in resupply. The broken terrain and steep slopes made hand-carrying ammo and food very slow and methodical, and nearly one-third of the men in the battalion were used on the supply chain.

On the morning of November 21, around 5:15 A.M., the Japanese unloaded a barrage of artillery on the 8th Marines for more than forty minutes. Every few seconds, a round landed near Griffith, and the resulting explosion was often followed by the screams of soldiers and then the silence of death, lasting a mere second before another round landed. When the attack subsided, the Americans counterattacked, but during the ensuing firefight, an army battery of 105-millimeter howitzers fired thirty-three rounds mistakenly on the 3rd Battalion, killing two soldiers and wounding another.

At 6:00 A.M., Walter Griffith was found riddled with holes, whether by enemy or friendly fire the first of Wallace Wade's boys to pay the ultimate sacrifice. His remains were interred later that day in the 1st Marines' cemetery, Row 64, Grave 6, adorned with a wooden cross in deference to his Lutheran faith (he was the first member of his church, Trinity Lutheran, back in Pennsylvania, to be killed in the war).

The fight for Guadalcanal would last another three months and sent a message to all Americans that the Pacific war would be brutal and costly.

The form letter from the commandant of the Marine Corps reached Levi and Dorothy Griffith in early December:

> *Deeply regret to inform you that your son Private Walter L Griffith was killed in action in the performance of his duty and in the service of his country. To prevent possible aid to our enemies, please do not divulge the name of his ship or station. Present situation necessitates interment temporarily in the locality where death occurred and you will be notified accordingly.*

In January, they received some of their late son's belongings—a fountain pen and Bulova watch among them. It would be two years before they received Griffith's final paycheck of $49.75 and six years before their son's body was returned and buried in the United States.

The decision had been made by Roosevelt and Churchill in 1942 to fully engage the Americans in the fight for North Africa, electing not to open a second European front—yet. As early as July 1942, 48 percent of Americans favored a European attack, fearing every hour of delay was in the Germans' favor. Still, the decision to focus first on North Africa was made, and General George C. Marshall ordered Dwight Eisenhower to take control of the African invasion, leaving his post in England to head to Gibraltar. Army troops were trained in amphibious landings and warfare in a matter of months, and they sailed directly to the Atlantic coast of French Morocco, near Casablanca. Allied troops from England landed in nearby Algeria as part of a strategy to control Morocco and Algeria before pushing east into Tunisia.

Word had been circulating around Fort Bragg that the 60th Field Artillery and the rest of the 9th Infantry Division were headed overseas to engage the enemy in late 1942. Wallace Wade Jr. had an emotional good-bye with his mother and Sis and even coaxed a warm, seemingly final farewell from his father.

The journey across the Atlantic for Wade Jr. and his fellow soldiers lasted sixteen days, with a safe arrival in Morocco on November 8. The Germans, aware of an incoming assault, flooded Tunisia with troops in December. For the next seven weeks, the 38 officers and 505 enlisted men of the 60th made their way south and bivouacked in Mamora Forest, near the south city of Port Lyautey, in the closing days of 1942.

War is like a football game, he remembered his father telling him. But Wade Jr.—who had yet to see the enemy, fire his weapon in battle, or experience war—knew he was far away from home and that his father's name would provide neither safety nor favor.

As the calendar turned to 1943, Roosevelt and Churchill and their advisers met in Casablanca to approve the invasion of Sicily and initiate Operation Pointblank, the strategic bombing of Germany—a "second front in the air." The meeting, code-named Symbol, also resulted in Roosevelt's declaration of unconditional surrender by the enemy. While the leaders looked ahead, Wallace Wade Jr. was taking it one day at a time.

On February 17, 1943, Wade Jr. and the 60th Field Artillery participated in one of the most famous actions by American artillery in World War II—the forced march, in vehicles, by the 9th Infantry Division's artillery over eight hundred miles of mountainous terrain from its bivouac at Tlemcen, Algeria, to Tébessa, Tunisia. The division artillery—two battalions of 105-millimeter howitzers of the 60th and 84th Field Artillery, one battalion of 155-millimeter howitzers, and the 34th Field Artillery, along with infantry cannon companies and antitank guns—marched in cold, windy, and wet weather and poor road conditions to help defend the Allied front in Tunisia that was crumbling under a sudden attack by German and Italian forces commanded by Erwin Rommel. The 9th Division's artillery unit arrived on February 21 and joined a group of British infantry, tank, artillery, and antiaircraft units hastily thrown together to defend the vital pass.

Under cover of darkness and based on what would prove to be faulty British intelligence, the 60th and attached units headed toward the town of Thala, where members of the German 10th Panzer Division, under Rommel's personal command, were steadily driving back the British. At approximately 1:00 A.M. on February 22, a few enemy rounds fell on the Anglo-American positions. Then at daylight, German artillery and tanks bombarded the British and American positions while occasional German dive-bomber sorties—only slightly deterred by bad weather—dropped bombs on the hastily prepared Allies.

Wade's shallow slit trenches on the front line gave little shelter, while his assignment as a forward observer put him in the most dangerous of positions for an artilleryman, at the very front line with the infantry serving as their only means of communication to the artillery batteries firing from the rear. Bombs shook the ground and pummeled his ears and did even more damage to his psyche. He heard the screams of fellow soldiers and the calls of "Medic!"

However, despite suffering forty-five casualties, including eight killed, the 9th Division Artillery and its British companions didn't budge. Instead, the Germans withdrew, and the 9th Division Artillery was awarded a distinguished unit citation for conspicuous gallantry and heroism for the battle of February 21–23, 1943. The Battle of Thala was America's first land victory—however minor—over the Germans in World War II.

On March 17, the battalion marched fifty miles on a long, muddy, and narrow mountain road to a spot twenty-three miles northeast of Gafsa. The rainstorms continued, slowing their progress and forcing the battalion to spend several hours moving their vehicles from the quagmire to solid ground. They were headed to confront the enemy in Maknassy.

The Germans and Italians were heavily armed and supported by a large number of dive-bombers. On March 22, the engagement began with the Stuka dive-bombers hitting battalion headquarters as the

Americans unleashed their .50-caliber machine guns on the incoming planes, knocking one out of the sky. The Americans then trained their heavy guns on tanks, vehicles, and mortar emplacements in a showdown that would last for eighteen days.

The 9th Infantry Division was victorious again in the battle at Sedjenane-Bizerte over rugged terrain, capturing Bizerte and signaling the end of the eighty-one-day Tunisian Campaign. The Allies had not only killed or captured a quarter of a million German and Italian troops but they had control of North Africa, which opened the door to the Mediterranean and southern Europe.

Yet despite the successful campaign, Wade was rattled, as were so many of his fellow green soldiers, despite a respite from the fighting. The man on the outside had served valiantly; the boy on the inside was shaken to his core. Ironically, he was the first of the Wades to see death in war up close, and it was nothing like he'd thought it would be.

Horrific. Jarring. Bloody. Murderous. Wade—even if he'd been allowed by army censors to describe war—could not accurately use words to convey the horror. He and his fellow soldiers were mere boys witnessing life's most horrific endings. Heads blown off, men walking around looking for lost limbs, intestines held inside a body by a makeshift rag, teenagers losing their minds and any sense of morality. The moments of quiet were but a facade; the silence gave Wade more time to think about the horrors of war. Wade grew up fast in war—all boys do.

On July 22, the 60th sailed from Bizerte Harbor to Licata, Sicily, to continue the American pursuit of the enemy. On July 10, British troops had landed on Sicily's southeast coast while General Patton's Seventh Army waded ashore near Gela on the southern coast. The Sicilian Campaign was difficult for Wade, but the toughest was still to come. Along with elements of the division, the troops made their way through the treacherous mountains north of the Sicilian town of Randazzo and then to Messina, chasing the Germans for close to forty miles. There were narrow near misses over cliffs, and imposing boulders to navigate. The fighting was sporadic for the Americans, with no single engagement large enough to be considered a battle by the time Sicily was in Allied hands. The 60th moved to positions near Floresta and then Cefalù, where they would remain for almost three months, enjoying the Sicilian countryside, food, and women. Wade was promoted from second lieutenant to first lieutenant in September.

"Outfit entered the active phase of the Tunisian campaign in February," Wade wrote to the *Duke Alumni Register* in August 1943, "and from then till now we have been constantly at the front except for three or four breaks of a few days. I won't go into any details, but I will say that Sherman's description of war was a great understatement."

12. CAMPUS AT WAR

In February 1943, Duke was selected as one of the nation's first hosts of a navy V-12 program, an engineering program for men between the ages of seventeen and twenty with a high school or prep school diploma. A month later, the program would raise the maximum age limit to twenty-two and expand to include an army V-12 program. It was not a coincidence that Duke was selected, as Duke and North Carolina government officials lobbied at the highest levels of government to host the new program.

The program began in July on a three-semester system, with another class starting in September on a two-semester cycle. When the first V-12 class began at Duke, 1,763 trainees in uniform inundated the campus and affected student life as a whole. All fraternity houses were taken over by the V-12s or Army Finance School soldiers, and many classrooms and laboratories were filled to capacity from sunup through sundown. V-12 students were allowed to participate in sports and student organizations, and Eddie Cameron announced that varsity athletics would continue, with both traditional Duke students and V-12s, but that sports would in no way interfere with the war effort.

The disconnect at Duke between students and soldiers that was evident in 1942 grew deeper in 1943, as more soldiers took up residence at Duke and in Durham and more Duke students left for war. The uniformed men were considered outsiders and not real Duke students by the others. The majority of soldiers were middle- to lower-class, from blue-collar towns or rural enclaves, contrasting with the mostly upper-class Duke students, though this was not necessarily reflected in the football team.

The remaining Duke men on campus felt threatened by the attention the soldiers paid to the coeds, and the soldiers inspired caution among young ladies' parents. The Durham Defense Recreation Committee scheduled a dance to entertain the soldiers, but of the nearly 900 Duke female students, just 244 had permission from their parents to attend the dance as dates, and only 71 of those volunteered to go.

As America became more entrenched in the life of a nation at war, more and more Duke faculty members were in uniform or supported the effort as civilians. By the end of 1943, thirty-four members of the faculty were in the army, fifteen were in the navy, and seventy-nine were engaged in some type of government work or research as civilians. By the end of the war, more than three hundred would serve their country in some capacity.

They researched the psychological effects of high-altitude flying, worked with the navy on avoiding the fouling of ships by marine animals, played a large role in the Office of Price Administration (OPA), provided interpreters and translated letters and documents, developed a plastic-shelled plane nose for practice, replicating those used in aerial gunnery, and developed infrared mesh for the navy that protected against poisonous smoke. And both before and during the war, several physics professors also played major roles in the development of the atomic bomb.

The professors' patriotic contributions did not lessen the debate on campus over the curriculum and course offerings that had begun in the spring of 1942; it only intensified with the addition of the navy V-12s. Duke University was not the same place that many students had entered in 1941 and years prior. In the spring of 1943, not only were course subjects at the center of debate, so was the awarding of "war degrees" to those students who had not yet completed the full degree requirements but who left for war. Those in favor believed it was the right thing to do for men going overseas to sacrifice their lives. Those opposed believed it devalued the Duke degree, insisting that cutting corners was not what Duke was about. *The Chronicle* weighed in with a compromise, suggesting the awarding of "war degrees" only to those seniors in their last semester who were called to war.

On the other side of the country, Oregon State was selected as one of seven schools for the Army Specialized Training Program (ASTP), which provided advanced military training in engineering, communications, and foreign languages to soldiers, along with instruction in chemistry and mathematics. Professors didn't mind the ASTP students, as they had high IQs, and the program kept them employed. The students enrolled in ASTP got to remain safe stateside and received deferments. ASTP consisted of eleven courses over twelve weeks, with hundreds of troops rotated in and out every three months. To accomodate the influx of students, Oregon State made accommodations in Snell Hall and Waldo Hall and in empty fraternity houses, with the other frats housing OSC coeds. OSC even used some offices and classrooms as lodges. The physical education component of ASTP was led by Lon Stiner and focused on not only conditioning but swimming and first aid. By the fall of 1943, there were 1,971 civilians registered for classes (1,529 women) at Oregon State and 1,295 soldiers enrolled in ASTP.

Oregon State's Cooperative Extension Service was called on to assist in food production in the state, in the collection of scrap metal and rubber, in the dissemination of information to rural communities, in support of county 4-H programs, and in dozens of other, smaller tasks. With so many able-bodied men headed off to war, the farms in

Oregon were devoid of a much-needed labor supply, and OSC Extension organized new labor pools, including OSC students, migrant workers, soldiers on furlough, and the largest pool—children between the ages of eleven and seventeen. In April 1943, the United States Congress passed the Farm Labor Supply Appropriation Act, which provided $13 million to states to recruit, train, and place farmworkers. Oregon's share was $124,000. Meanwhile, the Women's Land Army (WLA) placed 135,000 women in farm jobs from 1943 through 1947.

Sixty-seven Oregon State faculty members served in the military, with another thirty serving in civilian positions in the armed services. Fourteen OSC engineering faculty members consulted on the construction of nearby Camp Adair. Like their Duke counterparts, faculty assisted in the war effort in all areas, from developing techniques for combating and evading enemy radar to working on the atomic bomb.

For all intents and purposes, Oregon State was a military academy during the war. Though at times the number of civilians equaled the number of soldiers, the campus buzzed with military maneuvers, rumors of battles won and men lost, and with a single-minded purpose.

Duke Rose Bowl starter Jim Smith did not take any shortcuts in earning his degree in business administration in May 1943, reported to the University of Notre Dame for four months for his initial naval training, then boarded a train from South Bend to New Orleans to join the USS *Richmond* as a gunnery officer. The ship headed out to the North Atlantic for six months, serving on antisubmarine patrols and escorting ships in and out of the British Isles. The *Richmond* returned to shore in the spring of 1944, and Smith was ordered to Key West, Florida, for sonar training. His girlfriend, Elsie Crone, traveled to Florida, and the two were married before Smith returned to Norfolk, waiting for his next assignment.

At the same time as Smith was awarded his Duke degree, Oregon

State's Bob Dethman was awarded his degree in absentia, four years after college officials had warned him he might not even be able to earn a junior certificate due to academic shortfalls. In January, Dethman became a father. His wife, Margaret, gave birth to little Delores, and life changed in a moment. Dethman kissed his wife and daughter good-bye in May and boarded a train to cross the country again, this time for basic training at Parris Island, in South Carolina, as a United States Marine.

Parris Island was not a resort. The Marines' basic training was meant to save their lives, and encouraged instructors to push the rookies well past their limits. Dethman's experience as a hunter, outdoorsman, and football player came in handy. He wanted to become an officer, which meant not only surviving basic training but flourishing, which is just what he did. After officer training at Quantico, Virginia, Dethman was commissioned as a second lieutenant on September 23, 1943, and spent the next three months as a reserve officer.

In January 1944, Dethman headed west for Camp Pendleton, where he was assigned to the 1st Battalion, 26th Marines, 5th Marine Division as a company and athletic officer. En route, he was granted leave to visit Margaret and Delores, who were living on the Dethman homestead in Hood River.

On occasion, he would write to his former coach and boss, Lon Stiner, back in Corvallis. Stiner was too old to be drafted, and elected not to volunteer based on his age. In his office at Oregon State, Stiner kept a large world map on his wall, placing pins to identify the locations of his former players and coaches at war. He worried about his boys.

On a half acre out in back of his house, Stiner planted a victory garden with carrots, cabbage, lettuce, and tomatoes and pears, which young Betty canned and put in reserve in case of an attack. The family saved string, bacon grease, and aluminum foil from gum wrappers and Hershey bars to contribute to the war effort. A retired nurse, Caroline Stiner volunteered in a hospital, and since many Americans believed it was not patriotic to take vacations, the Stiners did little traveling during the war. But there were limits to Stiner's patriotism, as he became overly concerned about his daughter mingling with the sons of army officers who were stationed at nearby Camp Adair. Betty was the bond sales chairwoman for her high school, selling bonds or, for those who couldn't afford a bond outright, stamps for fifty cents each to students, who would fill up a book and trade it in for a bond.

In mid-September 1943, Oregon State, Washington State, and Idaho canceled their football seasons, joining Oregon, which had just done the same in the month earlier. Travel restrictions made away games difficult, rosters were gutted by enlistments, and the army soldiers on campus were prohibited from participating. The navy permitted those soldiers in various V-programs on campuses to play, so USC, California, and Washington continued their competitive schedules.

At Duke, the war wreaked havoc on the football slate for the 1943 season, but the season would go on, with games against Pittsburgh, Colgate, and Vanderbilt postponed until after the war. Under travel restrictions, Duke and North Carolina were scheduled to play twice. Since the conclusion of the 1942 season, twenty men were lost to military service, but with the navy V-12 program in full operation, Coach Eddie Cameron had many capable players out for football. In fact, returning player Ernest Beamer was the only true "civilian" on the roster, the other players either already active in the military or enlisted but deferred. Cameron's roster had constant turnover during the season, as players transferred in and out of Duke. The day before Duke faced Georgia Tech, twenty-three players received orders to report for duty the following week, including Bob Nanni and Tom Davis.

Despite the ever-changing lineup, Duke played one of its most successful football seasons in history, finishing 8–1, with its only loss to Navy in Baltimore on a missed extra-point attempt. The team won by massive margins (40–0, 61–0, 42–0, 75–0, 29–0) and beat UNC twice in winning the Southern Conference title. Duke finished as the highest-scoring team in its history and ranked seventh in the nation.

Wallace Wade Sr. was able to catch a few of the home games after returning from Fort Sill in Oklahoma to Camp Butner in North Carolina, where he took command of the 272nd Field Artillery Battalion. In November, Wade was riding in the passenger seat of a jeep during blackout maneuvers when the driver lost control and crashed. Wade sustained a broken leg and was sent to Oliver General Hospital in Augusta, Georgia, to rehabilitate. At the time of the injury, Wade's 272nd was among the finest in the army during maneuvers in the States and was now ready for battle. Wade believed that the broken leg—just as the army football assignment had—would prevent him from joining the battle.

As he lay in the hospital bed, Wade was asked yet again by a news reporter about the prospect of continuing football during the war. "I know of nothing that is a better preparation for a young man who is going into the army than football. The greatest benefit that football gives to a young man is that it teaches him to be a competitor, to never give up, to get back up after you're knocked down. Success in both football and war depends on morale, loyalty, and sound fundamentals."

The coach's words never rang more true than in the case of his former player Hugh Miller.

There was little doubt that Miller, who was born in Tuscaloosa, would play football at the University of Alabama, as his athletic prowess became known throughout the state. So when it came time to select a college, Miller indeed fulfilled his destiny, becoming a football star at his hometown university under Wallace Wade, and winning a national title on the undefeated 1930 Rose Bowl championship team. Thirteen years later, Wade was still coaching Miller—this time on an enemy-infested beachfront in the Solomon Islands.

On July 4, 1943, Miller was serving as a gunnery officer on the destroyer USS *Strong* in the Kula Gulf when it was sunk by a Japanese torpedo. After helping to evacuate men from the sinking ship to the USS *Chevalier,* which would soon have to escape an enemy bombardment itself, Miller jumped overboard. He spotted two sailors tangled in a line pressed against the quickly sinking ship and swam to free them with his knife. He did his best to hold the seriously injured men above water. When the *Strong* finally went under, it sucked Miller and the men so deep that two underwater depth charges exploded, injuring Miller and knocking him temporarily unconscious. In the chaos on the surface, men floated dead or screamed for help or found floater nets as safety. The nets were ropes tied together with corks attached serving as a floatation device. After coming to, Miller somehow kept the two injured men alive and in his grasp and helped them onto the net.

The raft drifted back and forth in the currents of the gulf for days, as one by one, badly injured sailors died. Miller and five others eventually reached a small island, no more than fifty yards wide by two hundred yards long. One man died on the beach. Miller knew they couldn't stay. They hesitantly boarded the floater net and kicked and swam their way to Arundel Island, their best shot at survival but an island heavily manned by the Japanese.

The remaining five—including Miller—began to move through the daunting and dangerous jungle, one careful step at a time. It wasn't long before they lost another member of the group and it seemed Miller might be next, his internal injuries, including hemorrhaging, too severe for him to continue on. He ordered the three enlisted men to move on without him. He gave them a parka and his shoes and kept with him a broken pocketknife. The sailors reluctantly obeyed and left their officer to bleed to death. As Miller lay in the hot sun on the hot earth sure to be his coffin, a familiar voice came into his head. *Never give up! If you believe you can win, nothing can stop you! You can always do more than you think.* The voice belonged to his college coach, Wallace Wade, the words echoed many times by the coach on the football practice field. Miller summoned the strength to get up and soldier on.

He eventually came across a dead Japanese soldier and took his weapons and put on his uniform. When he encountered a five-man Japanese patrol, he killed all five with grenades and then took their weapons. He would go on to reportedly kill more than thirty Japanese soldiers on his more than forty days on Arundel, sustaining himself on water and coconuts, evading capture, disabling machine-gun posts, and—after his rescue—pinpointing key locations for the Allies. He was awarded the Navy Cross and Purple Heart by Eleanor Roosevelt on behalf of her husband as he recuperated in the hospital.

Wallace Wade had saved his player's life, and for the rest of his days, Miller credited his old coach as the inspiration for his survival.

13. AN ORDINARY HERO

The map in Lon Stiner's office was full of pins tracking the locations of his players serving around the States, and in bases around Europe and North Africa and in the Pacific—Martin Chaves, George Zellick, Orville Zielaskowski, and Bob Dethman among many. Stiner was fortunate that after almost two years of war, not one of those pins came down because of death—that is, until November 1943.

Douglas MacArthur was focused on the southwest Pacific region while Chester Nimitz was tasked with taking back the central Pacific, and after the ultimate American success on Guadalcanal, morale was high. But Nimitz believed that Guadalcanal had been too costly and that attempting to retake every island would have consequences, deciding instead on an island-hopping strategy, using large-scale American forces to take select enemy islands, cutting off supplies to the others. The next island on his list was the atoll of Tarawa, on the eastern end of the Gilbert Islands, and headed to the islands was Oregon State player Everett Smith.

Smith played as a reserve for Stiner in the 1941 pre–Rose Bowl season, scoring a handful of touchdowns from his halfback position. With two years of ROTC training complete and facing significant financial difficulties, Smith left Oregon State in 1943 and entered the

Marine Corps, having already enlisted in 1942. The private first class left the States on July 29, 1943, a proud member of the 3rd Battalion, 2nd Marines, 2nd Marine Division headed to New Zealand.

The largest island in the Tarawa atoll was Betio, just one and a half miles long and eight hundred yards wide but a strategic target for the Americans because of a small Japanese airstrip, well defended by soldiers. The 2nd Marines trained in amphibious landings on and off New Zealand in preparation for the assault.

On November 20, the 2nd Marines sailed on landing craft toward the smoke-filled beaches, bombarded by heavy exchange of artillery from the Japanese encampments and from navy warships. The plan was to motor the crafts right onto the beachhead and to get the Marines off the sand as fast as possible. But as the landing craft reached the edge of the shallow lagoon adjacent to Betio, coral reefs exposed by a dangerously low tide halted their progress. The Marines had no choice other than to disembark and wade to shore under enemy fire. Man by man, Marines climbed over the high sides of the boats with as much gear as they could carry and dropped into the blood-soaked water below. As their plans evaporated, each man, Everett Smith included, created his own path to the beach.

After hitting the water, Smith noticed the dark brown and red spots around him. There were muffled screams and cries of "Help!" that he at once acknowledged and ignored, as pausing for only a second could mean death. Smoke lay heavily in the air, and he struggled one stroke at a time toward shore, his equipment and rifle dragging him down. When large-caliber bullets hit the water around him, he could hear a *shump* as the bullets pierced the surface.

Everett Smith may have ultimately been gunned down by a sniper while still in the water, or he may have made it to the beach only to be blown away by the heavy defensive power. The records are inconclusive. However, what is known is that his remains, along with those of almost nine hundred other Marines, were buried on Betio Island, in the Tarawa atoll. The battle lasted just seventy-six hours, but one second too long for Everett Smith.

Recovered from his body on the day he was killed was a shiny ring, inscribed *Everett E. Smith. 44. Rose Bowl Champions—1942. Oregon State.*

One of the pins on Stiner's map tracked the overseas movement of lineman Stan Czech.

Before Rosie the Riveter, there was Big Anna Czech. Big bodied, big willed, she had big dreams for her two sons. She was a no-nonsense, Polish-speaking single mother who for more than twenty years was the only woman among 2,500 workers at the Buda Engine Company in Harvey, Illinois. Buda built engines for industrial, truck, and marine use. Despite being the butt of jokes and the subject of daily harassment from coworkers, Czech sought out jobs at the factory considered "men's jobs," and she pestered her supervisors until she'd worked on every machine in the plant. Before long, Big Anna was accepted as one of the guys and became an integral part of the factory. She did it for her sons, Ted and Stan.

Stan's football prowess took him out west to Oregon State to play for Stiner, and he would see significant minutes on the line in 1941. While in Corvallis, Czech fell in love with flying, taking lessons at nearby airstrips. He became proficient enough in the air that the Army Air Forces (AAF) were interested, but Czech passed on the opportunity multiple times, choosing instead to play football and to appease his mother, who, despite her own toughness, did not want her youngest boy at war.

After the attacks on Pearl Harbor, all civilian planes were grounded in Oregon, meaning Czech's time in the air was over. After the Rose Bowl game, with so many of his teammates and classmates entering the service, Czech relented and decided to enter the army (not the Army Air Forces) in the late summer after finishing the semester—but not his degree. Before enlisting, he spent hours in the hot summer sun helping to build Camp Adair just outside of Corvallis.

In August 1942, he borrowed some money and married Ora Lea Vannice, whom he had met on a blind date. They married on the twenty-first in Seattle, and Czech was inducted into the army in Chicago six days later. He spent the next two years on American soil, first in basic training and then at Fort Sill for artillery course work, and finally in Battery Officer's School, assigned to the Battery B, 3rd Battalion, 6th Field Artillery, 35th Division. When Czech finally left for Europe, Stiner moved the pin on the map.

Planning for the invasion of Europe had been under way since the spring of 1942, after the decision by Roosevelt and Churchill to focus first on North Africa and Italy and defer a cross-channel invasion of France. By the fall of 1943, U-boat attacks had been greatly diminished, and Allied troops and supplies began to pour into the British Isles, aided by the recent breaking of the German communication codes. In secret conferences in Quebec and again in Tehran, Churchill and Roosevelt fine-tuned the invasion plans.

In the spring of 1944, 1.6 million troops stood ready in Britain while Allied bombing campaigns on positions in Germany and in France took away many of the Germans' supply routes and transportation hubs, thereby slowing the potential replenishment of German troops after the invasion. When General Eisenhower took command in January 1944, the decision was made to land at Normandy and to secure the port at Cherbourg, assemble the armies, and begin to move toward Germany. The Germans assumed the landing would be in Pas-de-Calais and assembled their reserves there, fooled by elaborate deceptions by the Allies, including an entire fake army under General Patton. The Soviet advances on the eastern front forced Germany to keep divisions in the east instead of moving them to France for the expected assault.

The 9th Infantry Division, with Wallace Wade Jr. and the 60th, were ordered from Sicily to England, the soldiers having no idea of what the next objective was, though they knew it would be in Europe. They arrived at Camp Barton Stacey in Hampshire County, England, on November 26, 1943, after fifteen days at sea. It would be their home for the next six months.

Three months later, Wallace Wade Sr., having recovered from his broken leg suffered in the jeep accident, reassumed command of the 272nd Field Artillery. The unit was ordered overseas in April, as its 240-millimeter howitzers, the heaviest in the U.S. Army, were needed for the coming invasion of Europe. Unlike Wade Jr.'s 60th Field Artillery, the 272nd was not assigned permanently to a single army division but rather served as a separate artillery battalion assigned to wherever army and corps commanders thought the big guns were needed. The 272nd arrived in Packington Park, Warwickshire, England, on April 27. Father and son would be based just ninety miles from each other. As plans for the invasion developed, the 272nd would not be a part of the initial D-day invasion of France, but rather as a part of the following forces, which would land later in the summer.

On June 5, 1944, after days of uncertainty and one cancellation, favorable weather was forecast for June 6, and Eisenhower ordered the invasion to commence. Before dawn on the 6th, American paratroopers dropped behind enemy lines, and with the rising of the sun came their arrival on the shores at Utah and Omaha beaches. The British and Canadians landed farther east. At Omaha, the 1st and 29th Infantry Divisions and 2nd and 5th Ranger battalions gallantly fought to secure the beachhead as German pillboxes pummeled them from atop the cliffs. By midafternoon, the Allies had begun to advance.

The distance over water from Southampton, England, to near the commune of Sainte-Marie-du-Mont in northwest France is approximately 146 miles, but crossing it was like moving from one world to another. For months, the soldiers of the 60th had avoided direct enemy combat while training in seclusion and secrecy for an invasion of France. As D-day approached, the tension mounted, and the soldiers' memories of Tunisia and Sicily became more vivid as another battle inched closer. The 60th learned that they would not be a part of the initial invasion on Omaha and Utah Beaches or dropped behind lines like the 82nd Airborne and the 101st. Rather, they would sail in the days after the invasion to an area three miles northeast of Sainte-Marie-du-Mont near Utah Beach. They would be part of a force to secure an area in and around the commune and support the initial invasion troops. They landed on the tenth and began marching forward.

Cherbourg, a town on the Cotentin Peninsula, was a deepwater port vital to Allied supply lines, surrounded by daunting yet beautiful cliffs and small meadows. American and British military leaders knew they had to wrestle the town and port away from the Germans yet had originally planned to avoid the area in the initial incursion. But the decision was reversed, and in mid-June, First Lieutenant Wallace Wade Jr. and the 60th found themselves in a ferocious battle outside of Cherbourg. On June 23, 1944, the leading battery of the battalion was overwhelmed by intense small-arms fire and pounded by heavy artillery rounds.

Wade Jr., of his own volition, scampered to a forward observation post to provide better intelligence and to at least provide resistance. Armed with only a small gun, he valiantly exchanged fire with the Germans as their snipers did their best to take him out, but the young soldier proved capable and agile enough to duck behind the walls of earth. He stood his ground, and soon the battery moved forward.

It was a remarkable display of courage for a small-sized, ordinary young man who, like millions of others, was thrust into unimaginable circumstances. He pushed beyond his fear—beyond his limits—to do more than what was necessary. To do what was extraordinary.

As the battle for the Cotentin Peninsula continued as part of the Normandy Campaign, the 60th bivouacked near Les Pieux, but their fighting was not over. They continued to battle to secure the full range of land and key positions around Normandy, crossing fields, dodging from tree to tree, and making their way, inch by inch, into France. Wade Jr. began to suffer from flu symptoms—fever, vomiting, and chills. He had battled the enemy in North Africa and Sicily and France, but it was influenza that took him off the battlefield, forcing a stay in an army field hospital away from the front lines.

On August 7, the 272nd under Wade Sr.'s command unloaded its equipment on Utah Beach before moving to an assembly area near Montebourg, France. The 272nd was sent close to the front lines and dug in, in the vicinity of Mortain, where Hitler ordered a major German offensive to break through the American line. The 272nd engaged the enemy for the first time, in general support of the XIX Corps, on August 10.

The officers and enlisted men serving in the artillery units were often some of the best and brightest the army had to offer. A position in the artillery was a coveted spot for many soldiers, if only because the casualty rate was so low compared to that of the infantry. In fact, though the artillery comprised roughly 16 percent of an infantry division, it accounted for just 3 percent of casualties. Wade Sr.'s battalion was responsible for providing heavy-artillery support for a variety of army divisions, using his six 240-millimeter howitzers to pound dug-in enemy positions. It was one of only fifteen 240-millimeter howitzer battalions in the army. The howitzers were enormous and complex, requiring a well-trained crew of almost fifty men to simply move and emplace each one and prepare it to fire. The guns were so large that they weren't moved as single loads like most artillery pieces, but each one was broken down into two separate loads, hauled by a massive 27.5-ton, fully tracked prime mover. Roads and bridges had to be carefully scouted to determine if they were strong enough and safe enough to withstand the massive loads.

In combat, forward observers from the battalion or—more rarely—from the infantry would identify targets, including fortified positions, tanks, command posts, and infantrymen, and direct the fire at them. The observers would often attempt to find an abandoned building for better long-distance sight lines. They would call the target coordinates into a fire direction center, or FDC, at the battalion headquarters, situated well behind the front lines. The FDCs were "war rooms" filled with soldiers relying on maps and specialized instruments who would seek input from their commanding officers to decide which guns would fire where and when. The weather, the urgency, and the target all factored into the ultimate directives to fire. The FDC would transmit the coordinates by radio or field telephone to the firing batteries. Then the 240-millimeter howitzer would unleash a massive 360-pound shell up to fourteen miles, which could hurl killing fragments over three hundred yards from where it landed and could penetrate a half inch of steel at one hundred yards. However, like all artillery firing indirectly—that is, with the gun out of sight of the target—a trial-and-error process between the observers, the FDC, and the gun crews was required to get a hit.

As the battalion commanding officer—and with his penchant for perfection—Wade was often intimately involved in firing decisions and, at times, in forward observation posts helping to pinpoint targets. As the unit moved from one site to another, Wade played a vital role in assigning observation posts, verifying a zone of fire, and surveying maps while staying in regular touch with higher commands.

Throughout the late summer and fall of 1944, the 272nd provided critical support to many different units of the U.S. First and Third Armies. It was often attached to one unit for only a few days before moving to assist another. There were days when the battalion fired no rounds and others when it fired regularly throughout an engagement. Fortunately, as expected with the large artillery battalions, casualties were few for the 272nd. For now.

The Allies entered Paris on August 25 after fast-moving advances by the First and Third U.S. Armies, and there was much optimism that the war would end in the coming months. Wade confessed to Eddie Cameron in a letter that he had witnessed some "horrible" sights in war, but he expressed his hope that the fighting would be over before winter weather blustered in. Yet enemy resistance strengthened as the Allies approached Germany, the Allies ran short of fuel and ammunition, and inadequate transportation of supplies from the beaches in Normandy slowed the advance.

As for Wade Jr., by September 1, he had recovered from influenza and was back with the 60th Field Artillery as the 9th Infantry Division assembled in an area west and south of Versailles, joining the First Army as they marched through France and into Belgium in the fall of 1944. He crossed over into Belgium under heavy fire, which continued for thirteen days. By the sixteenth, Wade Jr. entered Germany. The action continued to take its toll. More carnage. More losses. More longing for home.

After battling the enemy in North Africa and then Sicily and then France and Belgium, Wallace Wade Jr. had had enough. The short, rail-thin kid with glasses was beat-up and ready to give up. The physical and emotional toll of war had finally brought him to the verge of a breakdown. His commander in the 60th contacted his father with the 272nd and implored him to come visit his son. They had seen one another on occasion in Europe, and at times had been stationed just a short drive from one another. So Wallace Wade Sr. reluctantly left his men to go to the son who needed him. Young Wallace was in neither good shape nor good spirit, and his father gave him the best pep talk he could, just like he had motivated so many of his players. But this was not football.

"He is still intact," Wade Sr. wrote home to Cameron after visiting his son in France, "although he has taken an awful beating."

The visit by his father gave Wade Jr. both strength and hope—strength that he would make it through this ugly war and hope that it would soon be over.

Late in September, Wade Jr. was transferred from the 60th to the 32nd Field Artillery Brigade, currently in southern Holland. The 32nd was an artillery headquarters that coordinated fires for the U.S. First Army's heavy-artillery battalions, including occasionally Wade Sr.'s 272nd Field Artillery.

On January 31, 1944, Second Lieutenant Charles Haynes left the United States bound for North Africa, where he would remain until July, attending various warfare schools and taking a four-week course in leadership and battle. Without having seen actual battle, Haynes was still a leader among men. He routinely volunteered to go first in drills and rarely complained about the heat or the cold or being away from home. He had the same gratefulness and tenacity in the military as he did playing football. The difficult training in some of the courses led Haynes to write to his mother that "you'd think Wallace Wade was running this place with all the exercise we got yesterday."

Haynes was the leader of the 2nd Platoon, Easy Company, 349th Regiment, 88th Division when the 349th boarded steamships in July headed to Italy. The dining room tables on board were covered in white tablecloths with shiny silver utensils for use during the six-course meals; female nurses and administrative assistants were plentiful on the decks. The boys forgot about the war, if only for a short time. They were heading to a battle in Italy that had been ferocious for months.

The Italian High Command, backed by King Victor Emmanuel III, entered into secret negotiations with the Allies while Germany added troops to its contingent in Italy. The more Adolf Hitler had to focus on Italy and keep his troops mired there, the less defense in Western Europe the Germans could support.

On September 9, 1943, the U.S. Fifth Army had landed on the beaches near Salerno under heavy fire, while British troops sailed into Taranto. One week later, the Allies met up, and two weeks after that, they entered Naples. The Allies began the march up the spine of Italy, through rugged mountain terrain and against heavily fortified German positions near rivers and high mountains. In October, the Allies crossed the Volturno River and advanced to what was known as the Winter Line, at the mountains near Cassino. After multiple attempts to take Monte Cassino, the Allies were successful and fought eastward until they entered Rome in June 1944.

Arriving in Italy in July, Haynes saw the destruction of war. The tiny villages reduced to barely recognizable rubble; the countryside littered with craters and the remains of bodies. The more he saw, the more grateful he was.

> *I'm always thankful for being an American and having had the opportunities that you and Dad gave me when I was growing up. We are lucky, too, that we are fighting "Gerry" in someone else's country before he got to ours. I suppose Italy is the first country in history that every town and farm has been fought over, bombed and blown up. I'm sure if the few Americans who bitch about shortages of materials and rationing for civilian use, could see this first-hand, they would easily forget their little petty wants. The depression of '32–'33 etc. was a time of prosperity compared to what some of these people have left.*

Haynes and his company were not the first Americans in Italy, and they would not be the last. The battle for Rome had already been fought, and the Americans were working their way along the Arno River when Haynes joined the fray. When the 349th engaged the enemy, Haynes did not shy away or cower behind others. Quite the opposite. There was never a time when Haynes *didn't* want to be the first one in. Some fellow soldiers thought he was reckless; others saw courage and bravado. The first kill is always the hardest, as it was for Haynes. The Eagle Scout had taken another man's life. But that is what he was asked to do, and he got very good at it. In one early close engagement, his 2nd Battalion chased retreating Germans down a hill as Haynes "pump[ed] carbine bullets as fast as he could pull the trigger," killing four. Despite his ferociousness in battle, at night, under the cover of darkness, he retreated to being just a boy, writing long and loving letters home to his mother, while occasionally sneaking puffs of his tobacco pipe, hidden upside down under his combat jacket to prevent the light from giving up his position.

While Haynes was already engaged in the fight, Frank Parker was just headed to it. On July 1, Parker packed his gear in Fort Meade, Maryland, professed his love one more time in a farewell letter to his wife, Peggy, and then boarded a ship bound for Italy. It had been a long twelve months for Parker, first stationed at Fort Benning in Georgia and then at Fort McClellan in Alabama, where he became a replacement officer and platoon leader in Company F, 2nd Battalion, 349th Infantry. Parker and the others on board the vessel were replacements and supplements for those troops wounded or killed and were sent to reinforce the Allies for a final push through Italy.

By the time Parker joined the 349th on the ground in Italy, they were engaged in the rugged hills and soft countryside valleys near the Arno River. Though a large and gruff leader, Parker was reserved in establishing connections and friendships with his fellow soldiers—quite the opposite of Haynes, who never could resist the opportunity to strike up a conversation. And Haynes did just that with the new arrivals on July 27. It didn't take Haynes and Parker too long to realize they had seen one another before on a field far, far away. Opponents on New Year's Day 1942, they had been brought together two and a half years later to fight on the same team. Haynes thought enough of the brief encounter to share the news with his mother in a letter home, though it was only a brief mention that he "met a Lt. yesterday who is here with me, who played guard for 'Oregon State' against Duke in the 'Rose Bowl' game at home in '42."

Neither realized at the time that their meeting was not coincidental but an act of fate.

Rodman Henry saw his first action in March of 1944 in Cassino, assigned to F Company, 349th, as a radioman and advance scout. At first blush, it might seem that Henry had no place in war. The eighteen-year-old was not physically imposing (standing just five-foot-five), and he aspired to become a concert pianist or violinist. He was smart and could put others at ease with a joke. Henry grew up in Pittsfield, Massachusetts, and enlisted in the army in September of 1943. He was first sent to Fort Devens in Massachusetts and then ultimately to Fort Meade in Maryland, before he sailed for five weeks across the Atlantic to North Africa.

In May 1944 in Italy, Henry was advancing with fellow soldiers to establish a roadblock to trap retreating Germans when the group was pinned down by German tanks and guns. With five of his fellow soldiers severely wounded and the rest of F Company retreating to safety, Henry stayed with the five wounded men and provided cover and a solo nighttime patrol of the nearby areas to protect the men. Help arrived the next morning, and Henry earned a Bronze Star for his actions. The underdog's heart and belief had been underestimated.

But just weeks later, Henry found himself in the hospital for six weeks, unable to shake the combat shocks that often left soldiers incapacitated. Frayed nerves, slow reaction time, and an inability to be "in the moment" were common occurrences among the soldiers in Italy who had experienced the horrors of war. The sights and sounds of war were in stark contrast to the introspective nature of a musician. In his frequent letters home to his sister and parents, Henry often shared poems, stories of his early tastings of alcohol and tobacco, his company's adoption of a porcupine as a pet, and his desire to escape the hell of war.

In late July, Henry was out of the hospital and back with F Company with a new commanding officer, Lieutenant Frank Parker, six years his senior. It didn't take long for Parker to adopt Henry as his charge, sensing a vulnerability in him and deciding it was his duty to serve as Henry's protector. Maybe it was the fact that Parker saw heroism in a scrawny kid whose God-given talents would be wasted on a battlefield. Regardless, the two men grew quite close—as close as a soldier could get to his CO, especially one who tended to keep to himself, like Parker did. They talked about life and, on occasion, music and family and, yes, war, and the lieutenant would check on Henry every time shots were fired. Parker took great care to keep tabs on him during enemy engagements. "Peanuts," as Henry was nicknamed, was seemingly always in danger, not because of bravado but because of his assignments. Parker vowed to get him home safely to his family.

On September 15, the Fifth Army renewed its assault on the Germans' Gothic Line north of Florence, and on the twenty-first, the 349th was ordered to create an opening in the line. The next day, in fog and rain, the 2nd Battalion moved to relieve the 3rd Battalion, which had been battered by the fighting. Parker was given the assignment of making face-to-face contact with the 3rd Battalion. Three times, he and his patrol of six men identified German soldiers lying in wait and cleverly encircled the enemy. They killed twelve and took fourteen as prisoners before finally reaching their objective. Parker never flinched.

The coming days were filled with American movements and German shellings, a battle waged hill by hill, often in close-range firefights. The 2nd Battalion had helped crush the spine of the German defense, but not without heavy casualties. The advance picked up again as they fought their way to the village of Sassoleone.

On October 4, on an unnamed hill held by the Germans in the Po Valley, just outside of Sassoleone, Charles Haynes led an assault of the 1st and 2nd Platoons of Easy Company. There was nothing remarkable about the hill, just another of the hundreds of numbered hills in the Allies' way. The terrain was rocky but with an occasional patch of weeds, grass, or vegetation breaking up the monotony of the earth. Not surprisingly,

Haynes was out in front of the platoon and began to make his ascent to the top.

He could hear sounds of enemy fire in the distance, but it did not appear to him that the Germans were holding the ridge. If they were, surely they would have fired upon him on his way up. As Haynes approached the ridge, he could hear the familiar sounds of the enemy cocking their guns and even muffled whispers. Clearly, he had misread the situation or been expertly deceived, but either way, in that frightful moment of recognition, the Germans opened on Haynes and the platoon with machine-gun fire, leaving no time for the boy from Durham to get off a shot, let alone retreat. He collapsed to the ground as blood poured from his bullet-ridden arms and legs and a two-fist-sized wound in his chest that had missed his heart by a mere quarter of an inch. The bullet had destroyed the surrounding arteries, yet his heart still beat . . .

Haynes could barely muster enough breath to call for help, and of course he was drowned out by the continuing spray of machine-gun fire and mortars. Under the cold drizzle and strangely receding pain, which contrasted with the devastation he saw by glancing down at his body, Haynes nearly accepted that he was in the last realm of consciousness, and he turned his thoughts over to his mother, Alice; his friends; his teammates; and his childhood horses. As he contemplated this last image, he began to let go.

Bullets and artillery continued to whiz overhead, the firefight so intense Haynes's company comrades could not get to him without being shot themselves. The seconds turned into minutes. The minutes turned into hours. The hours turned into overnight. He lay there on the wet ground atop the ridge, drifting in and out of consciousness for almost seventeen hours before waking to the sounds of American voices and a familiar face looking down at him.

With the assistance of another soldier, Lieutenant Frank Parker, who had learned that Haynes had been hit and headed over to save him, picked up Haynes's limp body and began to carry it down the hill to a small farmhouse serving as a medical station. The blood continued to drip as his body bounced up and down, the men carefully navigating their way down the hill.

"Parker, Parker," Haynes kept repeating as Parker urged his Rose Bowl opponent to "pipe down."

"We're almost there, Haynes," Parker said, incredulous himself as he automatically uttered his comrade's name. "Just hang on."

They got him to a stretcher and made it to the farmhouse, and medics immediately began tending to Haynes's wounds. Parker took one last look at the bloodied Haynes before turning around and hustling right back to battle.

As he always did, Parker held his breath as Rodman Henry went ahead to radio back locations of the German gunners. In the darkness of early morning ahead of the troops, Henry advanced on his own to get a clear position of the enemy, but the Germans spotted him, despite the darkness, and began a targeted assault. He was able to escape the early mortar and gun rounds, but at 5:00 A.M., his luck ran out. Bullets riddled his leg and exploded his cartridge belt, sending hundreds of pieces of shrapnel into his small body. One of the bullets ripped the pin off the grenade he was carrying—ironic, as Henry rarely carried a grenade but had been convinced by his fellow soldiers before this particular fight to bring one along. In a frantic effort to throw the grenade away from his body, Henry grabbed the device with his left arm, his right arm already shattered. The grenade exploded before it left his hand, and he watched in horror as it left his body.

Word quickly made it back to Parker that Henry had been hit. The lieutenant, who, in a twist of fate, had just hours earlier dramatically saved one life, sprinted between the mortars and reached the teenager, grabbing him by the back of his shirt while firing off rounds with his M1 to give them both cover.

"Captain Frank, it is a million-dollar wound," Henry proclaimed in pain, using the lieutenant's nickname and knowing that his wound was his ticket out of the hellhole of war.

Parker dragged him more than one hundred yards to a safe position and then gave him to Henry's best friend, Sergeant Roy Anderson, who carried him the rest of the way to a makeshift field hospital. On Anderson's way back to the front, he was shot dead by a sniper. Meanwhile, the medics in the field hospital did the best they could, doing emergency surgery on Henry's arms and legs while bullets flew through the hospital tent.

Frank Parker was racked with guilt. Rodman Henry, he felt, was his personal responsibility. Henry should not have been in war, and he should have protected Henry better.

By October 11, Parker and the 2nd Battalion finally took Sassoleone. After nineteen straight days of violence, the men received five days off the line, taking hot showers, getting plenty of much-needed sleep, and finally putting on clean—and dry—clothes.

The Po Valley, a large swath of beautiful, flat land, would be a welcome respite from the drudgery of the rugged mountains for the 349th, but Monte Grande and Della Tombe stood in the way. Parker and F Company's first objective was to take Della Tombe from the Germans. They engaged in a heavy exchange of fire on the south side of the mountain as they began their ascent, with Parker leading the charge, killing two Germans and wounding six others. They couldn't take the crest, as the Germans kept replacements and ammo coming at a furious pace, realizing that losing Della Tombe could be catastrophic to keeping Monte Grande.

In one final push, Parker and elements of the 349th destroyed two machine guns, killed eleven, and captured five in taking the hill. It was then on to Monte Grande, where a barrage of firepower weakened the German defenses, but not before the 349th was blasted by shells, MG 42s, and 88s. They took the ridge without huge casualties, surprisingly, and E and F Companies settled in. But just thirty minutes after securing the crest, the Germans counterattacked, killing four Americans and wounding many others. But the companies held, and a critical objective had been achieved.

The division headquarters decided to halt the drive in the Apennines and dig in for the winter, as casualties had mounted and morale had plummeted. The countryside was populated by the smell of dead bodies, littered with gaping holes in the hillsides, and riddled with destroyed or abandoned equipment. On November 7 and 8, the 2nd Battalion was relieved after fifty-four days of fighting. The battalion wearily climbed onto trucks and was transported to Montecatini Terme, a tourist area north of the Arno River, thirty miles west of Florence. It was safe, quiet, and untouched by war. The men settled into hotels with beds, running water, and electricity. There were haircuts and stage shows and movies and bars and women, and a Thanksgiving dinner complete with turkey, stuffing, and beer. But the men of the 2nd knew it couldn't last forever, and on November 27, they were back on the line, preparing to face a difficult winter.

Frank Parker had fundamentally changed as a man in the hills of Italy. He was now a killing machine, void of true reflection until the bullets stopped. Even in the midst of war, Peggy was never too far from Parker's thoughts, and when he could not pen a letter, he would ask a fellow soldier headed off the front lines to write to her and let her know that he was fine. But the letters became less frequent. He knew. He knew he had changed deep in his soul, and it created sadness in the boy from Astoria. Sadness that he would never again be the man that Peggy Prouty fell in love with.

14. CUP OF COFFEE

There was, of course, a whole other world war being fought far from the hills of Italy, and, perhaps not surprisingly, the men of the 1942 Rose Bowl were in the middle of it. The Americans had taken Guadalcanal, Tarawa, Bougainville, Kwajalein, Eniwetok, Saipan, and Guam and continued their advance toward the Japanese mainland. The tiny island of Peleliu in the Palau Islands was next.

At 6:30 A.M. on September 8, 1944, the 1st Marines began the trip to Peleliu, crammed into the holds of the USS *Warren* in steamy and irritating conditions, forcing many to grab their jungle hammocks and rest in the fresh air on deck. A week later, on September 15, the men were awakened and scarfed down breakfast. The landing craft, vehicle, personnel (LCVP), which were amphibious Higgins boats that could hold up to thirty-six men, were prepared for launch. Three miles from the island, the Marines could see the artillery exploding from sea and air bombardment, and, buoyed by reports that underwater demolition teams had removed potential hazards, they headed for shore at 8:32 A.M.

The ride was anything but smooth, and the Marines, even the toughest among them, were vomiting on the rough seas. Facing heavy resistance, Alfred Hoover and his 3rd Platoon of B Company, 1st

Battalion, 1st Marines of the 1st Marine Division, jumped out into the water, surrounded by both enemy and friendly gunfire and artillery, as well as by dead Marines floating in the water.

Born and raised in Toledo, Ohio, Hoover was the quintessential all-American kid. He followed the rules, attended Lutheran church services, and excelled on the playing fields. He was a member of the Hi-Y Club, a social and service organization for teens run by the YMCA, at Scott High School, the largest high school in the city, and he worked as a counselor at the local YMCA. As a fullback on the football team, Hoover was selected All-City his senior year and garnered the attention of college coaches—most notably, Wallace Wade.

At Duke, Hoover played football for four years and participated in track for two while majoring in economics and physical education. During the 1941 season, he was a substitute halfback but saw plenty of action, including a standout performance against Davidson, and held his own in the Rose Bowl loss to Oregon State. In the Davidson game, Hoover ran a reverse over left tackle from the opponent's twenty-five-yard line in the fourth quarter, scoring a touchdown, and eight minutes later, he scored again from ten yards out in the blowout win. His athletic ability was superior to that of many of the Duke starters, but football talent was at a premium for Wade.

But now, in the waters off Peleliu, Al Hoover was just a target.

Hoover made it to shore safely as bullets flew overhead, punctuated by the screams and moans of his fellow Marines. The beachhead was shallow, and small-arms fire was coming in from Japanese soldiers protected by a cliff seventy yards in front of Hoover.

The Japanese were judicious in their use of their weapons, not wanting to give away their fortified positions and aware of their limited ammunition. A Japanese battalion on the beach slowed down the initial advance but proved no match for the Americans, who began to make advances on the first day. The wretched smell on the island from already-decaying bodies in 115-degree heat was almost unbearable, almost as unbearable as the fire on the Marines from the enemy secured high above their positions. The casualties piled up, and medics bravely carried the wounded out under fire, with one unarmed soldier even killing a Japanese sniper with his bare hands.

On the first day of the invasion, the 1st Marines lost two hundred men, with another nine hundred wounded. As they fought a more disciplined and reserved enemy, they realized the battle on Peleliu would not be over in mere days. Less than twenty-four hours after landing, the Marines had secured the airfield, though the Japanese continued to fire, making crossing the airstrip a dangerous task for the next six days. At night, Marines exchanged hand-grenade lobs with the Japanese as pitch-black darkness set in, making targets difficult to identify.

Hoover and B Company fought slowly toward the center of the island, a range of high mountains topped by the highest point on the island, Umurbrogol. B Company was ordered to attack on September 18 at 5:30 P.M., on a hill tagged Bloody Nose Ridge by the Marines because of the amount of blood spilled there. The Marines were pinned down by mortar, artillery, and gunfire almost from the time they set off on the operation. They were able to pull back for the night and lick their wounds. The next morning, September 19, around 6:30 A.M., the mortars and artillery started to rain down on B Company, with Hoover's 3rd Platoon taking the brunt of it. At 8:00 A.M., what remained of the company was pulled back into reserve and placed in an open field near a command post. They were sitting ducks.

The Japanese opened fire and began launching six-inch shells at the vulnerable Marines, with blasts that shook the ground one hundred yards in every direction. Several of the men of the 3rd Platoon took cover near a donkey engine in a revetment, but it provided them little protection, as the Japanese targeted the engine with shells, wounding one of Hoover's men. Hoover jumped to his feet and started toward the injured soldier when a shell exploded just yards from him, shooting a fragment through his utility knife, canteen, and belt and ripping a gaping hole in his abdomen, blood splattering on his Rose Bowl ring. (Later reports state that he jumped on a grenade to save his fellow soldiers, though the official account differs.) Before his body made it to an aid station, Rose Bowl participant Second Lieutenant Aaron Alfred Hoover was dead, his blood dripping on Bloody Nose Ridge on an island of questionable strategic value.

In early September, Wallace Wade's 272nd FA Battalion was bivouacked near Versailles for two weeks before the order came to head into Belgium to occupy three positions in the First Army sector around Saint Vith. The British and Canadian forces moved into the Netherlands as the Americans marched from Macon to a position five kilometers southeast of Saint Vith on the seventeenth. For the next two weeks, the 272nd fired hundreds of 360-pound shells, while avoiding enemy artillery and recon planes at night. The 272nd was low on ammunition and was prudent in its use of the 240-millimeter guns.

As the advancing armies made gains toward the Siegfried Line, the 272nd encamped at Büllingen, Belgium. The railways and roads in France had been decimated by the pre-D-day bombing, and moving men and supplies along the line was a difficult task. It raised the question of where limited supplies should be used in trying to breach the line, with the British advocating for the north, the Americans for the south. Patton's Third Army drive, slowed by low supplies, including a lack of gasoline, picked up in November and began to breach holes in the Siegfried Line. The First and Ninth Armies slogged through the Hürtgen Forest as cold weather set in.

Hürtgen was in Germany on the border of Belgium, and intelligence had indicated that the armies would face moderate resistance in the area, falsely believing that the Germans were under duress after Normandy and miscalculating that the dense trees would prevent the superior Allied airpower and artillery from being as effective. Intelligence was wrong. The close-quarters fighting involved five American divisions and raged for months.

Wade and the 272nd provided as much support for the infantry as possible, trying to take out the German tanks and machine guns. But it was not easy. The Germans cut trees to block key roads and fired artillery over the heads of American troops, the rounds detonating on the tops of trees to eliminate Allied cover and creating barrages of lethal wood splinters. The forest was really nothing more than the remains of tree bases surrounded by burning embers. There were no leaves and very few branches, and when Wade left the command post to go into the field, everywhere he looked, wounded American soldiers lay wrapped in makeshift bandages. When the barrages of enemy artillery paused—momentarily—the soldiers assessed the damage to their bodies and to one another. Momentary relief from this hell was reduced to a quick drag on a cigarette for men in the field, many suffering from trench foot and surviving on K rations.

The Battle of Hürtgen Forest lasted for three months, into early December, with both sides claiming few gains. The First Army suffered more than thirty-three thousand casualties. The 272nd arrived in Rott, Germany, in early December, believing there would be some time for rest during the winter.

In the ashen skies above Wade Sr., Wallace Wade Jr. spent his time with the 32nd on board observation planes above France, Holland, Belgium, and Germany. In the closing days of 1944, he was awarded the Air Medal to go along with the Bronze Star he received for the incident in Cherbourg.

Though Hürtgen was a stalemate, the Allies were already in German territory. Surely, the war would be over in a matter of weeks.

Yet over the waning days of the fighting in the Hürtgen Forest, the Germans were already planning for the next phase of the war, unbeknownst to the Allies. The Germans built up troops south of Hürtgen

Forest in an area known as the Schnee Eifel, not for defensive maneuvers—as American generals believed—but rather as preparations for a counteroffensive that Adolf Hitler expected would turn the tide of the war in his favor. Against the advice of his military staff, Hitler had withheld much-needed reserves from the eastern front and amassed them on the lightly defended Ardennes front. The massing of the German forces was done under the cloak of darkness, the Germans using charcoal to reduce smoke when cooking, laying straw on the ground to muffle the sounds of moving vehicles and troops, and orchestrating low-flying German aircraft over Allied positions to drown out the sound of movement. Hitler believed the operation, code-named Autumn Mist, could allow the Germans to not only split the American and British front but to advance to Antwerp and capture the critical Allied port.

The Germans had attacked the same area in 1870 during the Franco-Prussian War, in 1914 during World War I, and in 1940 as the Germans used the advantages of the dense forest to surprise their foes. Eisenhower and Lieutenant General Omar Bradley had little reason to believe an attack was coming, with both sides having just emerged from a bloody three-month battle in the Hürtgen Forest.

Tens of thousands of American soldiers were still sleeping in the early dawn of December 16, many of them weary from the battles in Hürtgen. During the night, a heavy snow had begun to fall, covering the land in an ironic show of beauty. As patrols and a few early risers shuffled around, there was an eerie silence.

Boom! Boom! Boom!

The skies lit up from Monschau, Germany, to Echternach, Luxembourg, a sixty-mile stretch of the Allied front, at exactly 5:30 A.M. The eighty-three thousand American troops in the area were taken off guard and, outnumbered six to one at attack points, were under early duress. A good portion of the troops were replacements and inexperienced at war, while the veterans were visibly weary. In many areas, the Germans bypassed the infantry lines and attacked artillery units, scattering men and battalions. Brave artillery soldiers stayed on the guns and, in some cases, even called in strikes on their own positions. The 106th Infantry Division was in a difficult position from the start, and despite heroic efforts by the men under Major General Alan Jones's command, two regiments—totally encircled and hopelessly cut off—were surrendered by their commanders just seventy hours after the initial wave of attacks.

The German incursions had created a bulge in the American line. On December 18, Eisenhower ordered the 101st and 82nd Airborne Divisions held in reserve in France to come to fight, and they swiftly moved ninety miles overnight, with limited lighting, to assist troops holding out at Saint Vith and Bastogne to prevent a German seizure of the town. Saint Vith fell to the Germans; Bastogne held out but was surrounded.

The 272nd Field Artillery Battalion under Wallace Wade was in high demand during the early days of the battle near Bastogne, with constant calls for the 240-millimeter howitzers to support the troops. In the month of December alone, it fired 1,311 rounds.

"Eagle, this is Eagle Crow 2. Fire mission. Azimuth 2,500. Coordinates 234-146. Enemy tanks 4. Destruction. Will adjust."

The call came over to the fire detection center from the forward observers using their battalion commander's scope mounted on a tripod.

The young soldiers in the FDC were surrounded by sandbags and covered by a well-worn tent as they studied the detailed maps on wooden boxes serving as makeshift desks. As the transmissions came in fast and furious, Wade listened closely to the calls and issued corrections when necessary. After a few minutes of calculation by the FDC team, the order went out to one of Wade's firing batteries.

"Battery adjust. Base deflection right 140. Shell HE, range 8,500!" a lieutenant ordered the firing battery over the field telephone.

A few moments later, the phone crackled in response. "On the way! On the way!" repeated the lieutenant to the observer. After another moment, the observer responded.

"One hundred over! Fifty right!"

After a few more adjusting rounds bracketed the German tanks, the order went out.

"Battalion. Fire for effect. Five rounds."

And thirty massive 240-millimeter rounds went downrange to pummel the Germans. Moments later, the observer called.

"End of mission. One tank destroyed; others withdrawing."

This was the routine for Wade and his men, hour after hour, day after day, as they met the request of units in desperate need of his battalions' deadly firepower.

The temperature dipped to nineteen below with knee-high snow covering the ground. Soldiers in the 272nd slept in tents buried in snow or near the guns or, for the lucky ones, in a barn. On one of the many cold and wet December days shortly before Christmas, Wade ventured into the field toward the front lines, leaving the relative safety of the command post well behind. The woods were dense with trees and snow, and American soldiers near the front lines hunkered down in rapidly made foxholes. As he walked through the snow, tired and hungry, his socks soaked, he came across members of the 35th Infantry Division, a part of Patton's Third Army, some of whom were novices in battle, short on sleep, food rations, and ammunition, making for a combustible climate. In December, with the 101st Airborne pinned down at Bastogne, the Third Army was ordered to relieve the encircled garrison by punching through German lines, and the 35th Infantry was right in the middle of the fight.

They were huddled in foxholes, seeking the slightest bit of comfort and reprieve. One soldier was slumped over a small pot, making something resembling coffee. Wade asked if he could have a sip. The soldier not only obliged, pouring the old man a generous cup, but also found him some bits of food and a blanket to warm him up.

Wade thanked him, and the foxhole partners gave an account of what had brought them to this specific spot. The young man revealed that he had been sent ahead to scout enemy positions, and he introduced himself.

"Czech, sir. First Lieutenant Stanley Czech. Field artillery observer."

"Lieutenant Colonel Wallace Wade of the 272nd."

The young soldier stared at him. Of all the foxholes in all the war, the great Duke coach Wallace Wade had fallen into the foxhole of Oregon State's Stan Czech.

With the Allies making progress on Bastogne, members of the 35th began to move into an area a few miles south of the city center, Villers-la-Bonne-Eau. On December 27, Czech and six others made their way through to a two-story farmhouse outside of the village with clear sight lines of the enemy. The observers radioed to the tanks behind them, which fired over the farmhouse and hit some German tanks and troops. The American tanks scored some direct hits, and killed a German captain, but they could not stop the advance.

Within minutes, the farmhouse was surrounded by German troops, many of them members of the SS, the most ruthless in Hitler's arsenal. There was nowhere to run.

"*Raus!*" a German soldier shouted to the men surrounded in the farmhouse, ordering them to come out. "*Jetzt!*" (Now!)

Czech looked at his soldiers. He knew what he had to do. He quickly took apart his .45 and threw the pieces across the floor and began to walk down the steps to surrender. His men followed him out the door. As soon as his head emerged from the doorway, the Germans began shouting, "*Gegen die Wand!*" (Get against the wall!)

Czech and the men took each step as if it were their last as they walked the short distance to what they thought would be their execution site. He thought about Ora Lea, Big Anna, and his brother. He wondered if there was any way to escape.

The SS soldiers put a tripod in the snow just a few feet in front of the men and attached a machine gun to the top, pointed right at the soldiers. Each second that passed felt like a lifetime. One of the soldiers approached Czech.

"Pis-tal!" he demanded in broken English. "Pis-tal!"

It took the lieutenant a moment to decipher the order and then to remember his dismantled .45.

"Pistol? Yes, I have a pistol," Czech replied with confidence. "I will send a man inside to get it." He motioned to one of the sergeants to retrieve the gun. The German reluctantly nodded.

The sergeant left the wall and, trailed by a soldier, stumbled up the stairs and within seconds reemerged holding the pieces of the pistol. He handed them to Czech. And then the boy from Illinois had an idea.

"Watch?" he asked, lifting up his jacket sleeve to reveal a watch. "Do. You. Want. My. Watch?"

Czech had heard stories about fellow American soldiers bribing Germans with watches, jewelry, even clothes. He figured he had nothing to lose.

"*Ja,*" the man replied.

So Czech took his frozen left hand and clumsily removed the watch on his right wrist. He handed over the watch and the .45 to the SS.

Czech took a glance at his men shivering against the wall. He looked back at the German and exchanged a look of hopelessness. The German turned his back and walked toward the machine gun tripod. He paused.

"*Nehmt sie fest!*" (Take them!) he ordered.

And with that, the American soldiers were now not KIAs but POWs and marched with their hands at their sides toward an unknown fate. Stanley Czech's quick thinking had saved their lives.

Within days, the captured Americans were on a train with fellow POWs en route to Hammelburg, Germany. Just outside of Hammelburg was a training facility being used to house more than 1,500 Serbian, Russian, and American POWs, with the officers and enlisted men kept in separate camps. Known as OFLAG XIII-B, the POW camp had been flooded with new POWs during the Battle of the Bulge. This would be either Stan Czech's final resting place or a test of endurance on his journey home.

On New Year's Day 1945, Wallace Wade Sr. was granted a few hours "home." He rarely used his rank to pull strings, but he decided he would use his bars to get the War Department to carry the Duke-Alabama Sugar Bowl game broadcast on the Armed Forces Network (AFN). So, thousands of miles from New Orleans, the old football coach huddled next to a radio, a cup of coffee in hand, for just a few hours of reminiscing.

The story of the 1944 Duke football season is really the story of two different teams wearing the same uniform. One of Wade's 1941 standouts, Tom Davis, returned to the team after an early discharge from the Marines and joined the mostly V-12 players but did not lead them to early wins, as Duke started the season losing four of its first five games. But then they won the next four to finish 5–4. In a development almost as shocking as the Rose Bowl coming to Durham three years earlier, Duke was invited to take on Alabama in the Sugar Bowl, despite its mediocre record. Duke's strength of schedule helped. The invitation set off wild celebrations in Durham, though not nearly as robust as those in 1941.

Alabama finished the year 5–1–2 coached by Frank Thomas, who had replaced Wade in 1931. On January 1, 1945, seventy-two thousand fans in Tulane Stadium, including twenty thousand men in uniform, witnessed one of the greatest college football games ever played, with four lead changes and the game coming down to the final play.

Alabama led 19–13 at halftime, but a third-period touchdown by Davis put Duke up 20–19. It was temporary, as Hugh Morrow intercepted a Duke pass and returned it seventy-eight yards for a touchdown to give Alabama back the lead, 26–20. The Alabama defense rose to the occasion, stuffing Duke at the one-yard line with under three minutes to go. Thomas called for Alabama to take a safety, willing to give up the two points in exchange for pinning Duke much deeper down the field with precious seconds left. But Duke was not done, and on just their second play after the safety kick, Duke's George Clark scored on a twenty-yard touchdown run, giving Duke a 29–26 lead. Alabama had one last gasp, but Duke tackled the ball carrier to end the game.

Wade listened with pride and then turned off the radio; his moment of reverie had passed.

Shortly after New Year's Day, German troops were driven back from the Bulge, as the Soviets headed toward Berlin from the east. Hitler began to pull his troops, as it was clear that he would not achieve the objective of capturing Antwerp. The Allies pushed the Germans back to the December 16 lines by the end of January.

The Battle of the Bulge was the bloodiest battle in American history, with nineteen thousand American soldiers killed, close to fifty thousand wounded, and between twenty thousand and twenty-five thousand taken as POWs. It was also an incredible failure of intelligence for the Americans. But they were back on the offensive, and both Wade Sr. and his son were still alive.

Wade Sr. returned to the battlefield and spent January in Rott, Germany, with the 272nd, pummeling enemy artillery positions and protecting a key road for the V Corps as they advanced toward the Roer River dams. In early February, the unit moved from a location near Camp Elsenborn in Belgium to a bivouac area in Oirsbeek, Holland. They were there for a few hours after the fifty-mile march before being ordered to the vicinity of Freialdenhoven, Germany, to support the upcoming Ninth Army offensive. The 272nd engaged in numerous missions prior to the launch of the offensive on February 23, delayed due to flooding of the Roer.

In the skies above, Gene Gray, the Oregon State hero of the 1942 Rose Bowl who had broken so many Duke hearts with his late touchdown catch and run, was delivering bombs as part of the 646th Bombardment Squadron (Light), 410th Bomb Group, 9th Air Force.

After graduating with a degree in dairy manufacturing in 1942, Gray sweated out the draft until August, when he was finally released to apply for the Army Air Corps and scored well on his initial screening tests and physical. In March of 1943, Gray went into active service and began a series of flight schools, which took him from California to South Carolina and finally to battle in late January 1945. Gray proved himself a more than capable pilot in more than thirty sorties against the Germans over France, Belgium, and Germany. The steadiness of his hands earned him three Air Medals and one Bronze Star. The ordinary kid was anything but yet again.

Charles Haynes, like his football coach, listened to the Sugar Bowl game radio broadcast. But unlike his coach, Haynes was in the comfort of a hospital room in Naples, Italy, still recovering from his wounds in the Po Valley in October 1944. He was supposed to have been flown back to the States, but bad weather had prevented that from happening. He spent his days reading magazines and newspapers and, on clear days, looking out his hospital window at the snowcapped mountains. He thought about the German soldiers he had killed and the others he had not. They were just scrawny kids in uniforms—much like Haynes himself—he thought, and the prisoners captured at the front looked defeated. Surely, the war would be over soon. But Haynes was determined to heal and to continue to fight if needed. The voice of his college football coach was always in his head, always pushing him beyond the boundaries of his mind.

In January, just three months after being wounded and after many surgeries, Haynes had recovered enough—though not fully—to be recalled to duty after a desperate call came for replacements to go back on the lines. By the time he rejoined E Company in the 2nd Battalion of the 349th Infantry, his troops had advanced just three miles in the ninety days he had been recuperating.

Ironically, as Haynes was released from the Naples hospital, his savior, Frank Parker, was admitted with a severe case of hepatitis. In December of 1944, Parker had briefly transferred as an "exchange officer" to the 15th Air Force in southern Italy, flying in a B-17 bomber as a waist gunner, dropping bombs over Linz, Austria, when he fell ill. But by late February, both men were back with their companies in the 349th.

Oregon State punts against a heavy Duke defense. *(Courtesy of the 1942 Duke University Yearbook)*

Rose Bowl MVP Don Durdan (#39) looking to pass. *(Courtesy of the 1942 Duke University Yearbook)*

Oregon State's Stan Czech alongside coach Lon Stiner during the Rose Bowl game. *(Courtesy of Debra Czech Lorenzen)*

Duke bench during the Rose Bowl game. *(Courtesy of Duke University Archives)*

Rose Bowl champions returning to Corvallis. *(Courtesy of Harriet's Photograph Collection, OSU Libraries Special Collections and Archives Research Center)*

Major Wallace Wade Sr. *(Courtesy of Duke University Archives)*

Wallace Wade Jr.'s military photograph. *(Courtesy of Betsy Wade Kerley)*

Wallace Wade Jr. leaving for Fort Bragg in 1942. *(Courtesy of the Associated Press)*

Wallace Wade Sr. and Wallace Wade Jr. in Germany in 1944. *(Courtesy of Duke University Archives)*

Bob Dethman (second from left) just minutes after departing the fight on Iwo Jima. *(Courtesy of Robert Dethman Jr.)*

Bob Dethman *(bottom row, third from left)* on boat leaving the Battle of Iwo Jima. *(Courtesy of Robert Dethman Jr.)*

Charles Haynes in front of the Leaning Tower of Pisa *(Courtesy of Charles C. Haynes Papers, Southern Historical Collection, Wilson Library, The University of North Carolina at Chapel Hill)*

Frank Parker in the Army in Europe c. 1945. *(Courtesy of Heidi Parker Morris)*

Charles Haynes and wife Jane Barry c. 1948. *(Courtesy of Charles Haynes III)*

Oregon State's Stan Czech and nephew Alan Zehntbauer postwar. *(Courtesy of Debra Czech Lorenzen)*

Bob Dethman fishing in the Oregon waters postwar. *(Courtesy of Robert Dethman Jr.)*

Rose Bowl Team 1941
20th Anniversary
Nov. 4, 1961
Oregon State University

Oregon State Rose Bowl team twenty-year reunion. *(Courtesy of Alumni Relations Photographs, OSU Libraries Special Collections and Archives Research Center)*

Charles Haynes and Frank Parker at the fiftieth reunion in Corvallis. *(Courtesy of Terry Parker)*

15. UNCOMMON VALOR

STAN CZECH WAS FREEZING in OFLAG XIII-B outside of Hammelburg. In the harsh winter of 1945, one of the coldest on record, the suffering inside the barbed wires of the camp was felt not just by the prisoners but by their German guards as well. Food was scarce, with small tidbits of soup and bread for every meal, served by Czech, among others who were chosen to dole out the portions. Contrary to expectations, the Germans were generally civil and kind to most of the POWs. Still, conditions were harsh, with the prisoners jammed into seven five-room buildings. Many prisoners contracted influenza or dysentery in the camp, and almost all experienced significant weight loss. Czech, the big man who'd played guard for Lon Stiner, would drop fifty pounds.

On January 23, almost a month after her husband's capture, Ora Lea Czech received a telegram from the secretary of war declaring that her husband was missing. A few weeks later, she received a letter from Captain John Porter of the 35th, expressing his sincere hope that she would receive "good news" in the future. It would be another month before the army informed her that the Red Cross had located Czech in a POW camp. For forty-nine days, Ora Lea Czech had believed the worst—that her husband had been killed in a faraway land.

In late January, the Germans had shut down a POW camp in Schubin, Poland, and marched 1,200 prisoners to Hammelburg, creating even more crowded conditions and less food for everyone. Among the prisoners relocated to OFLAG XIII was Lieutenant Colonel John K. Waters, a POW for two years, having been captured in Tunisia in February of 1943. He was also the son-in-law of General George S. Patton.

In early March, Patton assigned Combat Command B, 4th Armored Division, under the command of Lieutenant Colonel Creighton Abrams, an unusual wartime task: drive fifty miles behind enemy lines and liberate hundreds of American POWs, including Waters.

Abrams wanted to bring two battalions and artillery on the trek but was ordered to send just three hundred troops, manning medium and light tanks along with infantry. Captain Abraham Baum was given the assignment of leading 294 men and 53 vehicles on the mission, dubbed Task Force Baum, which was vastly underequipped and had little intelligence on the location of the camp and too few maps to navigate to it.

The group set out on the night of March 25, and twenty-four hours later, they reached Aschaffenburg, where they took heavy fire from the Germans, rendering some of their tanks useless. They pressed on and broke past the German line on the morning of the twenty-seventh. As the column rumbled—not so quietly—through the countryside, a German plane followed its path and radioed its location to troops on the ground. When Task Force Baum reached Hammelburg, they knew they were close, but they still did not have an exact location of the camp. It wasn't until Baum spotted the camp from a hillside that they had their target in sight. Because there was little evidence of strong defenses at the camp, Baum ordered the tanks to amass side by side across a hill, with the infantry protected behind the tanks. At a rate of five miles per hour, the tanks headed toward the camp. *One thousand yards. Six hundred yards.* The men's adrenaline reached a fever pitch.

With two hundred yards to go, the first German bullets began to hit the task force, which returned fire with power, despite the fact that many of Baum's men were no longer in fighting shape after the rough path behind enemy lines. But the Americans mistakenly focused their guns on the Serbian part of the camp, as POWs were dressed in gray coats and thought to be German guards. With the vicious onslaught, the view of the tanks amassed on the hill, and rumors that the Third Army was on the move, the German commanding officer believed that the entire Third Army was on his doorstep and surrendered the camp to Colonel Paul Goode.

Inside the camp, the men were awash in celebratory hugs, hearing the exchange of gunfire and artillery shells and with word spreading about the German surrender. As the fighting grew closer to the front gates, John Waters volunteered to walk over to the Americans to inform them that the Germans had surrendered inside the camp and that the Americans were hitting the Serbs. Waters left the camp with three American officers and a German, carrying a white flag and an American flag. As they passed through the camp gates, a German soldier who had not been briefed on the situation falsely believed Waters and the Americans were escaping and shot him below his right hip, causing severe damage.

Baum and the surviving members of the task force finally entered the camp with both elation and pause, as they quickly realized that the intelligence that indicated the camp held three hundred men had been vastly deficient. There were more than fifteen hundred Americans. After internal discussion among the command, Baum ordered only senior officers to climb aboard the tanks, while offering the remaining POWs the opportunity to walk behind the column, to escape on their own, or simply to remain at the OFLAG. Many of the POWs were simply too weak and frail and chose to remain behind as Task Force Baum left the camp around 8:00 P.M.

Stan Czech was weak and just wanted to go home. But an opportunity presented itself for him to fight—and to expedite his journey home. So Czech and three others decided to make a run for it. After sunset, the foursome scurried into the unknown of the darkening German forest,

Czech reverting to his football training to stay light on his feet and avoid detection. The temperature dipped significantly, and with no moonlight, the escapees struggled to find a place to rest for the night, finally coming across an old barn. Czech gave one of the men the thick Russian coat he had acquired in the camp to prevent frostbite. At daylight, the men knew they had to move. They made their way through the forest until they spotted the outskirts of a small town. Perhaps there would be food, clothes, and safety.

Though they approached the town with the diligence and carefulness of fugitives on the run, the Germans were waiting. Two of the POWs took off running, but Czech saw no opportunity. He had been free for a little over twelve hours.

Czech was sent with many former and new POWs on a train to camps much deeper inside Germany, far away from the American lines. He would remain a prisoner for another six weeks before the German surrender.

His fate was not much better than that of the members of Task Force Baum. With news spreading of the camp breakout among German commanders, they flooded the area and pounded the column as it attempted to move back toward Allied lines. Baum and his men retreated to a safe area for the night, but in the morning, at the first sign of movement, the Germans pounced. Baum suggested many of the remaining men, too weak to fight, make their way back to OFLAG XIII while others were left to fend for themselves.

There were slightly less than three hundred men who set out on March 25 on a heroic yet flawed mission to free their fellow soldiers. Only a reported thirty-five returned safely. Though no one can be sure, authorities believe more than fifty-five were killed or wounded in the attempt and most of the rest captured as POWs. Every American vehicle was either destroyed or captured. The mission was viewed as a colossal failure by General Dwight Eisenhower, and he was furious at Patton's orders.

In early April, just days after the failed attempt, the Allies finally liberated OFLAG XIII as they rapidly advanced toward Berlin.

The 442nd Regimental Combat Team, comprising Japanese Americans, finally saw action in Italy in 1944, and would go on to fight in southern and northeastern France. The 552nd Field Artillery detached from the 442nd and was one of the first military units to liberate a sub-camp of the Dachau concentration camp. The members of the 442nd and its attachments distinguished themselves on the battlefield, with twenty-one Medal of Honor recipients and eight Distinguished Unit Citations. Jack Yoshihara had tried to enlist in the 442nd in 1944 but could not pass the medical exam because of his injured knee from playing football at the University of Utah in the fall of 1943.

Instead, in December 1944, the same month that the WRA announced that all internment camps would be shuttered by the end of 1945, Yoshihara packed two suitcases, put twenty-five dollars in his pocket, and headed to Detroit, where he took a job in a carburetor manufacturing plant. He kept a low profile during a summer of race riots in the city. His young wife, Elsie, and their daughter, Lynn, joined him in March 1945, but the stay in Michigan lasted just a year, as the family returned to Oregon to live with Yoshihara's parents, Roosevelt having officially revoked the mass exclusion orders in January 1945. The Yoshiharas were part of the less than 30 percent of the Nisei who returned to Oregon after the war.

Though they were free from barbed wire in Idaho, they were not free from discrimination, as many locals in the West made life downright inhospitable for those of Japanese descent. So Yoshihara began his life again. And while a sense of normalcy came and went, finishing his degree at Oregon State was not in the cards for his future.

Mount Suribachi soars above the ash shoreline of Iwo Jima, which lies some 530 feet below its peak. Its shape against the relatively flat land surrounding it is the most striking feature of an otherwise mundane volcanic island, if one can be mundane. Seven hundred and fifty miles south of Tokyo, Iwo Jima, also known as Sulfur Island, is just eight square miles, but its relative proximity to Japan made it valuable real estate during the war.

With approximately one thousand residents who mined sulfur and farmed sugarcane, the island before World War II was quiet, laid-back, and poor. But with the arrival of the war, the Japanese saw the strategic value of the island and used its two airfields and began building a third. The airfields on the north end of the island provided Japanese fighter planes with a takeoff location to strike American bombers headed toward Japan.

After the capture of Guam, Saipan, and other Japanese strongholds, the Americans set their sights on Iwo. If the Americans could gain control of the island, the United States could not only prevent the air attacks but set the stage for an invasion of Japan, launching air raids from the island.

The Japanese navy had a small garrison on one end of the island, but as the expectation of an American invasion took hold in 1944, the Japanese empire flooded the island with fifteen thousand troops and weapons. Lieutenant General Tadamichi Kuribayashi was put in charge of Japanese defenses on Iwo Jima, and he designed a defensive strategy not to confront the Americans as they landed on the beaches but to wait in ambush as thousands came ashore in order to kill as many enemy soldiers as possible. The Japanese spent days and nights digging an elaborate system of miles and miles of tunnels throughout the island, creating steel gun emplacements and fortified bunkers at key locations. The system allowed Japanese guns to reach every inch of Iwo Jima.

The initial timing of an attack on Iwo Jima was held up for a month as the naval fleet supported the invasion of the Philippines in the fall of

1944. But with a new target in early 1945, the U.S. Navy and Army Air Forces began a sustained bombardment of the island to minimize the resistance to the landing forces that lasted for months. The American military command believed the enemy had been decimated—or, at the very least, declawed.

On November 15, 1944, senior officers of Marine Landing Team 126, including former Oregon State Beaver star Bob Dethman, were briefed on the pending assault on Iwo Jima and immediately began planning both the landing and the necessary training schedule in Hawaii. Fourteen battalion officers prepared lectures on everything from the sequence of the landing to potential terrain issues on Iwo, to be delivered to the enlisted men aboard the ship transports using aerial reconnaissance photos that, of course, did not reveal the unknown bunkers hiding within the earth. The 5th Division trained at Camp Tarawa on the main island of Hawaii, scaling cliffs, working on demolitions, and practicing camouflage tactics and protections against chemical warfare and enemy mines.

The division began loading onto ships on December 16, and all were out by January 4, sailing to Pearl Harbor and then Maui to engage in the first of several rehearsals of the planned amphibious landing. On January 15 at high noon, LT 126 landed on Maui in a mock assault. The Marines returned to Pearl Harbor on the eighteenth and enjoyed nine days of limited training, recreation, and liberty passes. It was a distraction at best. At 11:00 A.M. on January 27, Dethman and the Marines headed out to sea.

The ships arrived on Saipan on February 11 and conducted one last rehearsal on the thirteenth before joining 450 ships sailing to Iwo Jima on the sixteenth. Vehicles were combat-loaded four days before D-day. In total, Landing Team 126 consisted of 40 officers and 993 enlisted men.

The initial plan for LT 126 had it landing in a second assault wave in support of a Combat Team of Corps Reserve, but that was changed a few days before the landing, when LT 126 became a reserve for the

5th Marine Division. LT 126 was to be at the Line of Departure 150 minutes after the initial landing on the nineteenth and to be prepared to land on any of the beaches assigned to the 5th. The Marines' boats rocked in choppy waters seven miles offshore as the armada of hundreds of large and small ships prepared to approach the island.

The first Marines to arrive on the southern beaches were shocked at the relative lack of resistance and enemy fire, allowing them to believe that the months-long bombing campaign had wiped out the enemy. There were a few shells and bullets sent their way, but nothing like they had expected. The island was smoldering ash with no water, no animals, and black, hot sand. There was a distinct smell of sulphur. The Marines cautiously but confidently began to head off the beachhead, approaching a fifteen-foot-high ridge, unknowingly right into the path of Japanese guns. General Kuribayashi gave the signal, and the bloodiest battle in Marine history began. Japanese guns opened fire from well-hidden and camouflaged foxholes near the beach while heavy artillery poured down on the Marines from seemingly every other direction. Many of the Marines never even got off a shot. The gravel and sand were too hard or too loose to dig holes for safety, and it was only after more waves of Marines arrived onshore that the Americans were at least able to secure the beach, aided by naval gunfire and air strikes.

LT 126 was ordered to land on Beach Red One and attach to Combat Team 27. At 2:15 P.M., they received orders to land, and by 3:00 P.M., they were on the sand and moved quickly to an assembly area, establishing defensive lines for the night on the western beaches. Dethman had been training for more than a year to fight, and his heart beat fast as he walked across the black sand amid the smell of burning human flesh.

Dethman's unit went on the attack for three straight days and nights and was often a sitting duck in the low, open terrain of Iwo, with the enemy watching every move from above. His orders were to inch forward, and Dethman screamed directions to his platoon as they moved slowly inland like crabs. The fighting was intense in the early days of the battle, and the Americans had to pull back several times under heavy fire. The number of troops, the small size of the island, and the tactics of the enemy made hand-to-hand combat a regular occurrence. On February 20, the advance had all but stopped, with staggering casualties along the front lines. Continued assaults by artillery seemed to be having little effect, but by the twenty-second, Mount Suribachi was in friendly hands.

The Marine Corps released the news that there were more than five thousand Marine casualties on Iwo Jima in the first few days of the assault. Americans read the accounts in newspapers and associated columns and began questioning the tactics and true strategic value of the tiny island, raising both concern and debate over the staggering costs of the battle. However, after the capture of Mount Suribachi and the indelible image of Americans hoisting the American flag atop its peak on February 23, the tide turned, buoyed by the news of MacArthur's triumphant return to Manila.

But capturing Suribachi was a false indicator of success. Close combat battles raged for days on end, with Dethman fighting off bullets, bombs, hunger, fear, and the loss of his platoon commander and many friends. Though Dethman had always assumed war would be rough, he never could have imagined the differences from the game of football. His eighty-one-millimeter mortar platoon was shelled heavily on February 24 and 25, with devastating casualties. Though the Japanese were outnumbered and now low on supplies, they continued to fight hard and were not afraid to undertake suicide infiltration missions to inflict harm. When the platoon did get a brief respite off the line, they were treated with hot coffee and doughnuts and visited by the in-demand chaplains.

Every night, no matter his condition or safety, Dethman would scamper behind the lines to another battalion of the 26th, of which his younger brother, Wendell, was a member. Wendell had enlisted in the

Marines out of high school and wanted nothing more than to be a hero in his older brother's eyes, but Wendell, like so many others, had it tough on Iwo Jima and struggled to maintain his mental well-being. Every night, his older brother would make his way to Wendell's unit to check on him and to provide encouragement.

Despite his fragile state, Wendell never failed in his duty. In fact, between March 12 and 16, Wendell displayed unique courage in taking out small enemy pockets, and in one instance, on the fifteenth, he ran up to a cave entrance full of Japanese snipers and threw white phosphorous and fragmentation grenades into the cave while unleashing his Browning automatic rifle. The Marines thought so highly of his actions that he would later be awarded a Bronze Star.

Bob Dethman was on the front lines for seventeen days and eighteen nights. By March 10, the 5th Marines had exhausted the supply of replacements—many of whom were very green, having never been in battle and who were less effective on the front—and battalions in the field were on their own.

Dethman assumed command of the 1st Platoon after the loss of its senior officer and was immediately ordered to fill an urgent gap in the front lines, which protected a command post, turning his mortar platoon into riflemen. Japanese snipers and artillery were buzzing in the air in the late afternoon of March 18, and Dethman kept losing men.

"Move it! Now!" he screamed to what was left of the platoon over the sounds of explosions and bullets. "Get your asses down!"

Dethman exchanged fire while pressed behind a rock that hid a foxhole, though it wasn't much more than a very shallow trench. The lieutenant alternated between exposing his position to get off shots and retreating to the safety behind the earth.

"Get off the guns!" Dethman relayed to two soldiers he could barely make out to his right.

Just then, a loud screaming sound rained down from the sky—a piercing whistle with which Dethman had become all too familiar. A

Japanese shell was headed his way. Before Dethman could even move, his runner, Private First Class Henry C. Costley, a nineteen-year-old from Saint Louis, dove into Dethman's foxhole, knocking Dethman off his knees. The artillery shell landed just feet from the foxhole a moment later, sending shrapnel and fragments of heated metal in every direction. Dethman and Costley were lucky to avoid injury, but a fragment broke the operating rod on Costley's rifle, leaving him with just one bullet that could be salvaged in the chamber. Dethman's supply of ammo was low, and he gazed quickly at his knife, perhaps his best chance.

The artillery and small-arms fire continued to come at a faster and faster pace. Dethman could not see the men left in his platoon, though an occasional shout or the sound of American gunfire was a welcome noise. The sun set on Iwo Jima and plunged the battleground into darkness before clouds gave way to a partial moon.

"What are we going to do?" the private innocently asked Lieutenant Dethman.

"Shh! Keep your voice down, Costley! Just sit tight and keep your head down," Dethman instructed in a heavy whisper.

And that's what both men did—sat still and quiet, fearful of moving or making a sound, of exposing their location to snipers ready to pounce. Costley's heart beat loudly, and his commander could see the fear in his eyes.

In the silence of the night, Dethman's ears picked up the tiniest sound of footsteps and whispers of Japanese soldiers encroaching on the foxhole. His adrenaline was running high, and he clenched his palm around his knife, sweat dripping off his fingers. He was ready to kill. The enemy got closer. Ten feet. Then eight feet. Then six feet. Dethman prepared to jump. Somehow, by the grace of God, or perhaps by the curse of darkness, the Japanese soldiers did not discover the Americans. Dethman and Costley listened as the sounds of the footsteps grew faint.

Though they had avoided one near miss, Dethman knew they could not stay in the foxhole much longer. Come daylight, they were sitting ducks. Besides, he and his platoon had an order to follow: fill in the gap on the line. Members of the platoon were still alive, spread out among foxholes and hiding behind boulders, but trying to confirm their whereabouts could expose Dethman and Costley.

Around midnight, Dethman decided that they would make a run for it.

"You stay right next to me, and move as fast as you can!" he told Costley, and the private acknowledged his order with a slight nod.

Dethman clutched his knife once again and put one hand on Costley's shoulder.

"Go!"

And with that, the pair burst out of the hole. They had not run more than five steps before Japanese bullets began to fly, the moon now illuminating their every move. Like he had done so many times on the football field, Dethman shot for an opening, jumping over jagged rocks as if they were tacklers, Costley three steps behind. Dethman spotted a foxhole with what looked like American soldiers. He took one last big step and leaped through the air, crashing into the hard dirt and sand. Costley came down next, landing on Dethman's leg. There were two Marines already occupying the hole, and they were on such an edge, ready to shoot anything that moved, that they almost killed their mates.

Over the next twenty-four hours, Dethman loosely organized the remaining men in the platoon in darkness and in light, and he continued to lead them in a brutal firefight at close range. They survived a constant barrage of grenades, close-in shoot-outs, and multiple suicide attacks by the enemy. Undermanned and under-armed, the men of the 26th Marines were able to repel the attacks and hold the line.

Bob Dethman was not the only member of the 1942 Rose Bowl club to be shuttered on Iwo Jima. Among them was Bob Barnett, the captain of the Duke squad and a veteran of the battles in Bougainville and Guam, who came ashore days after Dethman, as did Oregon State's Warren Perryman. Dethman's teammates Norm Peters and Joe Day remained offshore in the supply chain. And Duke's Bob Nanni disembarked on Iwo Jima around 2:00 P.M. on February 24, five days after D-day.

Nanni had had an inauspicious start on the Duke freshman football team when, in his first game, he was ejected after amassing 170 penalty yards in just five minutes for his violent outbursts and lack of understanding of the rules of the game. While on the team, Nanni would learn discipline from Wallace Wade, though he didn't always exhibit it. He developed into a more than capable substitute by 1941, his junior year, and saw action in many games, even recovering a key fumble for Duke in the third period of the Rose Bowl game.

He enlisted in the Marines and saw his first action on Guam. In a moment of quiet solitude while in his tent, Nanni took the time to write to Eddie Cameron:

> *Dear Coach,*
> *Sitting here on my bunk and thinking what foolish things I have done while playing. At that time I didn't realize that I was hurting the team, also myself. Pig-head as I am it seems that we wake up to the fact that all was in vain what I have done. I guess I didn't appreciate the things you and the rest of the coaching staff was trying to do. I know it's to[o] late now to repent, but I can thank you and your assistants [for] what you have done that helps me now, more than ever. You have given me that spirit never to quit while the chips are down, and to go on trying to give your best at all time[s]. I remember what Coach Wade use[d] to say "you always have a little left, even though [you're] very tired." To do that I realize one must be in condition and have fortitude to carry on. The years I have spent under your guidance and tutoring, I believe I have acquired it. Again, the credit goes to you and "Dumpy" [Hagler]. What I am*

trying to say is you have taught me never to quit or let your team mates down. I guess war is the same as a football game. The one that hits the hardest first, will win. I want you to know that if I had the chance again, things would be different. I hope all misunderstandings we had are forgotten.

I would like you to tell "Dumpy" that he has done a good job in teaching me to hit and hit hard. That has come handy in this outfit. I'm sure that he is continuing to do the same to the boys he is coaching. Some day, they will realize and be thankful for what he has done for them. You can tell him for me that I miss his voice and howling at me, yet if I had that same chance now, it would be heaven to be near. I do hope he doesn't think to[o] badly of me.

I'm trying to keep up with each game and I'm pulling for you and the boys, win or lose.

I have seen Bob Barnett and we really had a long talk together. He is the same Bob, but a little thinner. I guess we would all be if we have [sic] *gone through those campaigns. It was darn good to meet him.*

I have written nearly three pages and didn't say much, so I wish you a successful season. Some day, with the help of God we may see each other again, and have a place on your team. My best regards to "Dumpy" and "Stanley" and again I shall say, thank you for what you gave me and taught me. I do hope you find time to drop me a line, when your [sic] *not to[o] busy.*

Your Former Pupil,
Bob Nanni

Nanni remained on Guam after the fighting ended and underwent training in rifle and scout sniper shooting, flamethrowers, and bazookas as he prepared for his next assault.

The 1st Battalion consisted of 33 officers and 759 enlisted men when it received word on February 23, four days into the fight for Iwo Jima, that the battalion would land the following day in landing craft mechanizeds (LCMs) on Beach Yellow Two and assemble near Motoyama Airfield No. 1. The LCMs could hold up to one hundred troops and made for easy egress. The Marines were armed with high-level maps, which turned out to not always be accurate, and they were joined by a Japanese American who served as an interpreter. The Marines had been well trained for the operation, both on Guam and on board, and were armed with flamethrowers and rocket launchers in addition to their guns, cargo carriers, and trucks.

The initial objective was to seize the high ground over Motoyama Airfield No. 2. They launched the assault on the morning of the twenty-fifth on Hill Peter, as it was designated. Peter was riddled with elaborate tunnels and secured pillboxes, difficult to penetrate. Initial attempts to make progress up the hill were rebuffed, and the battalion suffered heavy casualties under small-arms and mortar fire. At night, less fighting was done, as there was little illumination of both the enemy and the objective. The men hunkered down, lit up a Coleman gasoline stove, and ate their B and C rations.

After three intense days of fighting, the 9th Marines were able to secure the hill on the evening of February 27. They were held in reserve for twenty-four hours before resuming their offensive to take the last remaining hill on the northern end of the island.

Bob Nanni set out with the platoon that afternoon in search of Japanese soldiers, his eyes constantly scanning his surroundings. Yet his vigilance didn't matter. He never heard or saw it coming. The bullet pierced his skin in a clean hole on the side of his head, ripping through his muscle and through a cranial bone that protects the brain. It went through his tissue and sprayed fragments of mass throughout, all in a fraction of a second. His comrades picked him up and carried him to a makeshift battalion aid station, where Bob Nanni officially died, though he was dead the moment the Japanese soldier pulled the trigger. Nanni was one of three from his battalion killed that night and one of 157 killed on Iwo Jima.

The only nonmilitary possession on his body was his Rose Bowl ring, which was mailed to his father six months later, his last reminder of his son.

The Battle of Iwo Jima officially ended on March 26. With 6,140 Marines dead and more than 17,000 wounded, the Americans sacrificed 700 young men for roughly each square mile of land captured. But the ability to land planes on Iwo Jima greatly increased the Americans' range and ability to defeat the enemy. Admiral Nimitz remarked, "Among the Americans who served on Iwo Jima, uncommon valor was a common virtue." His words are now memorialized in the Marine Corps Memorial in Arlington.

Across the world, the late winter and early spring of 1945 exposed some of the most vicious battles in Italy, with the Allies on the offensive but the Germans holding the line. The race across the rugged mountains of Italy was slow and methodical and deadly. For three weeks in March, the 349th, with Frank Parker and Charles Haynes, moved off the lines and stationed at La Croce, where they trained for an anticipated final push into Germany while enjoying free time, taking side trips to Montecatini, Rome, and Florence, playing card games, listening to the radio, and writing letters home.

They moved out on April 2, headed north, with an initial objective of Furcoli Ridge, where the Germans were dug in and bunkered in caves. On April 15 at 10:00 P.M., the front lines erupted, and war returned to the men of the 349th. But after nearly a month of training and refreshment, they were ready. They quickly took the ridge, secured the town of Le Braine, and marched forward at an accelerating rate. Lieutenant Colonel John W. Lyon ordered Haynes's platoon to mount tanks and head toward Decima, the last main German resistance before the Po River.

The tanks rumbled—not quietly—down the main road toward town, and it wasn't long before the Germans opened fire.

Haynes jumped off the moving tank and found safety in a ditch on the side of the road, and many of his platoon soldiers did the same. The German machine guns never stopped. Haynes ordered heavy return fire, but because of the platoon's distance from town, it proved to be ineffective.

"Men, we must get closer!" he screamed over the sounds of war. "Keep your knives close!"

And with that, Haynes began to scramble toward town, finding cover every few feet with his men trailing behind. One by one, they made it to town and engaged the Germans in hand-to-hand combat, with knives and bayonets the preferred methods of attack. It was chaos and every man for himself.

Haynes killed five Germans in the first few minutes and then another after a vicious hand-to-hand battle. His wrestling and football training proved useful in a life-or-death situation.

In all, the platoon killed more than forty Germans, took seventy as prisoners, and destroyed a German tank for good measure. The fiery horseback rider from Durham had earned himself a Silver Star.

Within days, the Americans reached the Po River, and from the time they headed out on April 2 until April 18, the 349th had advanced one hundred miles, grabbing 10,557 prisoners and killing hundreds more. The German resistance was scattered, their will defeated. The Americans moved quickly for the deathblow and were headed into the Alps when word came that the Germans had surrendered in Italy. The 349th, including both Parker and Haynes, were in the Brenner Pass when they received word of the surrender. Their work was not done, however, as troops spent the month of May securing buildings and roads but also enjoying the free time in fancy hotels and boardinghouses after morning training sessions. They participated in organized athletic activities, attended dances with the locals, and caught up on news from back home.

It was unremarkable how it happened, that last good-bye in the

Brenner Pass in Austria in May 1945. Soldiers were being relocated all over Europe and some sent home or to the Pacific, and the passing goodbyes between soldiers came quickly and often unexpectedly.

Charles Haynes and Frank Parker had left the States as opponents, boys from different sides of the country, whose exceptional actions on the battlefield and on one day in the Arno Valley had pulled their fates together, now, as men. They became close friends in the context of war and even spent a few days in a rare respite from the battlefields, enjoying the luxuries of the Excelsior Hotel in Rome, the headquarters of the U.S. Army. Parker, who never believed his heroic actions in saving Haynes were worthy of even a mention, calmly wished Haynes well, shook his hand, and then immediately turned and walked away to his next assignment. For Haynes, it was more emotional. He would return to see his mother and family because of Frank Parker, and for that he would be eternally indebted to him. As Parker walked away, Haynes paused for a moment, and then it was back to duty.

Parker, by now the recipient of three Bronze Stars, was soon ordered to Rome to participate in a military football game to help boost morale. However, he injured his knee during practice while in Rome and would live with pain the rest of his life. He could have requested a return to the United States for active duty, to reunite with Peggy, before a likely trip to the Pacific—but he didn't. Peggy also could have joined him in Italy like many other soldiers' wives—but she didn't. The clues were perhaps visible in the exchange of letters as the war came to an end—Frank more hesitant in offering the invitation, Peggy less enthusiastic about accepting.

Simply, Frank Parker believed he was a changed man. His killing of men and witnessing of war had forever altered his soul, and he believed that the love of his life could never truly love the monster he had become. He was battling demons before even stepping off the battlefield. So instead of heading home, Parker accepted an assignment to oversee German POWs in southern Germany, a task that would keep him in Europe for more than a year.

As for Haynes, in the months after the end of hostilities, he served in a variety of capacities for the army in Italy and traveled to Florence and Rome. His letters home to his mother reflected a changed man from the eager Duke student in 1942, and after stopping by an American cemetery, the preciousness of life came into focus.

> *I can well appreciate coming out of the war with just a few scars and when I think of all of those boys who never will be going home—my delay in going home seems awful trivial and makes me ashame[d] of myself thinking solely for my own interest instead of doing whatever I can to prevent or to help prevent it happening again.*

Haynes would end his service in Italy in charge of feeding fifty thousand German POWs and with the keys to the largest German wine warehouse in the country. He earned a Silver Star, a Purple Heart, and three battle stars for his service to America before coming home in October to an uncertain future.

PART V

HOME

I firmly believe that any man's finest hour, his greatest fulfillment to all he holds dear, is that moment when he has worked his heart out in good cause and lies exhausted on the field of battle, victorious.

—Vince Lombardi, coach, National Football League Hall of Fame

16. THE NEW NORMAL

THE USS *BRIGHT* WAS a DE-747 Cannon-class destroyer escort commissioned in September of 1943, with William McMahan in command, when Duke's Jim Smith was assigned to the ship in 1944. The *Bright* sailed from San Diego to Pearl Harbor and then on to Eniwetok and Saipan, escorting convoys through the dangerous waters of the South Pacific, protecting them from submarine and air attacks. Though trained in sonar, Smith was moved to gunnery officer after a previous one had died. In 1945, the *Bright* anchored off the shores of Okinawa as part of the last major military initiatives by the Americans, the assault on Japan. Along with its fellow ships, the USS *Bright* was under constant threat of kamikaze attacks, suicide missions by Japanese pilots. (In fact, 40 percent of the American casualties in Okinawa were the result of kamikaze attacks.)

On one fateful night, as Smith stood watch, an enemy plane approached the ship, flying just above the horizon, a clear sign it was headed on a one-way trip. As the plane flew closer, the *Bright* opened up its guns, striking the left wing but not impeding its progress. The captain steered the vessel to the right, but the massive ship took too long to turn. The pilot of the aircraft maintained enough control to hit the ship near its fantail, which limited but did not eliminate American casualties. Five sailors were killed, and seven more were injured. Other ships were struck by kamikazes that night, and the *Bright* floundered in the Pacific waters. Even after it came into the bay for repairs, the threat of attacks remained, and crews were fearful of rafts filled with bombs exploding next to the resting ships.

President Harry Truman made the final decision to drop the atomic bombs on Japan—the same bombs that Arthur Compton, Enrico Fermi, and Duke and Oregon State professors had helped build. The first bomb fell on Hiroshima on August 6 and the second on Nagasaki on August 9. Days later, Japan surrendered, and World War II had mercifully come to an end.

More than seventy players and coaches from the 1942 Rose Bowl served in the armed services during the war, some in battle, others in support roles in the States. They stormed the beaches of Normandy and Iwo Jima and flew over Germany and Guadalcanal. They fought in Europe and in the Pacific, and they did so with valor and courage.

Twenty-nine of the thirty-one players on the Oregon State Rose Bowl roster served their country. Rose Bowl captain Martin Chaves flew sorties over Europe and Africa. Orville Zielaskowski was wounded twice on Saipan, while Warren Simas took up arms in New Guinea. Glenn Byington navigated planes in the South Pacific, while Norm Peters served with the Marines in China and Guadalcanal. George Zellick was part of the Okinawa invasion force. So many more made sacrifices for America.

Like their counterparts in Corvallis, the men of the 1942 Duke Rose Bowl team served their country on land, in the air, and on sea. Floating in the waters off Okinawa as a member of the United States Navy was Tommy Prothro. Clyde Redding signed up for the Marines just hours after the Rose Bowl loss and served in the Solomons and on Guam. Ralph Felty was wounded while fighting in Saipan but returned to action in Okinawa. And they were just a few.

There were so many on both squads who served and sacrificed.

Four players from the Rose Bowl would make the ultimate sacrifice: Walter Griffith, Everett Smith, Al Hoover, and Bob Nanni. Many others would carry the burden of war with them for the rest of their lives. They were not the boys who had played the game on New Year's Day and who thought that war was just another game to be played. They returned home to find that the world was different.

Historian Tom Bennett later would repeat the notion, started in the 1920s, that Oregon State was "the West Point of the West," in praise of its large turnout of soldiers and leaders. More than two thousand students trained in Oregon State's ROTC programs were commissioned as officers, more than from any other nonmilitary academy in the country. Of course, the pride in the boys' service in the world war was prevalent in Corvallis but was tempered by the loss of 275 members of the Oregon State family. Even as the war began to wind down, America's military leaders wanted to prepare a new generation of soldiers and sailors and selected Oregon State, Stanford, Utah, and Idaho for additional naval ROTC work, and an Army Air Corps training branch was soon added.

More than seven thousand Duke alums and students served in the war. A total of 245 were killed. They died in training accidents in America, in forests in Belgium, and in the air over China and Italy and Germany and on the beaches of France. A service in the Duke University Chapel on August 12 commemorated the conclusion of hostilities and honored the Duke students and faculty who had served. It wasn't long before the navy V-12 school closed its doors, and the military presence on campus dropped by almost 50 percent from July until November 1945 as the army began discharging one million men a month.

Servicemen returning from war matriculated at Duke, some picking up where they had left off in their studies, others enrolling for the first time, most supported by the GI Bill, which funded their education. Many of the returning students requested academic credit for their time in the armed forces, which was determined on a case-by-case basis by Dean Herbert J. Herring.

From 1945 on, veterans at Duke earned better grades than non-veterans. Perhaps they understood the value of an education more, or perhaps they were simply older and more mature. Duke officials estimated that 4,800 veterans applied for the 1946–47 school year, with the admissions committee giving preference to veterans over standard high school applicants and placing a higher priority to returning veterans who were previously Duke students. The freshman class consisted of four hundred men, half of whom were former soldiers.

Wallace Wade Sr., at the age of fifty-two, fought in the European campaign without a day's leave, in constant range of enemy fire for nine months. He fought in the Battles of Normandy and on the Siegfried Line, in the Battle of the Bulge and the crossing of the Rhine. For his actions, Wade was awarded a Bronze Star and a Croix de Guerre with Palm from France. In the spring of 1945, he was named the athletic director of the Twelfth Army Group, comprising 1.5 million soldiers. He finally arrived back in North Carolina on July 5, and shortly thereafter, he announced he would return to Duke as the director of athletics—but not as the head football coach.

Upon his return, he spent his days in public and private reminiscences on war. Like his son, Wade had witnessed the atrocities of war and the seemingly unimaginable violence of the battlefield. To one audience, he noted that the lesson he had learned about war was that "we don't want to have another." War was "wasteful, horrible, and senseless," and he insisted that electing officials who were intelligent and honest was the best way to prevent discussions of war from making it a reality. He encouraged folks to attend church more often, stressed the new connectivity of the world, and insisted that families spend more time together. Wade, now a true philosopher, had indeed been changed by war, and football took its place in his new worldview.

He spent his first year back focused on building a newly strong physical education and intramural sports department at Duke, believing they were essential to students' development, yet he still had the urge to compete. As the 1945 season played out, Eddie Cameron led Duke to its third consecutive Southern Conference championship with losses only to Army and Navy. Wade began to have an itch for the hands-on coaching experience again, and after the season's conclusion, Duke announced that Wade would resume his duties as football coach, perhaps buoyed by rumors that the University of Kentucky had offered him a large sum of money to coach its football team.

Spring practice in 1946 felt familiar to Wade, but there were very few faces he recognized among the players. Only Clyde Redding, Leo Long, and Bob Gantt were back from the last team he had coached in 1941, as most of the players out in the spring were returning war veterans on government-funded educations.

Duke was favored to win the opener against North Carolina State during Wade's return to the sideline in September 1946 but they lost 13–6, followed by a 12–7 loss to the University of Tennessee. They lost to Army 19–0 at the Polo Grounds in New York in front of fifty-nine thousand fans. Ultimately, Wade suffered his worst season as a head coach, finishing at 4–5. It was the only losing season he was ever a part of, as a player *or* as a coach, since high school. There was some local chatter about whether Wade—and his system of run and punt—could still be effective, but the coach was not rattled.

His wife, Frances, had been battling cancer and was in declining health in 1946, in and out of Duke Hospital, with her husband tending to her needs when he was not at practice. They had been married almost thirty years but separated for much of the previous four because of the war. Frances was the only person with whom Wade ever let his softness show—not unexpected from the man who'd waved good-bye to his daughter through a fence on the practice field as she headed off to college.

On June 2, 1947, Frances passed away, and two days later, hundreds of mourners jammed into the Duke University Chapel for the memorial service, officiated by Dr. Kelsey Regen, pastor of the First Presbyterian Church of Durham. Pallbearers included Eddie Cameron, Herschel Caldwell, Ellis "Dumpy" Hagler, and Bob Barnett. Sis was there with her young daughter, Barbara, as were young Wallace Wade Jr. and one of Frances's sisters, Claire Bell. The diminutive yet strong woman had survived as the wife of a soldier, as the mother of another, and to a lesser (though many in the South might say greater) extent as the wife of the football coach at Alabama and Duke.

Frances's spirit lived on in quiet moments that her husband found during the 1947 season. Along with assistants Ace Parker, Jack Hennemier, Dan Hill, and Bob Cox, Wade coached the boys to a 4–1 start and a national ranking of ninth, relieving some of the angst of alumni who believed that Wade had lost his touch. The coach was fully engaged, routinely getting down in a stance on a hot day to demonstrate a blocking move or a tackle. But when Duke went winless (including one tie) the rest of the way, including a shutout loss to North Carolina, critics began to blame the lack of depth on Duke's waning attitude toward football. Defenders insisted the poor depth was due to Duke's refusal not to entice recruits with cash, like their opponents did, and to stick with their much tougher academic standards. Either way, the heat was on Wallace Wade.

By the time college football returned to Oregon State in the fall of 1945, after a two-year absence, the enthusiasm generated by the remarkable 1941 conference championship and Rose Bowl–winning season had dissipated. Folks still talked about Bob Dethman and Don Durdan and that day in Durham, but it had long since been relegated to the background of war. Still, 1945 saw the return of football, and with a roster comprising both young veterans and fresh-faced boys only slightly younger in chronological years but much younger in life experience, Lon Stiner led his team to a respectable .500 record of 4–4–1.

Some football diehards understood that circumstances meant that a .500 record in 1945 marked a highly successful season, but those skeptical that Stiner's magic had survived the war were proven wrong in 1946 when he fielded perhaps his best team at Oregon State—better even than the 1942 Rose Bowl champs. OSC posted a 7–1–1 record, losing only their opening game to UCLA, who would go on to win the conference title. After the season, Stiner reportedly turned down a lucrative offer from Yale.

But Stiner was a football coach, which meant job insecurity when the wins and championships stopped coming, and despite leading Oregon State to the Rose Bowl victory in 1942, his job was never safe. He would soon be gone.

Frank Parker was still in uniform as many of his former teammates returned to civilian life. In December 1945, after agreeing to stay on assignment in Europe with Peggy still in the States, Parker became ill and, on Christmas Day, was admitted to a hospital. His appetite greatly diminished, he vomited what he was able to swallow, and he felt fatigued all the time. He stayed in the hospital for ten days before being released but returned on January 11 with jaundice. The jaundice subsided more slowly than expected, and further complications kept Parker in the hospital until March 1946, when he returned to his duties in Italy. He finally arrived back in America on Christmas Eve 1946, more than two and a half years since he'd last stepped on U.S. soil. In his possession were a few German lugers and P-38s.

He arrived on the East Coast, and almost immediately upon his return, he took a train to Pittsfield, Massachusetts, to visit an old friend—Rodman Henry. After suffering the loss of most of his left arm and hand in Italy in 1944, Henry was transported to a hospital ship and then to hospitals on Staten Island and in Atlantic City for recovery. His dreams of becoming a concert musician died on the battlefield in Italy, but he was not deterred in his pursuit of the arts and learning. He would go on to earn a Ph.D. in philosophy, studied and taught art history for years, and even worked for the Boston Symphony Orchestra. Parker and Henry would remain in touch for the rest of their lives.

Parker remained in the army as a captain and was assigned to the 717th Tank Battalion stationed in Washington State, near his home. He reunited with Peggy, of course, but their marriage would never be the same. How could it be? He was finally relieved of active duty in May 1948 and returned to Astoria.

The emotional scars of warfare were seared deep in his soul as he set about earning a living. He never stopped loving Peggy or caring for her, but he lived in fear that he could no longer be the man that she had married. The world had changed too much since he'd left Oregon State, and though he thought about teaching and coaching, he never finished his degree. He reverted to what he knew—driving a dump truck. He picked up where he had left off before the war and ran garbage, rocks, and construction materials in and around Astoria. But when his brother Wilder wrecked the truck, Parker had little choice but to join his brother Eben as a fisherman.

The man whose life Frank Parker had saved returned to Durham after the war and left the army in January 1946. Charles Haynes was the same likable and friendly guy that his friends had known before he'd gone to war. He married the daughter of an editor at *The Durham Sun,* a Broadway actress named Jane Barry, who acted and directed in playhouses in North Carolina and Pennsylvania, with the occasional job in New York. The Hayneses began a family, first with John, and then Charles III, and finally Wendy. Haynes partnered with his friend Bill

Whitt to form Whitt-Haynes Construction in 1947 and continued on alone when Whitt dropped out two years later. Haynes was one of the first builders in the region to construct prefabricated houses, churches, and schools, and the business did well until a recession in 1957 shut its doors. (When the military asked him to serve in Korea in the early 1950s, he declined, believing—rightfully so—that he had sacrificed enough and that his children needed him.)

Haynes had always been interested in food, but he fell in love with cooking while dining with the French Foreign Legion in North Africa in 1944, partaking in the preparation and consumption of seven-course meals served with an assortment of wines. In 1946, along with friend and Duke alum Thomas Huckabee, Haynes constructed a restaurant by the stables on Hillsborough Road near the Hillandale Golf Course in a rural part of Durham. His mother and father helped run the Saddle Club while their son built homes in the Carolinas, but in the early 1960s, Haynes took over the restaurant and renamed it the Saddle & Fox. There was an orchestra pit and small stage that welcomed big bands and singers to town, becoming a "big dine and dance place." Diners were seated by a large rock fireplace, a wagon wheel, and a wall decorated with framed pictures of Haynes's beloved horses, including Pandora, his childhood favorite, whom he tragically had to put down with a Colt .45 when he came up lame during Charles's college years.

The restaurant became Haynes's passion.

The man who caught the winning touchdown pass in the Rose Bowl, Gene Gray—who had earned accolades as a pilot for his bombing runs in Europe—returned to the United States but remained a pilot in the Army Air Corps. He continued his training and teaching of young cadets on the finer points of aviation combat. Gray served as a test pilot with the 23rd Tow Squadron and then the 60th Airways Division.

Later, he was with the 5th Base Camp stationed at Howard Air Base in the Panama Canal Zone and then at Río Hato in Panama. His wife joined him, and their daughter was born.

Gray was qualified to fly a variety of aircraft, but the primary aircraft flown at France Field in Panama was the new Lockheed FP 80A-5, which presented two critical problems for the pilots. First, there were no two-seat training planes available, so pilots taking off in the 80A-5 had no experience in a two-seat plane. Sure, they could read the training manuals and be briefed by other pilots, but the lack of flight time in a similar plane was an issue. Second, the 80A-5 was operated much differently from other military aircraft, with a top speed of more than 600 miles per hour, faster than any plane the test pilots had flown, and with an acceleration that they had never experienced.

On May 4, 1948, Gray buckled himself into the front seat of an 80A-5 for a routine test flight. A few days earlier, he had almost crashed on takeoff but had been able to avert catastrophe. (He had flashbacks to four years earlier when his plane was caught in the prop wash of a preceding plane and took a hard landing at Mather Field in California.) The runway acceleration in Panama went as expected for Gray, with a thrust of power moving the plane forward and Gray taking the nose of the plane into the sky. He had just started climbing when a cloud of white vapor appeared out of the tailpipe at one hundred feet, a typical sign of an engine flameout. Gray struggled to maintain control of the plane and attempted, at the very least, to return it to the field.

Instead, the jungle swallowed Gray's plane five thousand yards from the runway.

Because of the density of brush surrounding the accident site, it took rescue crews several minutes to reach Gray, who lay unconscious in a flaming coffin. The plane had hit a tree, and the pilot had no time to escape before gasoline exploded in a fireball. Gray was burned over one-third of his body, with severe burns on his face, chest, and arms. When rescue personnel finally extricated Gray from what was left of the body of the plane, they injected him with morphine and wrapped him in lily-white sheets before transporting him to Gorgas General Hospital.

Doctors and nurses were astounded that Gray had survived not just the crash but the effects of the severe burns. Once again, Gray's resolve had been underestimated. The next morning, the pilot was again breathing on his own and chewing soft foods but suffered severe pain in his arms. He could move his hands but could not feel them. The patient developed a temperature of 103, and doctors huddled to discuss what to do next. Their decision would save his life, but not the life that he knew. On May 17, in a surgical room steps from the jungles of Panama, Gene Gray had both of his arms amputated. They were the arms that had caught the winning touchdown pass in the Rose Bowl game. The arms that flew dozens of sorties against the now-conquered enemy. And the arms that gave Gray a fighting chance throughout life.

After his return to Oregon from Michigan in 1946 with his wife, Elsie, and daughter, Lynn, Jack Yoshihara took classes at Multnomah College in Portland. He never returned to study at Oregon State, and in 1948, the twenty-seven-year-old Yoshihara started a refrigeration installation and repair company, making a decent living supporting his family, which now included a son, Jay. When the store on Oak Street in Portland burned down, he operated the business out of his home.

Yoshihara had lived in the United States since 1924, yet the process of acquiring citizenship took him until 1957, at which time he also built his first house in the Portland suburb of Montavilla. The Yoshiharas settled into a routine, and every year removed from the world war, Americans became more accepting of Japanese Americans. Yet Yoshihara never forgot what his country had done to him and his family and what his university had not done for him. He carried his sadness and anger with him the rest of his life.

Despite never being a star on the Oregon State football team or winning medals in battle, Jack Yoshihara was extraordinary. He endured the pain of internment with dignity, never turning his back on his country despite his treatment. To then have a family and build a career, a home, and a life is perhaps as much of an accolade as his teammates received on the fields of battle.

Wallace Wade attempted to change with the evolving game of football by trying T-formation plays in practice in 1948 and using full platoon teams for offense and defense, strategies other squads had already implemented. Wade also called for more passes, a far cry from the ground-and-pound teams that had played in previous Rose Bowls. Again, Duke started off strong at 3–0–2 but floundered down the stretch, finishing at 4–3–2. In 1949, the team went 6–3, with Wade having recruited many of the athletes on the basketball and baseball teams to play football. By 1950, Wade had lost a great deal of interest in coaching at Duke. He was never really the coach he had been before the war. As he would later reflect:

> *I was whipped down. I got back into coaching before I should have, and I didn't do very well. But I had been in a bigger game over in Europe. Coaches always talk about plays like they're life and death situations, but I had been in a position where my moves really did involve life and death. Football just didn't seem as important anymore.*

He found a new love in his life, Virginia Jones, and spent a lot of time on the local golf course, shooting in the high seventies, sometimes lower. He did not share his plans with most, but 1950 would be his last season on the Duke sideline. Still, his constitution dictated that he take the 1950 team for a ride, and he hired Billy Hickman, a T-formation specialist from the University of Virginia, to sharpen the Blue Devil attack. There would be losses to Tennessee, Maryland, and Wake Forest in 1950, but no game was perhaps more significant to Wade—and to the South—than the second game of the season, at home against Pittsburgh. The Panthers had a star in their backfield, Flint Greene, who, in addition to scoring touchdowns, was black. Duke alumni and Southern segregationists were in an uproar about Duke hosting an opponent with a black player. It was one thing to travel to Syracuse to face a black player, as Duke had done in 1938; it was another to face one at home in Durham. Wade and Director of Athletics Eddie Cameron did not back down, releasing a statement that said in part:

> *Yes, we have heard that the Pittsburgh team has a Negro on the squad. When we schedule a team we of course expect to play on fair and even terms. The coaches of each team have the unquestioned right to play any eligible man they choose to play. We have neither the right nor the desire to ask a coach to restrict or limit his team's participation because of creed or color. Duke fans and students have a fine record of treating visiting teams courteously. We have every reason to believe that this record will be continued.*

Duke beat Pittsburgh that day 28–14, but the inclusion of Flint Greene marked an important step in the integration of college football in North Carolina.

Four days after the end of the season, Wade and Jones were married in a small, private ceremony and honeymooned in New York. Upon his return, he announced his resignation from Duke to become the first full-time commissioner of the Southern Conference. The conference headquarters would be in the Carolina Theatre complex in downtown Durham. Duke selected Bill Murray, a former player and 1931 Duke graduate, to replace Wade. Wade's twenty-year association with Duke was over.

Bob Dethman returned from war in November 1945 with a Bronze Star for his heroism on Iwo Jima and with a more aggressive and hard-charging soul, and was stationed in San Francisco before his ultimate relief from active duty in late December. He reunited with Margaret and Delores and enrolled in graduate classes at Oregon State. In 1946, his son, Robert Jr., was born. He coached the backfield for Lon Stiner with none other than Don Durdan—the Double Ds back in action. Dethman fulfilled his duties as an assistant, helping recruit new players and traveling the country scouting upcoming opponents. During games when he was in Corvallis, he watched from the press box, sending information and plays down to Stiner on the bench.

Coaching football was not his only means of income in the ensuing years, however, as Dethman became a co-owner of Les and Bob's Sporting Goods on South Fourth Street in Corvallis. He also worked for some of the logging mill owners and for Richfield Oil, whose owners knew him as a local hero for the Rose Bowl win and for his war exploits.

His temper could explode at any moment over a slight; his patience and laissez-faire attitude he'd carried with him since childhood were now gone. Like many fellow veterans, Dethman turned to alcohol as a coping mechanism to numb the memories of war. It likely did not help that he was still a celebrity in Corvallis and routinely stayed out late with his boys, some nights never bothering to come home. The anger, the alcohol, and the late nights put stress on his marriage. Despite their difficulties, Margaret gave birth to John Dethman in 1950, who joined his much older sister, Delores, and Bob Jr. However, any progress toward rekindling their love affair was halted by tragedy.

On April 12, 1952, Margaret was backing the family car out when John, who was twenty-two months old, ran across the driveway just as his mother put the car in reverse. The impact crushed his head, and John Dethman was dead.

The tragic loss crippled both husband and wife. Margaret felt guilt, while her husband struggled with sadness. A year later, they divorced.

Margaret first moved with the kids to Eugene, where Bob would pick up the kids, the ex-spouses bursting into tears every time their eyes met out of sadness that their love could not make marriage work. Then Margaret and the kids returned to her family in New Meadows, Idaho. Dethman carried on, working for Wilson Motors, as a roofer, and in the mills, but his reliance on alcohol and medication only intensified as he dealt with the loss of his son, the scars of war, and his other demons.

On weekends in the summer, he returned to the homestead in Hood River, where Bob Jr. would visit him, and they would fish on the Columbia River and toss a football. His relationship with his daughter, however, was nonexistent.

In 1956, Dethman was spending more and more time at the local hospital, trying to overcome his addictions. He met a nurse, Lucille. She loved the outdoors and loved to fish, and the two quickly fell in love and married. Lucille was patient, doing her best to help her husband deal with his demons, so much so that a rift developed with his parents, who believed that the love was smothering.

On Sunday, August 25, 1957, Bob and Lucille went for a hike with their Labradors along the Willamette River. Dethman spent the afternoon watching the dogs retrieve sticks in the water. Suddenly, as they passed behind the Corvallis Sand & Gravel Company building, one of the dogs seemed to be in distress and, recalling his lifeguard days on the Marys River, Dethman immediately sprang into action, fully clothed.

The waters were rushing that Sunday at sunset, and Dethman was in trouble.

"Get help!" Dethman cried out to his wife as the water rushed around his face. "Go!"

Lucille took off to find the nearest phone.

The athlete, the war hero, the guy who always came out on top, was fighting for his life, gasping for air as he fought the current. By the time Lucille returned to the spot where her husband had been struggling, he was gone.

Word spread quickly, and Dethman's younger brother, Wendell, came down to the scene to help authorities search. They scoured the river for days until Wendell spotted his brother's body floating facedown in eight feet of water, fifty feet from where he was last seen. His body was taken to the Benton County coroner's office for an autopsy, with the conclusion that he had drowned. The coroner suggested that "overexertion to save [his] life caused heart attack and subsequent drowning."

Hood River buried its favorite son in a small cemetery in Pine Grove, just a stone's throw from the Dethman homestead. Bob Dethman's grave is marked by a nondescript marker for him and Lucille. Just feet from his final resting place sits the marker for his young son, John. And a few steps away is the gravestone for his brother Wendell, who could never overcome the loss of his older brother. Wendell fell into a deep depression and, combined with the untreated scars of Iwo Jima, also turned to alcohol. Financial struggles and a divorce were simply too much. The Bronze Star winner committed suicide in 1965.

Bob Dethman's life was cut short not on a battlefield but in a river, flowing near the football fields that had given him one hell of a life.

17. THE LAST DAYS

CHARLES HAYNES SPENT EVERY day at the Saddle & Fox restaurant, where he could always be seen glad-handing table to table, smoking a cigar, and jamming on the drums at closing. He divorced Jane Barry in the late 1950s and remarried twice more before spending his sunset years with companion Patsy Ashby.

Haynes's love affair with Duke continued until his last breath. He took classes through the Duke Extension, mastered new languages, including Italian, and earned his certification as an executive chef. He discovered the joys and benefits of physical fitness late in life and was frequently seen around town in Duke athletics apparel. Haynes told folks his hometown was "Duke, North Carolina," not Durham. Everyone in Durham knew "Charlie."

He returned to the battlefields of Italy with some army buddies on a reunion trip in retirement and even found time to do some creative writing based on his days outside of Sassoleone, Italy, during the war. In a lined spiral notebook, in journals never published, he wrote:

> *An objective to the Army is like a gold* [sic] *in football. Yea—that's it I thought—just like football—today's a crisp October Saturday*

afternoon back home, perfect game conditions—not too cold for the spectators, not too hot for the players. The cool autumn wind blowing the flags atop the press boxes situated higher in the stadium. The roll of the drums. The clang of the symbols [sic] *to the beat of that heart quickens, throbbing, cheer and "We want a touchdown! We want a touchdown!" And back across the field accompanied by more drums beating—the old familiar "Hold that line! Hold that line!"*

Yea, war is just like a football game you keep telling yourself, at least today anyway—anything to get you through one more day and still be alive.

Charles Haynes Jr. died of a massive heart attack on January 20, 1994, at the age of seventy-two. His funeral was held in the Duke University Chapel, officiated by his son, Charles III. He was buried next to his father with full military honors, including the symbolic riderless horse, with his old polished saddle and cavalry boots turned backward, a final military salute to his "troops" as he rode off into the sunset. It was a proper passing and burial, unlike the one fate had had in store for him on a bloody battlefield in Italy fifty years before. He repaid Frank Parker by living with an appetite for life and enjoying what the world had to offer.

Frank Parker reluctantly joined his brother Eben fishing for cod off the coast of Oregon, as there were mouths to feed, with Parker and Peggy becoming parents to Keith, born in 1948; Frank Jr. in 1950; and sisters Becky in 1952, Terry in 1955, and Heidi in 1958. The Parker brothers bought and sold various-sized boats until securing the *Tom & Al,* and they continued to disappear into the arms of the water for weeks at a time, leaving Peggy to raise the children by herself. At times, she would get reports that her husband was lost at sea in storms, but she never believed them. Her husband was too strong. And he always returned.

The brothers' distributor, Bio Products, purchased a ninety-millimeter harpoon gun from a Norwegian whaling operation and mounted it on the *Tom & Al* for the Parkers to hunt whale, a much-in-demand mammal in the early 1960s, as NASA used whale oil in many capacities because of its ability to withstand wide-ranging temperatures. Mink breeders in Oregon also used whale products to provide large quantities of cheap protein for their animals. Captured whales would be dragged onto the beaches of Astoria, stripped down to the bones, and displayed to local schoolchildren—including Parker's—who would take field trips to see the vanquished mammals. But in 1963, synthetic oils came on the market and significantly lowered the demand for and price of whale products. Bio Products wanted the brothers to buy the harpoon gun from them; they declined, so the company replaced it with a smaller, much less effective sixty-millimeter gun. They continued to fish the waters off Oregon, Washington, Alaska, and Canada but returned to more mundane catch. Always on the well-worn fingers of the fisherman was Parker's 1942 Rose Bowl ring, and always in his mind were the memories of war.

Nightmares. Guilt that he made it home. Guilt that he could not protect Rodman Henry. A continued belief that he was some sort of monster and not worthy of his wife. Parker never talked about war with his family and rarely shared his emotions with his brother. But they knew he was haunted. For example, when firecrackers went off at one of Keith's high school football games, Parker believed they were gunshots and reacted with urgency, his mind racing to the blood of Italy. Parker, like so many of his fellow veterans, turned to alcohol, a problem exacerbated by the lifestyle of a fisherman, whose routine included heading to the bars after surviving yet another outing at sea.

There were days when he would leave his two youngest daughters, Heidi and Terry, in the car for "just a minute" and hop into the Mermaid

Tavern, disappearing into the day. Terry wrote him a letter as a young child, pleading with him to stop drinking, but her father refused to open it, knowing what was likely inside.

"If you have something to say to me, say it to me," he chided Terry.

Ironically, he never even liked fishing and thought about completing his college degree to get a better job onshore. In fact, in 1964, Parker reached out to his former Oregon State teammate Orville Zielaskowski, who was now the director of adult and vocational education for the Corvallis school district, to see if he could help. Turns out, Parker was forty-two credits shy of his Oregon State degree. He never went back.

In 1967, Parker moved to Kodiak, Alaska, and focused on shrimp fishing. He had been sailing to Kodiak, working out of there on and off through the years, but he decided to move there permanently, without his family. He returned to Astoria two or three times a year and always on Christmas, and when back in his hometown, he was "Captain Frank," with a stroll downtown taking two hours, friends and fellow fishermen all wanting his time. Peggy and the children visited Kodiak in the summers when the kids grew older, working in the canneries and making fishing trips with Parker.

Kodiak was all dirt roads, no streetlights, and ash filled the air. It was a typical remote fishing town, with the local bars serving as the center of life, filled with a cast of characters, many of whom had too many stories to make them believable and some of whom Parker let crash on his sofa or floor. The days on land were spent sleeping or drinking or lining up the next sailing trip. The days on the water were grueling. Shrimp fishing was tough. From 4:00 A.M.—when the sun rose in Alaska—until midnight, when it set, fishermen would shrimp, forcing Parker to become a master at the twenty-minute catnap.

He worked on the *Tom & Al* for just a year before finances got tough, whereupon he sold it and moved on to other boats as a worker until returning to the *Tom & Al* for a bit as an employee of the new owner. For the last half of 1976, Parker was a deck boss on the *Chief William*

Schimmel in the rough waters of the Bering Sea. The close calls on the water continued, as did the seemingly annual Mayday calls, when a ship would be lost at sea or flooded with water or stuck on rocks. But always, Frank Parker made it through.

As the fishing business was drying up for Parker, he applied to no avail for jobs with the state of Alaska and worked seasonally on the boats. In 1977, after his youngest child, Heidi, graduated from high school, Peggy finally moved to Kodiak to be with her husband. Though they shared nice times, going for hikes and picking berries in the hills, the difficult nights became far too frequent. Their financial woes and marital strife were compounded by nagging pain from the knee he had injured playing football in Italy in 1945. He took prescription medication to ease the pain. Just as the Rose Bowl ring served as a constant reminder of a day of glory, his knee pain reminded him of the dark days of war.

Peggy, meanwhile, joined the women's bowling league in Kodiak, which was as competitive for the participants as shrimp fishing was for their husbands. Sure, there were laughs, cocktails, and a few cigarettes, but these ladies wanted to win, including Peggy, whose tiny frame somehow managed to lift a twelve-pound ball.

It was a Friday night in 1994 when Frank sat among the bowlers, encouraging his wife, if only by his presence. At the time, the Parkers were entering a new stage in life as grandparents and were preparing to sell their house in Kodiak and return to Astoria. After a five-mile hike in the hills to pick berries with a friend, Peggy had spent part of the day preparing the house to go on the market. She was in a great mood as she stood to grab her ball to bowl her frame.

"My head," she said almost in a whisper, putting both hands to the sides of her head. "I think I need to go home."

The diminutive woman changed her shoes and grabbed her ball and then swayed for a second before collapsing into her husband's lap with severe head pain. Frank had seen men have their heads blown off, arms shattered, and death strike them down, but this was different. This was Peggy. Parker held Peggy steady as they walked to the car, Frank laying her in the front passenger seat. After a series of vomits, Peggy suggested they go to the hospital. She lost consciousness by the time they arrived at Kodiak Medical Center.

Within hours, Peggy was taken by medevac to Anchorage, where she was diagnosed with a brain aneurysm and put on life support. Roughly forty hours after collapsing in the bowling alley, with her husband and love of her life by her side, Peggy Parker died. And as her children would later say, her husband died that day too.

A few days later, Parker stood over the open coffin at the funeral home in Astoria, barely recognizing the woman who lay inside. He touched her right hip.

"That feels like her," he said to no one in particular, finding comfort in the tiniest of details. "This was not the plan," Parker uttered, a mantra he would repeat often in the months ahead.

Parker returned to Kodiak, lost. The marriage had not been perfect, but Peggy had been a part of his life for more than sixty years. Instead of selling the house as planned, he invested the rest of his savings in a boat, against the advice of Frank Jr., christening it the *Margaret Ann,* his late wife's birth name. As it turned out, the boat was a lemon, with undetected cracks, unable to serve as a fishing vessel, let alone a recreational vehicle. His savings gone, his wife gone, Parker maxed out his credit cards and fell into despair.

He spent much of his monthly veterans' pay on booze and much of his time at the local bars or sitting alone in the house. His only companions were alcoholics and a few younger folks who lived nearby who would check on him.

When Peggy was still alive, Parker had considered suicide. He thought that Peggy would be better off without him and could use the life insurance benefit. But he never could go through with it. It went directly against his Catholic faith.

But now, in 1998, he thought a life in hell was better than the hell on earth. When he gave away some of his possessions, including a teddy bear that had been cherished by Peggy, his neighbors grew concerned—none too soon, as one evening Parker sat at the kitchen table in the empty house, one of the German pistols he had brought home with him from Italy resting inches in front of him. The Germans couldn't kill him with the gun, but he could. He would have pulled the trigger, but a neighbor interrupted him. Realizing what was going on and with grave concern for Parker, the neighbor removed all guns from the house.

Weeks later, when Parker asked for a return of one of the guns, the neighbor contacted his children. Parker was put on suicide watch in the hospital in Kodiak, and soon Terry flew up from Eugene. She returned to Oregon with her father, who was admitted to the Veterans Health Administration in Portland, where he was held in the psychiatric lock-down ward and evaluated for six weeks. Not surprisingly, post-traumatic stress disorder and depression were the diagnoses, and he was put on heavy medication. In therapy sessions in the hospital, Parker volunteered to talk about some of his demons, including his guilt.

When he no longer posed a danger to himself, in 1999 Parker moved in with Terry in Eugene, where he would spend the next five years slowly decaying. His eyes would light up when they would sit on the sofa and watch college football. And on occasion, he would speak fondly of Rodman Henry and the awfulness of what happened to him, yet he made no mention of his heroic actions in saving Charles Haynes.

His health declining, but his hopelessness not, Parker went so far as to write a farewell note.

After being moved to a nursing home in Astoria in 2002, Parker reached the end of his long journey. It wasn't a German bullet that killed him or a monster storm in the waters off Alaska but a bad heart. In his dying days, he asked his son Keith to take care of his boat, though the boat had been long gone. He also made it known that he did not want to be buried at sea.

"I spent my whole life on the water; I don't want to be buried under it."

So, according to his wishes, Frank Parker was cremated and his ashes buried in a small hole next to Peggy's resting place in a small cemetery in Astoria.

A stiff breeze ruffled the purple flower petals on the lei around Jack Yoshihara's neck, but he barely noticed. The crystal-blue sky, the glaring sun, and the thousands in attendance were mere afterthoughts for Yoshihara, now eighty-seven, as he was one of the Japanese American students finally receiving their degrees from Oregon State on June 18, 2008.

The day may have been sixty-six years in the making but was really the result of two Oregon State students, Andy Kiyuna and Joel Fischer, who pushed legislators in 2007 to award honorary degrees to Japanese American students who had been unable to graduate because of the war. The country had long ago taken steps to acknowledge the wrong done to many Japanese Americans. In 1976, President Gerald Ford had formally rescinded Executive Order 9066, and in 1989, President George H. W. Bush signed Public Law 101–162, guaranteeing reparations for internees from World War II, which amounted to approximately $20,000 for each internee—though almost one-third were already gone.

Yoshihara's lifelong partner, Elsie, had died in 1996 from cancer, and he had married his late wife's childhood friend a few years later, the two moving to Edmonds, Washington. He enjoyed fishing and gardening in his later years, grooming bonsai trees, and he remained a wood-carver until his hands would not allow it anymore. Yoshihara attended as many of his Oregon State team's reunions as his health would allow, as accepted and loved by his teammates as he was when he was yanked off the practice field in 1941.

In the hours before the graduation ceremony, Yoshihara shared laughter and tears with his fellow graduates and their families at a lunch reception, the thin and somewhat frail former football player proudly wearing a now well-oversize letterman's jacket and gleefully showing off the Rose Bowl ring he had received in 1985 during the 1941 team's induction into the Oregon Sports Hall of Fame.

"This is the commencement ceremony that you should have had so many years ago," Oregon State president Ed Ray shared with graduates and others in attendance in Reser Stadium. "And this is the opportunity for all of us to tell you publicly how sorry we are for your pain."

One by one, Ray called out a name of a living or deceased Japanese American student. Only five were present.

"Jack Yoshihara," Ray announced as Yoshihara's student photo was displayed on the large screen inside the stadium.

The crowd in attendance stood proudly and clapped enthusiastically when Ray announced that Yoshihara had not been allowed to play in the Rose Bowl game, prompting the former player to hold up his Rose Bowl ring for all to see. His smile was as broad as the Oregon sun.

Less than twelve months later, Chiaki "Jack" Yoshihara passed away.

Shikata ga nai.

Wallace Wade ruled over the Southern Conference for ten years, which included the secession of 1953, when seven schools, including Duke and North Carolina, announced they were leaving to form the Atlantic Coast Conference. Despite his disappointment at the breakup of the Southern Conference, Wade lent his wisdom about the schools to the leaders of the new conference. In 1955, he was inducted into the College Football Hall of Fame, the first of multiple inductions in the coming years, including to the Alabama Sports Hall of Fame, North Carolina Sports Hall of Fame, Duke Athletics Hall of Fame, Brown Athletic Hall of Fame, and the Rose Bowl Hall of Fame.

By 1960, Wade had had enough of the working life and retired to Wade Hill Farm to raise Hereford cattle and enjoy retirement with

Virginia on the 120-acre farm they had built in 1952. It was located in Bahama, six miles from Durham, on Snow Hill Road. The main house was set back from the public road, and accessed by a winding gravel path lined with trees and a wooden fence. There was a large white feed and storage barn and a smaller shed near the house. Wade loved to sit in the library just off the main hallway in the house, flooded by sunlight shining through many windows. He had his favorite chair, a walnut desk for writing correspondence, a coffee table, and dozens and dozens of books and magazines, most of them focused on the military or current affairs. On the walls of the library was a framed cover of a *Time* magazine cover story from 1937, a plaque recognizing his induction into the College Football Hall of Fame, and the certificate he was given by the Tournament of Roses in 1942 in appreciation of his contributions to the Rose Bowl.

Wade spent his twilight years walking or driving his truck around the farm, feeding the animals, mending fences, cutting grass, competing in livestock competitions, reading military histories, and serving on the national football rules committee. He took the raising of cattle seriously but joked that it was good for seniors, as "you always are aiming toward the future in looking for calves."

In 1967, former Duke player Arthur Vann wrote to Duke president Douglas Knight with an idea:

> *You are, of course, aware of the contributions made by Coach Wade to our University, to the athletic world in general, and to this community over his long tenure as Athletic Director and Head Football Coach at Duke University. More important than these, however, is the contribution he made to those of us who were his former players, in that we learned from him excellency was to be achieved over mediocrity, discipline instead of indulgence, sacrifice above self.*
>
> *It has disturbed me that no fitting testimonial has ever been given in his honor . . .*

Among the ideas suggested by Vann was naming the Indoor Stadium or Duke Stadium in Wade's honor.

On September 30, 1967, Wallace Wade Senior Day was celebrated in Durham, and at halftime in the Duke–South Carolina football game, the stadium was renamed Wallace Wade Stadium. The date was exactly thirty-six years after Wade's first game at Duke against South Carolina, in 1931.

The night before the dedication, a dinner was held in the Great Hall at the Duke Union, with menu items including Crimson Tide Punch, Single-Wing Wafers, and Southern Conference Baked Potatoes with Rose Bowl Garnish.

"I have had a lot of pleasant experiences," Wade reminisced during his remarks at the dinner, "and some unpleasant experiences, but never have I been overcome as I have on this occasion. It's something to think that a former barefooted farm boy from Tennessee is being honored in this fashion tonight.

"What success we had can be attributed to the coaching staff and players. I'm thankful for the players and coaches and fans who are here tonight. Some of them have come from long distances. I'm thankful for what they have said about me. I'm thankful for the messages received from those unable to attend. In fact, I'm thankful for everything tonight."

The following day, hundreds of former players, coaches, and friends were present as former Wade boys Eric Tipton, Dan Hill, and Bob Barnett spoke from midfield about their beloved coach, who was driven around the field in an open convertible so that the masses could glimpse the man most had heard of but never seen. Of course, Sis and Wallace Jr. were on hand, as were the Old Man's five grandchildren.

That same year, the Knoxville Quarterback Club named Wade the recipient of the Robert R. Neyland Memorial Trophy, in memory of

Wade's friend who had earned a Distinguished Service Medal for service in the China-Burma-India theater.

Wallace Wade died of pneumonia in 1986, at the age of ninety-four, at Duke University Hospital. The funeral was held on October 8, and former players, assistants, colleagues, faculty, and friends filled the Duke University Chapel to capacity to say farewell. Pallbearers included former players Bob Barnett and Tom Davis, and attendees included Eddie Cameron, Herschel Caldwell, and Charles Haynes. "O World I Now Must Leave Thee" and "In Peace and Joy I Now Depart" emanated from the massive chapel organs.

"When Wallace Wade talked, I listened," remarked former Duke University president and North Carolina governor Terry Sanford. "He had complete composure in all circumstances. He is one of America's true compatriots, worthy of his honors. . . . He demanded of himself nothing short of perfection and demanded that of all around him.

"Thank God for sending Wallace Wade into the lives of each of us, and give us the guidance and dedication to live up to the life he expected of us."

Wade was buried in Durham's Maplewood Cemetery with full military honors, with soldiers from the 27th Engineer Battalion from Fort Bragg on hand.

On the occasion of the stadium dedication in Wade's honor in 1967, Duke professor Dr. Hersey Spence composed an ode for the man who had touched so many.

What means the sound of revelry and joy,
Where tens of thousands all their powers employ?
Where mingled shouts of Rah! Rah! Wade are raised,
And "Dear Old Duke" whose name is proudly praised?
What means the blaring of the marching bands?
The deafening sound of yells and clapping hands?

In the vast stadium joy and sadness blend;
Gloom that has a great career has reached an end;
Gladness at memories of the long ago;
Praise given one we love and honor so.

Why are they here with all their pomp and splendor;
Due honor to an "all-time Great" to render;
Whose prowess countless football fans has thrilled;
Whose sportsmanship with pride our hearts filled;
He feared no foe, now did he lightly yield
To foe, however strong, no football field.
With trivial easy tasks was discontent;
Built football empires wheresoever he went,
But more than empires men to man them trained;
Whose high ideals with them e'er remained,
He taught them taste of victory without vaunting;
To lose, without despair their memory haunting.
Who is this man by noble impulse swayed?
The greatest of the great, Coach Wallace Wade.

Old Glory floats high o'er the stadium walls;
The bands once more play "Stars and Stripes Forever"
In memory he again that day recalls
When he awhile his ties with sports must sever.
A soldier now, and for his country's sake
Must run great risk and fearsome chances take:
War's whirlwind, bursting bombs and screaming shell;
Foul and fierce furies, horrible as hell;
Answering the call of duty unafraid
The calm, courageous, Colonel Wallace Wade.

Back from the battlefields, the war now o'er,
The gridiron battles he returns once more.

But larger task was proffered, there was need
For one who through the conference maze could lead:
Vexatious difficulties to be solved;
Cool judgments needed for the task involved;
Tedious the task; decisions must be made,
Fair and yet firm, Commissioner Wallace Wade.

In quietude the great man wends his ways,
No longer dreading coming Saturdays;
Not troubled now with "talks between the halves"
His interests, mooing cows and bleating calves.
Still he at times must feel the football urge,
And long to see his warriors, stopless urge
A down the field, and hear above the low
Of bulls, the cry: "Go, Blue Devils, go."
However many cattle he possessed
He'll doubtless always love his football best.
Long may he live, triumphant, undismayed:
Coach, soldier, statesman, William Wallace Wade.

EPILOGUE

"Coach Wade is not here tonight, but he did want me to ask something," Charles Haynes remarked to the crowd of a couple of hundred when it was his turn to speak at the fiftieth reunion dinner in Corvallis in 1991, remembering his coach who had passed away five years earlier. Based on a conversation Wade and Haynes had had at a thirtieth reunion event in Durham years earlier, Haynes now asked, "Any of you ever fought in the Battle of Bulge?" Haynes and the guests turned as Stan Czech rose to his feet. "Coach Wade wanted me to thank you for that coffee."

Four weeks later in Durham, Duke University hosted its own fiftieth anniversary celebration, which included players parading in vintage cars around Wallace Wade Stadium before kickoff between Duke and North Carolina State. The game officials used a 1942 coin for the toss, and the field was painted with era-appropriate markings. Fans even received a replica of the 1942 Rose Bowl game program. Twenty-nine former Duke players showed up for the occasion, joined by nine Oregon State players, including Martin Chaves, Stan Czech, and Frank Parker. Bob Barnett was there, with Mike Karmazin, Tommy Prothro, and Jim Smith. It was an amazing weekend. The men took time during their visit to the stadium to pay their respects to Coach Wade at a bust of the coach prominently displayed in front of the stadium entrance, surrounded by beautiful red roses.

Charles Haynes and Frank Parker embraced one more time before Parker headed back to Oregon. They would never see each other again.

The 1942 Rose Bowl was a game remade by infamy, played by men too young to know the preciousness and precariousness of life, something they would soon learn the hard way. Despite the casually martial rhetoric often used to embolden a team, football, it turns out, is neither a matter of life and death nor a metaphor for battles and casualties nor fodder for war correspondents. And war, as it turns out, is not like football at all. Almost seventy-five years later, the 1942 game remains the only Rose Bowl ever to be played outside of Pasadena, an event memorialized in a patch of roses outside of Wallace Wade Stadium in Durham, in too many obituaries both then and now, and on the fingers of its now-dead participants. Football is play, its ramifications entirely symbolic, and while the 1942 Rose Bowl became the perfect receptacle for America's need to unify in a moment of national shock and mourning, it remained a game. The war these players and coaches scrambled to join—perhaps the last unambiguous war in U.S. history—was the opposite of play, and its consequences, both personal and global, were as real as blood and liberty.

The men who played in and coached the 1942 Rose Bowl game were admittedly not perfect. They were the sons of working-class men who were called upon by their team and then their coaches to do more than they'd ever thought they could. They were not heroes because of what they did on the football field or on the battlefield. They were heroes because, like so many others, they were ordinary boys who did an extraordinary thing by teaching us that heroic self-sacrifice should be an ordinary American virtue.

POSTGAME BIOGRAPHIES

Below are brief postgame biographies of some of the key players and coaches in the 1942 Rose Bowl

BOB BARNETT served in the United States Marine Corps in Bougainville, Guam, and Iwo Jima before being discharged in December 1945. He returned to Duke for law school while assisting Wallace Wade Sr. in coaching football. He worked in private legal practice for years in Wilmington, Delaware, and was a corporate executive until his death, in 2012.

EDDIE CAMERON served as the director of athletics at Duke until 1972. He and Wallace Wade first envisioned Duke's Indoor Stadium on the back of a matchbook cover, and the building was completed in 1940 and was named in his honor. Cameron died at home in 1988.

MARTIN CHAVES entered the Army Air Corps just days after the Rose Bowl victory and piloted planes over Africa and Europe during the war. He returned to Oregon State to complete his degree and suited up for Lon Stiner's team in 1946. He owned small commercial businesses in Corvallis and California, was an active member of the Oregon State alumni and booster groups, and helped organize many of the Rose Bowl team reunions. He died in 2000.

STAN CZECH remained an officer in the army after his release as a prisoner of war and was stationed in Japan. After his service, he returned to OSC and earned his degree while coaching the freshman team for Lon Stiner. Czech taught social studies and driver's education and coached football at Albany High School before eventually becoming a beloved principal, retiring in 1981. He died in 1997.

DON DURDAN was stationed stateside during his service for the navy, where he excelled as a multisport star for the branch. He would go on to play with the San Francisco 49ers and in professional basketball. When his sports career ended, Durdan became a funeral director in his wife's family business in Corvallis. Inducted into the Rose Bowl Hall of Fame, Oregon Sports Hall of Fame, and Oregon State University Athletics Hall of Fame, Durdan died of a heart attack at the young age of fifty, in 1971.

GENE GRAY underwent multiple surgeries after returning to the United States in the years after his plane accident in Panama. He moved with his wife and young children to Portland, Oregon, and then to a five-acre farm in Tigard. Gray earned a degree from Lewis & Clark College and sold insurance before retiring at an early age. He passed away in 2004.

QUENTIN GREENOUGH joined the United States Coast Guard after graduating from Oregon State and suited up for its football team. Upon his discharge, he worked as Lon Stiner's assistant and built a contractor business. He is a member of the Oregon Sports Hall of Fame and Oregon State Athletics Hall of Fame, to which he was inducted before his death, in 2005.

MIKE KARMAZIN joined the Coast Guard from Duke and served in the North Atlantic and South Pacific. After leaving the service, Karmazin coached at Duke, North Carolina State, and Tulane and earned his law degree from Tulane in 1960. In 1967, he assisted District Attorney Jim Garrison in New Orleans in the trial of Clay Shaw, accused of being a part of a conspiracy with the CIA in the John F. Kennedy assassination. Karmazin died in 2004 in New Orleans.

STEVE LACH served in the navy during the war but remained stateside, playing football at Naval Station Great Lakes and leading them to a historic upset against Notre Dame. Lach played for the Pittsburgh Steelers for one and a half seasons before returning to Altoona to finish school at Saint Francis College and opening a bar named Steve's Place. In 1960, while stopped at a red light next to the football stadium in Altoona with his two-year-old son with him in the car, Lach had a heart attack and died at the age of forty.

ANDY LANDFORCE, who had played only two games for Lon Stiner in 1941, after being plucked off the intramural fields as student body president, served in the U.S. Army in Europe and the Philippines. Landforce commanded an all-black trucking unit and survived attempts on his life by the men in his charge. He returned to Corvallis and worked for the Oregon Department of Fish and Wildlife for decades. The ninety-nine-year-old still resides in the house he shared with his late wife of sixty-plus years. Landforce hikes three miles every day.

TOMMY PROTHRO completed his service in the navy and returned to Memphis after the war, and despite his father's plans for a career in baseball for him, Prothro began a career as a college football coach. By 1955, he was the head coach, at Oregon State, leading the Beavers to six wins in his first season and to the Rose Bowl in 1958 for the first time since the transplanted game in Durham. He would go on to coach at UCLA and work in the NFL. Prothro died in 1995.

JIM SMITH thought about remaining in the navy after the end of the war but ultimately decided to head back to Hamilton, Ohio, where he worked with his father on parks and golf course maintenance. He earned a master's degree from Purdue University in industrial engineering and spent his career as an engineer in Indiana and then Louisville. Smith still lives in Louisville and plays golf three times a week.

LON STINER coached the Beavers to a 7–1–1 record in 1946, but in 1947 and 1948, Oregon State posted a 10–9–3 combined record, and despite a Pineapple Bowl victory over Hawaii, Stiner was fired at the conclusion of the 1948 season, ending a sixteen-year association with OSC. Stiner then worked as a corporate executive and lobbyist before passing away in 1985.

WALLACE WADE JR. was discharged from the army in 1945 with a Bronze Star and returned to Durham. He took a job with a trucking company in Charlotte and spent his career working sales and commission jobs in industry and finance in North Carolina. Wade suffered a debilitating stroke in the 1990s and died in 2004.

GEORGE ZELLICK joined the Marines after the Rose Bowl and spent much of his time in the Pacific. He would eventually return to the States and teach high school in Springfield, Oregon, before being recalled to duty in 1950 for service during the Korean War, where Zellick was one of the "Chosin Few" heroic and outnumbered American soldiers who valiantly fought off the Chinese and then marched seventy-eight miles to safety. Zellick went on to become a superintendent of schools and retired on the family homestead in Montana. He died in 2005, serenaded by "God Bless America" at his funeral.

ACKNOWLEDGMENTS

As the Enterprise rental car came to a stop on a quiet street in a suburb of Louisville, I paused to collect my thoughts for a moment, something I rarely do. I had interviewed hundreds, perhaps thousands, of men and women as a reporter and author, but rarely could I remember the nervous energy of such a routine sit-down. Leonard James Smith was the subject that day—"Jim," as he told me to call him over the phone. To most, Jim Smith was a ninety-two-year-old widower, living out his years in a house he had shared with his late wife, Elsie, and their children. He was not famous or even well-known for the reasons I was there to speak with him, yet my heart raced as I walked up the stone path to ring the doorbell.

The journey had not begun that morning but rather in the fall of 2012, in the most innocent of ways. I was skimming a quarterly newsletter from the Rose Bowl stadium when I came across an interesting fact: a Rose Bowl game long ago was not played in Pasadena. A lifelong sports fan and someone who has spent the better part of the last fifteen years in and around college sports, I was astonished that I had never come across this piece of trivia. I immediately went to Google and learned about the 1942 transplanted Rose Bowl in Durham. And the more I read, the more I learned, the more I was hooked. The thought of moving such a marquee event in a matter of days was astonishing in itself, but what really struck me were the men who played and coached the game.

Men like Wallace Wade Sr. and Bob Barnett and Bob Dethman, who walked off the football field on New Year's Day in 1942 and put on military uniforms for the United States of America. The boys from Oregon State and Duke—and many of them really were just boys—were sent to Guadalcanal and Iwo Jima, North Africa and Sicily, Normandy and Okinawa to fight a war that would claim so many lives and imprint the horrors of war on so many others. There was something so romantic to me about football players fighting in the most written-about battles in world history. It seemed so far-fetched when I learned about the coincidences that brought them together not only in Durham but on the fields of battle. These men were heroes in the truest sense of the word.

What began as a feature story in *Sports Illustrated* became an all-encompassing thirst to know more about the men of the 1942 Rose Bowl. After months and months of searching online and in archives, and of making cold calls, it became all too apparent that most of the men who played and coached in the game were no longer with us. And that is what brought me to Louisville and to Jim Smith. For as far as my research has taken me, he is the only man alive that I am aware of who actually played in the 1942 Rose Bowl game. There is one member of the Oregon State squad, Andy Landforce, still taking daily hikes at the age of ninety-nine in Corvallis, and I would visit with Andy as well, but Andy played in just a handful of games for Oregon State and was not in uniform for the Rose Bowl game. So a lot was riding on my interview with Jim Smith, for he and he alone could tell me firsthand stories of the game, of his Duke teammates, of Wallace Wade Sr., and of war.

Jim greeted me at the front door with a firm handshake and welcomed me into his home. In a small study rested pictures and mementos from football and war, and in the family room stood the gold Rose Bowl trophy given to every player and coach. Jim was bigger than I had imagined, and though he did walk gingerly, he appeared in great shape for a man of any age. After I accepted the offer of a glass of water, we took seats in his living room, and I pulled out my recorder and notepad.

My sincere gratitude to Jim and Andy, two men who served their schools and their countries and who are still inspiring others by their daily hikes, rounds of golf, and reflections on life. I enjoyed my visits with Jim and his family in Louisville as I did visiting Andy in Corvallis. Both men have been generous with their time in person and over the phone, and their honesty and openness have helped shape this narrative.

In the ensuing months, my journey took me to the hills above The Dalles in Oregon, where I evaded cattle on the dirt-and-gravel road to speak with the sons of a former Oregon State player; to the dark of night in Jefferson and the early morning of Hood River; to Corvallis and Eugene and Portland; to Altoona, Pennsylvania, where the temperature reached minus seven; to Durham and Pasadena and so many other places. There were phone calls to more than two dozen states and hundreds of failed leads in my search.

This book focuses on just a handful of the courageous and inspiring men who served their country, but every man who played or coached in the game deserves to have his story shared. There are many families, friends, and academics who graciously gave of their time and, in many cases, shared treasured documents, articles, and keepsakes from their loved ones. My special thanks to Patsy Ashby, Connie Felty Ashley, Robert Barnett Jr., Steve Durdan, Brad Halverson, the Haynes family, Betsy Wade Kerley, Debra Czech Lorenzen, the Markman family, Marlea Chaves Merikel, the Parker family, Gloria Chaves Solberg, Martha Uzzle, the Wade family, Diane Withrow, and Jim Zellick.

A project of this scope could not have been completed without the able assistance of researchers around the country, and my sincere thanks to Elizabeth Brake, Ph.D., at Duke University for her tireless efforts and to Amy McDonald, assistant university archivist at the Duke University Archives for her assistance. On the other side of the country, my thanks to Geoff Somnitz, who helped me scour the dusty boxes and fragile newspapers in the Oregon State University Libraries Special Collections & Archives Research Center, Chris Petersen, senior faculty research assistant, also at the Oregon State University Libraries Special Collections & Archives Research Center, and Michael Dicianna, who was tremendous in his research assistance there.

Todd Mayberry and the staff at the Oregon Nikkei Legacy Center in Portland were gracious with their time and assistance in helping me learn about the Nikkei experience, and Todd reviewed the manuscript sections on the Japanese American internment years.

Geoff Gentilini from Golden Arrow Research was invaluable in helping me retrieve dozens and dozens of military files from the U.S. National Archives and Records Administration, including personnel files, unit histories, and after-action reports, a task made especially hard since a 1973 fire destroyed many of the army files.

My sincere gratitude to Lewis Bowling, the biographer of Wallace Wade Sr., who not only shared his insights into Wade and others but whose fantastic book *Wallace Wade: Championship Years at Alabama and Duke* served as a critical resource for me in understanding the coach. Lewis also reviewed the manuscript to ensure accuracy, and I will always be indebted to him for his kindness.

My thanks as well to experts far smarter than I who reviewed the manuscript for accuracy: Mark Parillo, associate professor of history at Kansas State University; John Rossi, professor emeritus at La Salle University; Ronald Marcello, professor emeritus of history at the University of North Texas; Richard Anderson, senior analyst working for the Department of Defense and an expert in military history and defense analysis; Roger Cirillo, Association of the United States Army's Institute of Land Warfare; author C. J. Kelly, expert on the Battle of the

Bulge and World War II; Dr. Peter Mansoor, colonel, U.S. Army (Ret.); William King, former university archivist at Duke University; Larry Landis, director of Special Collections & Archives Research Center at Oregon State University, and his wife, Rebecca; and author and former sports information director Kip Carlson of Oregon State. Jeff Neuman and Adam Korn were gracious enough to read the early drafts and provide helpful editorial feedback. There were many others who assisted me in this process: Rachael Engler, Alan Golivesky, Zachary Hudak, John Schropp, and Ryan Thomas Smith.

My thanks to Jon Wertheim, executive editor at *Sports Illustrated*, for his initial interest in the story.

Gary Morris is a friend and my agent at the David Black Agency, and has believed in this project from the beginning, helping me to shape the story and finding us a great home at Flatiron Books. At Flatiron, Bob Miller's enthusiasm sold me right away, and he has been a great partner in this process. My sincere gratitude to Bob for believing in me and this story. Thanks as well to Jasmine Faustino at Flatiron for her editorial skills in shaping the manuscript and to Liz Keenan, Marlena Bittner, Steven Boriack, and the entire Flatiron team for their help.

Any author knows the immense amount of time and emotional energy put into a book project, and my family has been my inspiration and rock throughout in encouraging me and understanding the late nights at the computer. My wife, Tamara, is my best friend and biggest supporter, and, along with Emily and Daryn, keeps me laughing and smiling.

Finally, to the men of the 1942 Rose Bowl, who—like so many millions of others—faced the unknown, sacrificed their lives' canvases, and battled well after the last shot was fired: thank you for being anything but ordinary.

Brian Curtis
March 2016

NOTES

Author's Note: There are so many wonderful and comprehensive resources on World War II, on which I relied on for much of the well-known historical, political, and military histories of the war. Unless the information is not commonly known, I do not identify individual sources related to world history.

PROLOGUE: Description of fiftieth reunion: interviews with Gloria Chaves Solberg and Patsy Ashby; reunion dinner program, 10.18.91; *The Statesman Journal,* 10.19.91 and *Gazette Times,* 10.18.91; on veterans postwar: interview with Thomas Childers, professor of history, University of Pennsylvania; on Haynes in the Arno Valley: interviews with Charles Haynes III, David Haynes, John Haynes; *Durham Herald Sun,* 12.15.91, *The Durham Morning Herald,* 5.23.82; correspondence from Haynes to Haynes family, 10.22.44.

CHAPTER 1: On Wade Sr.'s early life: *Wallace Wade: Championship Years at Alabama and Duke,* Lewis Bowling, 2006; *Encyclopedia of Alabama; The Durham Morning Herald,* 10.7.86; *The Charlotte Observer,* 10.7.86; program from Wallace Wade Sr. Stadium naming dedication; on Tournament of Roses: *Rose Bowl: The History of the Granddaddy of Them All,* Malcolm Moran, 2013; *Rose Bowl Football since 1902,* Herb Michelson and Dave Newhouse, 1977; on Wade Sr.'s early coaching career: *Wallace Wade: Championship Years at Alabama and Duke,* Bowling; Raleigh

News & Observer, 1.18.76; *"[It is] our earnest desire . . . he will want,"* correspondence from William Wannamaker to Wade Sr., 2.15.30; *"If you decide to wait . . . basketball tournament,"* correspondence from Wade Sr. to Wannamaker, 2.18.30; *The Charlotte Observer,* 10.7.86.

CHAPTER 2: Early history of Duke: *Football at Duke,* A. A. Wilkinson; *"I have selected Duke University . . . and real ambition for life," Duke University and the War,* Duke Alumni Office, 1943; on Duke University Chapel: chapel facts distributed by Duke University; on Duke stadium: *Architecture Magazine,* Volume LXIX, No. 3, March 1934; on Wade Sr.'s early years at Duke: *Duke Alumni Register,* October 1948 and November 1948; *Wallace Wade: Championship Years at Alabama and Duke,* Bowling; *I Remember: Recollections and Reminiscences of Alma Mater,* Hersey Spence, 1954 *Duke Alumni Register,* January 1931; *The Charlotte Observer,* 8.7.79; *Football at Duke,* Wilkinson; *Durham Herald Sun,* 12.31.41; *Duke Alumni Register,* February 1939; *"So far, the University of North Carolina . . . the bugaboo of social equality," Wallace Wade: Championship Years at Alabama and Duke,* Bowling; on Rose Bowl history: *Rose Bowl Football since 1902,* Michelson and Newhouse; on 1938 Rose Bowl game: *Wallace Wade: Championship Years at Alabama and Duke,* Bowling; diary entries from Frances Wade, 1938; *A Story of Glory: Duke Football,* Ted Mann, 1985; *Duke Alumni Register,* January 1939; *I Remember: Recollections and Reminiscences of Alma Mater,* Spence; *Chronicle,* 10.12.95; *Football at Duke,* Wilkinson; *"Did he catch it . . . ," A Story of Glory: Duke University Football,* Mann; *"I've had enough of* him *for one day," Carolina Comments,* November 1991, XXXIX; on 1941 season: interview with Jim Smith; Duke University Sports Information Department 1941 preview; *Durham Herald Sun,* 12.31.41; *The Durham Morning Herald,* 9.1.41; *Duke Alumni Register,* August 1941; *"When a football player . . . in real trouble," The Charlotte Observer,* 8.7.79; on Haynes: interviews with Charles Haynes III, David Haynes, John Haynes (via e-mail), Wendy Haynes Connor; *The Durham Morning Herald,* 5.23.82; United States government military files; *"No Smoking, No Cursing . . . awake and morally straight,"* personal diary of Charles Haynes Jr., 12.31.38; on Wallace Wade Jr.: interview with Betsy Wade Kerley; United States government military files.

CHAPTER 3: Early history of Oregon State and football: *The Oregonian,* 9.24.93; *Oregon State Football,* Kip Carlson, 2006; on Lon Stiner Jr.: interview with Betty Stiner Ingram; *The Oregonian,* 2.5.59 and 12.11.39; on 1941 preseason: *Durham Herald Sun,* 12.31.41; *The Oregonian,* 3.27.41; on Donald Durdan: interview with Steve Durdan; United States government military files; OSC student record and transcript;

Oregon State Barometer, 10.21.41; correspondence from Bill McKallip to Arthur Durdan, 1.16.39; correspondence from Bob Conyers to Arthur Durdan, 2.9.39; telegrams from Philadelphia Eagles, 1941; on Gene Gray: *The Oregonian,* 6.11.48; United States government military files; interview with Karen Gray Mickel; on Bob Dethman: interviews with John Dethman, Fred Dethman, Gerry Dethman, and Bob Dethman Jr.; *Pine Grove Memories in the Hood River Valley,* J. Patricia Krussow, 1989; *Hood River News,* 1942; United States government military files; on Frank Parker: interviews with Terry Parker, Frank Parker Jr., and Heidi Parker Morris; United States Army Certificate of Service; OSC application; OSC student record; correspondence from OSC Registrar to Eben Parker, 12.4.40; on OSC season: *"It would be a miracle . . . three games," The Durham Morning Herald,* 12.31.41; *Gazette Times,* Special Edition, January 1942.

CHAPTER 4: Polling statistics on American views: *The New York Times,* 1938–1942; *"I profoundly sympathize . . . be of true gold," Chronicle,* 10.4.40; on Duke's ROTC: *Chronicle,* 9.16.41, 9.30.41, 10.3.41; *Duke Alumni Register,* July 1941; "Wartime Activities of Women's College 1941–1942," Duke University, Undated, Duke University Archives; *Duke Alumni Register,* August 1942; *"But now it has . . . assured of our liberty," Duke Alumni Register,* June 1941; on OSC prewar: *Bond Drives, Blood Donors and Bean Pickers,* Lawrence Landis, 1994; *Oregon Staters and the War in Europe,* George Edmonston Jr.; *Oregon Stater; Barometer,* 10.23.41; *The Durham Sun,* 12.31.41; *"But now it has been . . . on our liberty," Duke Alumni Register,* June 1941; on tensions with Japan: *A Brief History of the U.S. Army in World War II,* John Ray Skates and Wayne Dzwonchyk, 2011; *The 1942 Rose Bowl: A Story of War Adjustment and Southern Pride,* Michael Jacobs, 1987.

CHAPTER 5: *"Despite all other . . . never has sought, a bowl bid," Chronicle,* 10.28.41; *"This is a very inopportune time . . . remaining four games," Chronicle,* 10.28.41; on Duke late season: Duke University Sports Information statistics and play-by-play, 1941; *Duke Alumni Register,* December 1941; on Jack Yoshihara: interview with Lynn Yoshihara Kanaya; Japanese Relocation.org; intern declaration documents, 1942; *Los Angeles Times,* 11.22.08; *In This Great Land of Freedom: The Japanese Pioneers of Oregon,* Lawson Fusao Inada, Akemi Kikumura, Mary Worthington, and Eiichiro Azuma, 1993; *The Gift: The Oregon Nikkei Story Retold,* Deena Kei Nakata, 1995; on OSC football season: *Barometer,* 11.14.41, 11.18.41, 11.19.41; *Durham Herald Sun,* 12.31.41; *"There is no rule . . . was such a rule," Barometer,* 11.28.41; on the OSC-Oregon rivalry: *The Civil War Rivalry: Oregon vs. Oregon State,* Kerry Eggers, 2014; *Oregon State Football,* Carlson; on the Oregon game: *The Oregonian,* 9.24.93;

The Oregon Journal, 11.30.41; *Barometer,* 11.30.41; *"How does it feel . . . say after the game?"* NBC Radio script, 11.30.41; on Rose Bowl selection process: *Barometer,* 11.30.41; *Columbia Daily Tribune,* 12.6.81; *Barometer,* 12.2.41; on Wade Sr. and selection: *New York World-Telegram,* 12.1.41; "*. . . has no con-man . . . his effect upon others,*" *Los Angeles Examiner,* 12.3.41; *"I haven't seen . . . sixteen pigs," Barometer,* 12.2.41; on Rose Bowl financials and planning: correspondence from Hal Reynolds to Wade Sr., 12.4.41; *Barometer,* 11.26.41, 11.30.41, 12.2.41; *Carolina Comments,* November 1991, XXXIX; *Durham Herald,* 12.4.41; *Oregon Staters and the War in Europe,* Edmonston Jr.; *Blue Devil Weekly,* 1.4.92; various telegrams between Oregon State, Wade Sr., and Reynolds, Duke University Archives.

CHAPTER 6: On Pearl Harbor and campus reaction: *Santa Rosa Press Democrat,* 12.6.11; "When Willamette Went to War," Tom Wilson, d3football.com; *Pearl Harbor: Legacy of Attack,* National Geographic Ultimate World War II Collection DVD; *A Rose Bowl Transplanted,* Patricia Evert, 1983; *The 1942 Rose Bowl: A Story of War Adjustment and Southern Pride,* Jacobs; *Gazette Times,* 12.15.41; *Oregon Staters and the War in Europe,* Edmonston Jr.; *"The grim dance . . . down the land," Chronicle,* 12.9.41; *"Glad that we . . . no alternative," Barometer,* 12.9.41; *USA Today,* 12.18.01; on military law: *Oregon Staters and the War in Europe,* Edmonston Jr.; text of FDR speech, *The New York Times,* 12.9.41; *"We believe we . . . in the last war," Carolina Comments,* November 1991, XXXIX; *"In the light of . . . program or pleasure,"* "War and Roses," Michael Penn, 2011; *"No doubt the Rose Bowl . . . do their worst," Carolina Comments,* November 1991, XXXIX; on the days after Pearl Harbor: *"Boys, war is much . . .* hit hard," interview with Smith; *The Durham Morning Herald,* 12.11.41; "War and Roses," Penn; *Gazette Times,* 12.10.41; *A Rose Bowl Transplanted,* Evert; on cancellation of game: telegram from Governor Olson to Tournament of Roses, *A Rose Bowl Transplanted,* Evert; *Our State,* December 2001; *"I wonder if General DeWitt . . . the Rose Bowl lifted," Carolina Comments,* November 1991, XXXIX; on relocating the game: *Our State,* December 2001; *A Rose Bowl Transplanted,* Evert; *The 1942 Rose Bowl: A Story of War Adjustment and Southern Pride,* Jacobs; *Durham Herald Sun,* 12.31.41; *Carolina Comments,* November 1991, XXXIX; Wallace Wade's Recollections of Rose Bowl, undated, Duke University Archives; *"This is Coach Wallace Wade . . . Rose Bowl sanction," Durham Herald Sun,* 12.31.41; *"Now that military authorities . . . see it played here," The Durham Morning Herald,* 12.15.41; *The Charlotte Observer,* 11.15.91; on Jack Yoshihara and Japanese Americans at OSC: *"students of Japanese ancestry," Barometer,* 12.9.41; *Confinement and Ethnicity: An Overview of World War II Japanese American Relocation Sites,* Jeffery Burton, 2002; interview with Kanaya; *Los Angeles Times,* 11.22.08;

The Register-Guard, 12.29.11; *PBS NewsHour,* 7.29.08; *Oregon Stater,* August 1995; correspondence from Oregon State Japanese American students to President Gilfillan, 12.11.41; correspondence from President Gilfillan to Japanese American students, 12.18.41; interview with Andy Landforce; on Rose Bowl preparations: *Barometer,* 12.10.41, 12.11.41; *Our State,* December 2001; "Duke Athletic Officials Bar Negroes from Bowl Game But Will Admit Japs," *Carolina Comments,* November 1991, XXXIX; *"I hope you men . . . can have both," I Remember: Recollections and Reminiscences of Alma Mater,* Spence.

CHAPTER 7: On OSC train trip: *"We'll wait until . . . trip like this," The Oregonian,* 1.17.42; *The Oregon Journal,* 12.18.41; *The Oregonian,* 1.17.42; personal notes from James Busch, 11.21.91; *The Portland Rose* travel guide, 1941; interview with Ingram; *The Oregon Journal,* 12.20.41; *The Oregonian,* 12.23.41; *The Oregonian,* 12.17.42; *The Chicago Sun,* 12.24.41; *"I know little . . . against the Trojans," The Oregon Journal,* 12.20.41; *"Reflects the beauty," The Portland Rose* travel guide; on Compton and Fermi: United States Department of Energy website; *The New World: 1939–1946,* Richard Hewlett and Oscar Anderson, 1962; University of Chicago website; on Arcadia*: A Brief History of the U.S. Army in World War II;* Skates and Dzwonchyk; on OSC and Duke preparations: *"Our student body . . . would have been," The Chicago Sun,* 12.24.41 and *The Oregonian,* 1.17.42; *"Mr. Stiner, I work . . . I'll need two cars,"* The Associated Press, 12.24.41; *"I don't know . . . on the wrong foot," Lincoln Journal Star,* 12.26.41; *The Oregonian,* 1.17.42; official Christmas dinner invitation, 12.15.41; official list of player gifts, 12.25.41; *Lincoln Journal Star,* 12.26.41; on Pinehurst: *The Oregonian,* 12.28.41; *The Oregonian,* 1.4.42; *The Oregonian,* 1.17.42; "Aberdeen Man Dies of Polo Injuries," newspaper article, unidentified source and date; *Pinehurst-Outlook,* 12.28.41; *"Regardless of traffic, weather or other deterring conditions,"* Memorandum of Understanding between Tournament of Roses, OSC, and Duke, 12.29.41; *"We are going . . . coast this season,"* International News Service, 1.1.42; *"As The Sun Goes to American victory," The Durham Sun,* 12.31.41.

CHAPTER 8: On Pasadena: *Durham Herald Sun,* 12.31.41; *The 1942 Rose Bowl: A Story of War Adjustment and Southern Pride,* Jacobs; *"Match the tournament . . . for fifty years," The 1942 Rose Bowl: A Story of War Adjustment and Southern Pride,* Jacobs; on Rose Bowl game day: *The Durham Morning Herald,* 1.2.42; *"Regardless of who . . . stop the Americans," The Durham Sun,* 12.31.41; *The Oregonian,* 1.17.42; official Rose Bowl game program; *The Oregonian,* 1.17.42; "War and Roses," Penn; *Our State,* December 2001; *Durham Herald Sun,* 12.31.41; *The 1942 Rose Bowl: A Story of War Adjustment and Southern Pride,* Jacobs; *Blue Devil Weekly,* 1.4.92; *Carolina*

Comments, November 1991, XXXIX; *Chronicle,* 10.12.95; *I Remember: Recollections and Reminiscences of Alma Mater,* Spence; on bus driver incident with Stiner: *The Oregonian,* 1.17.42; *Carolina Comments,* November 1991, XXXIX; *A Rose Bowl Transplanted,* Evert; on coin flip and pregame: *The Durham Sun,* 1.2.42; *A Story of Glory: Duke University Football,* Mann; *"At some point . . . authorities in Washington,"* script from Rose Bowl game, Duke University Archives; interview with Landforce; on matchup: *A Story of Glory: Duke University Football,* Mann; *Durham Herald Sun,* 12.31.41; *Blue Devil Weekly,* 1.4.92; Rose Bowl game play-by-play from *The New York Times,* 1.2.42; official play-by-play, Duke University Archives; archived silent telecast of 1942 Rose Bowl game, 1942, Duke University Archives; on halftime: *A Rose Bowl Transplanted,* Evert; *"It looks like 1926 all over again,"* "War and Roses," Penn; *"I'm going in . . . means to a fellow," The Oregonian,* 1.20.42.

CHAPTER 9: On OSC trip home and arrival in Corvallis: Busch personal notes, 1991; *Barometer,* 1.9.42; *Barometer,* 1.10.42; official Oregon State train itinerary; interview with Landforce; *The Oregon Journal,* 1.8.42; *Gazette Times,* 1.8.42; *"And in this war . . . second of the game!" The Oregon Journal,* 1.8.42 and *Gazette Times,* 1.8.42; on Stiner coaching offers: *"Interim Move Starts Stiner Boom,"* unidentified source, 1942; interview with Ingram; on Rose Bowl financials: official financial report, Tournament of Roses, Duke University Archives, 1942; on OSC campus at war: *Barometer,* 1.7.42; *Barometer,* 1.10.42; *Barometer,* 1.13.42; *Oregon Staters and the War in Europe,* Edmonston Jr.; *Bond Drives, Blood Donors and Bean Pickers,* Landis; on Duke campus at war: *Chronicle,* 12.8.42; *Chronicle,* 1.7.42; *Chronicle,* 2.27.42; *Chronicle,* 3.3.42; *Chronicle,* 4.3.42; *Chronicle,* 4.17.42; on Durham air-raid drill: *Chronicle,* 4.21.42; *Chronicle,* 4.24.42; on FDR and war plans: *A Brief History of the U.S. Army in World War II,* Skates and Dzwonchyk; on the Wades' entry into service: *"You know, Coach . . . to call me, Ted,"* and *"My boys were going . . . in a different battle," Wallace Wade: Championship Years at Alabama and Duke,* Bowling; *"Naturally, we regret . . . of first importance," Chronicle,* 3.17.42; *"Best of luck . . . a true soldier," Chronicle,* 3.27.42; *"Put on uniform . . . after 11 ⅓ years,"* Wade Sr. diary entry, 3.27.42; *"Left home at 7:45 PM . . . Camp at 10:00 PM,"* Wade Sr. diary entry, 3.29.42; Wade Sr. at Fort Bragg: Wade Sr. diary entries, 1942; *Chronicle,* 3.24.42; *Wallace Wade: Championship Years at Alabama and Duke,* Bowling; *"In the past . . . a lot of contests," Duke Alumni Register,* May 1942.

CHAPTER 10: On Japanese American internment and Minidoka: *In This Great Land of Freedom: The Japanese Pioneers of Oregon,* Inada et al.; *Only What We Could Carry: The Japanese American Internment Experience,* Lawson Fusao Inada, 2000; *The Gift:*

The Oregon Nikkei Story Retold, Nakata; *Executive Order 9066: The Internment of 110,000 Japanese Americans,* Maisie Conrat and Richard Conrat, 1972; interview with Kanaya; *Oregon Stater,* August 1995; *Los Angeles Times,* 11.22.08; *Infamy: The Shocking Story of the Japanese American Internment in World War II,* Richard Reeves, 2015; *Confinement and Ethnicity: An Overview of World War II Japanese American Relocation Sites,* Burton; *"Destroy Japan and her Axis partner," In This Great Land of Freedom: The Japanese Pioneers of Oregon,* Inada et al.; *"Will you swear . . . power, or organization?," The Gift: The Oregon Nikkei Story Retold,* Nakata; on Wade Sr.: *"In order to have a better chance of getting combat duty,"* Wade Sr. diary entry, 6.8.42; *"I was terribly disappointed, about as low as any time in my life,"* Wade Sr. diary entry, 7.13.42; Wade diary entries, June–October 1942; *Wallace Wade: Championship Years at Alabama and Duke,* Bowling; *"Wallace and I left . . . at home alone,"* Wade Sr. diary entry, 10.5.42; on Wade Jr.: United States government military personnel record; on Army Finance School: *Chronicle,* 9.16.42; *Chronicle,* 11.3.42; *Chronicle,* 12.8.42; *Chronicle,* 12.11.42; *"Student jocular imitation . . . the utmost respect," Chronicle,* 9.16.42; on Duke women and war: "War Activities of Women's College," Duke University; College of Engineering Course List, 1942–1945, Duke University, Duke University Archives; *The Woman's College as I Remember It,* Alice Mary Baldwin.

CHAPTER 11: On Haynes: interviews with Charles Haynes III and John Haynes (via e-mail); *Duke Magazine,* October 1943; *The Durham Morning Herald,* 5.23.82; *"Hope I am not . . . a salute to you,"* correspondence from Haynes to Haynes family, 12.2.42; correspondence from Haynes to Haynes family, 1.2.43; United States military personnel file; on Bob Dethman: OSC student record; United States military personnel file; interview with Fred Dethman and Gerry Dethman; on Frank Parker: interview with Terry Parker; OSC student record; on 1942 Duke football season: *A Story of Glory: Duke University Football,* Mann; *Duke Alumni Register,* August 1942; *Chronicle,* 9.25.42; *Chronicle,* 9.29.42; on Walter Griffith: United States military personnel file; United States military after-action report, 3.18.43; *"Deeply regret to . . . notified accordingly,"* correspondence from commandant of Marine Corps to Dorothy and Levi Griffith, received 12.12.42; on war strategy: *A Brief History of the U.S. Army in World War II,* Skates and Dzwonchyk; *Great Battles of World War II,* John MacDonald, 2014; on Wade Jr.: United States military files.

CHAPTER 12: On Wade Jr.: *United States Military History of 60th Field Artillery Battalion for 1943;* 1.11.44; *"Outfit entered . . . great understatement,"* correspondence from Wade Jr. to *Duke Alumni Register,* August 1943; V-12 at Duke: *Chronicle,* 2.23.43;

Chronicle, 3.5.43; *Chronicle,* 3.16.43; *Chronicle,* 3.19.43; Duke faculty and war: "War Time Activities Faculty, 1943," Duke University, Duke University Archives; "Department of Physics During War," Duke University, Duke University Archives; "Department of Economics in WWII," Duke University, Duke University Archives; "Chemistry Department 1941–1947," Duke University, Duke University Archives; "German Department," Duke University, Duke University Archives, 1949; "Mathematics Department," 10.12.49, Duke University, Duke University Archives; on ASTP, OSC, and war: *Bond Drives, Blood Donors and Bean Pickers,* Landis; *Oregon Staters and the War in Europe,* Edmonston Jr.; on Dethman: interview with Bob Dethman Jr., Fred Dethman, and Gerry Dethman; United States Marines personnel file; on Stiner Jr.: interview with Ingram; on OSC 1943 football season: *Oregon Staters and the War in Europe,* Edmonston Jr.; on 1943 Duke football season: *Chronicle,* 3.5.43; *A Story of Glory: Duke University Football,* Mann; *Duke Alumni Register,* April 1943; *Duke Alumni Register,* July 1943; *Duke Alumni Register,* September 1943; *Duke Alumni Register,* November 1943; on Wade Sr. accident: *Wallace Wade: Championship Years at Alabama and Duke,* Bowling; *"I know of nothing . . . and sound fundamentals," Wallace Wade: Championship Years at Alabama and Duke,* Bowling; on Hugh Miller: *Milwaukee Journal,* 8.23.43; *United States Destroyer Operations in World War II,* Theodore Roscoe, 1953; *Wallace Wade: Championship Years at Alabama and Duke,* Bowling; *Lt. "Rose Bowl" Miller: The U.S. Navy's One Man Army,* Landon Miller, 2011.

CHAPTER 13: On Stan Czech: United States military files; interview with Deborah Czech Lorenzen; *Albany Democrat-Herald,* 10.19.91; *Albany Democrat-Herald,* 3.26.93; on Everett Smith: *World War II in the Pacific: An Encyclopedia,* Stanley Sandler, 2000; *Into the Rising Sun: In Their Own Words, World War II's Pacific Veterans Reveal the Heart of Combat,* Patrick K. O'Donnell, 2002; United States military personnel file; Everett Smith application to Marines Corps; on D-day planning: *A Brief History of the U.S. Army in World War II,* Skates and Dzwonchyk; on Wade Sr.: *Wallace Wade: Championship Years at Alabama and Duke,* Bowling; on Wade Jr. and the 60th: after-action report, 60th Field Artillery, 1944; United States military files; *"He is still intact . . . an awful beating,"* correspondence from Wade Sr. to Eddie Cameron, 8.27.44; United States military records; on Haynes: *"You'd think Wallace Wade . . . we got yesterday,"* correspondence from Haynes to Alice Haynes, 5.14.44; *"I'm always thankful . . . these people have left,"* correspondence from Haynes to Alice Haynes, 7.30.44; *A Brief History of the U.S. Army in World War II,* Skates and Dzwonchyk; *"Pump[ed] carbine bullets as fast as he could pull the trigger," History of 349th Regiment,* 88th Infantry Division Association, 1973; on Frank

Parker: *"Met a Lt. yesterday . . . at home in '41,"* correspondence from Haynes to Alice Haynes, 7.28.44; OSC student records; United States military files; Regimental History—349th Infantry Regiment, May–October 1944; on Rodman Henry: interview with Fay Henry; letters and documents from the Berkshire Historical Society; interviews with Terry Parker, Frank Parker, and Heidi Parker Morris; correspondence from Rodman Henry to Fay Henry, 1944; on battles in Arno Valley: Regimental History 349th Infantry Regiment, October 1944; *Durham Herald Sun,* 12.15.91; *The Durham Morning Herald,* 5.23.82; correspondence from Haynes to Haynes family, 10.22.44, 11.8.44, and 11.15.44; interviews with Charles Haynes III and John Haynes (via e-mail); correspondences from Rodman Henry to Henry family, October–December 1944; interview with Fay Henry; *The Blue Devils in Italy: A History of the 88th Infantry Division in World War II,* John P. Delaney, 1947.

CHAPTER 14: On Peleliu: *Into the Rising Sun: In Their Own Words, World War II's Pacific Veterans Reveal the Heart of Combat,* O'Donnell; *World War II in the Pacific: An Encyclopedia,* Sandler; *The Assault on Peleliu,* Frank O. Hough, 1950; *Last Man Standing: The 1st Marine Regiment on Peleliu, September 15–21, 1944,* Dick Camp, 2009; on Al Hoover: United States military personnel file; *Duke Alumni Register,* November 1944; History of First Battalion, First Marines, August–November 1944, 11.23.44; on Wade Sr. and Wade Jr. in Europe: 32nd FA after-action reports, 1944; 272nd FA after-action reports, 1944; 272nd FA 1944 Unit History; on Battle of the Bulge: *Red Legs of the Bulge: Artillerymen in the Battle of the Bulge,* C. J. Kelly, Merriam Press, 2014; *A Brief History of the U.S. Army in World War II,* Skates and Dzwonchyk; *Snow and Steel: The Battle of the Bulge, 1944–45,* Peter Caddick-Adams, 2015; Veterans of Foreign Wars, December 1944; on Czech and Wade Sr.: *USA Today,* 12.18.01; on Czech: telegram to Ora Lea Czech from secretary of war, January 1945; on 1944 Duke football season and 1945 Sugar Bowl game: *Wallace Wade: Championship Years at Alabama and Duke,* Bowling; *A Story of Glory: Duke University Football,* Mann; *Duke Alumni Register,* September 1944; on Haynes's recovery: *Durham Herald Sun,* 12.15.91; United States military files; correspondence from Haynes to family, 10.22.44; correspondence from Haynes to Alice Haynes, 11.8.44; correspondence from Haynes to Haynes Sr., 11.15.44; on Wade Sr. and Gene Gray: 272nd FA Unit History, 1944; United States military files; Air Medal Citation for Gene Gray.

CHAPTER 15: On Czech's capture and escape: United States military files; interview with Lorenzen; telegram from adjutant general to Ora Lea Czech, March 1945;

correspondence from Captain John D. Porter to Ora Lea Czech, 2.11.45; *Albany Democrat-Herald,* 11.7.94; *Albany Democrat-Herald,* 3.26.93; notes from Theodore Czech; *Los Angeles Times,* 3.23.13; Free Republic, 1.16.03; on Task Force Baum: *Raid! The Untold Story of Patton's Secret Mission,* Richard Baron, Abe Baum, and Richard Goldhurst, 2000; *The Longest Winter: The Battle of the Bulge and the Epic Story of World War II's Most Decorated Platoon,* Alex Kershaw, 2004; on the 442nd and Yoshihara's move: interview with Kanaya; *Intelligence, Internment and Relocation: Roosevelt's Executive Order 9066: How Top Secret MAGIC Intelligence Led to Evacuation,* Keith Robar, 2000; *The Gift: The Oregon Nikkei Story Retold,* Nakata; *In This Great Land of Freedom: The Japanese Pioneers of Oregon,* Inada et al.; *Only What We Could Carry: The Japanese American Internment Experience,* Inada; *Executive Order 9066: The Internment of 110,000 Japanese Americans,* Conrat and Conrat; on Iwo Jima: *Closing In: Marines in the Seizure of Iwo Jima,* Joseph Alexander, 2013; *World War II in the Pacific: An Encyclopedia,* Sandler; *Into the Rising Sun: In Their Own Words, World War II's Pacific Veterans Reveal the Heart of Combat,* O'Donnell; *The Pacific War: 1941–1945,* John Costello; *Marine Corps Chevron,* Volume 4, Number 11, 3.24.45; Bronze Star Certificate for Robert Dethman; 5th Marine Division, 26th Marines; 1st Battalion, February 1945; after-action report for 5th Marine Division, 4.28.45; on Bob Nanni: United States Marine Corps personnel file; *Chronicle,* 10.6.42; *"Sitting here on my bunk . . . your* [sic] *not to[o] busy,"* correspondence from Bob Nanni to Eddie Cameron, 10.9.44; after-action report, 1st Battalion, 9th Marines, 3rd Marine Division, 4.18.45; *"Among the Americans . . . was a common virtue,"* World War II Museum, Iwo Jima Fact Sheet; on final advance through Italy: Charles Haynes Silver Star Certificate, United States military files; *The Durham Morning Herald,* 5.23.82; *"I can well appreciate . . . it happening again,"* correspondence from Haynes to Alice Haynes, 9.18.45; 349th Infantry Regiment Summary, April 1945 and May 1945; *The Blue Devils in Italy: A History of the 88th Infantry Division in World War II,* Delaney; *The Final Campaign Across Northwest Italy, 14 April–2 May 1945,* Headquarters IV Corps, United States Army; interviews with Terry Parker, Frank Parker Jr., and Heidi Parker Morris.

CHAPTER 16: On Duke's war: *Wallace Wade: Championship Years at Alabama and Duke,* Bowling; program from chapel service, celebrating the end of war, 1945; "Educational Opportunities for Veterans," Duke University, March 1943; *Duke Alumni Register,* October 1945; *Duke Alumni Register,* April 1943; *Duke Alumni Register,* June 1947; *Duke Alumni Register,* August 1946; on OSC's war: *Bond Drives, Blood Donors and Bean Pickers,* Landis; *Oregon State Yank,* August 1945; *Oregon State Yank,* November 1945; *Oregon Staters and the War in Europe,* Edmonston Jr.; on Wade Sr.'s return: Certificate of Service; United States military files; *Wallace Wade: Championship Years at Alabama and Duke,* Bowling; *"We don't want to have another . . . horrible, and senseless," Durham Morning Herald,* 8.21.45 and 11.13.45; Duke University Athletic Communications release, 12.21.45; *Duke Alumni Register,* June 1947; *Duke Alumni Register,* July 1945; Duke football seasons, 1946–1950: Duke University media guides; *Wallace Wade: Championship Years at Alabama and Duke,* Bowling; *The Durham Morning Herald,* 7.18.45; *Duke Alumni Register,* September 1947; *A Story of Glory: Duke University Football,* Mann; *Duke Alumni Register,* September 1946; *Duke Alumni Register,* December 1945; on OSC football 1945–1947: Oregon State Football media guide; *The Oregonian,* 1.15.47; on Parker's return from war: interviews with Terry Parker and Frank Parker III; interview with Fay Henry; on Haynes's return from war: interviews with Charles Haynes III, John Haynes (via e-mail), Wendy Haynes Connor; *Durham Herald Sun,* 12.15.91; *Durham Morning Herald,* 5.23.82; United States military files; on Gene Gray's accident: *The Oregonian,* 6.11.48; Eugene Gray military medical and clinical records; *The Oregonian,* 12.9.56; United States military files; *Early Jet Aircraft Mechanic,* Richard Kamm; on Yoshihara's post-internment life: interview with Kanaya; *Los Angeles Times,* 11.22.08; *The Register-Guard,* 12.29.11; on Wade Sr.'s coaching and retirement: *Duke Alumni Register,* September 1947; *Wallace Wade: Championship Years at Alabama and Duke,* Bowling; *A Story of Glory: Duke University Football,* Mann; *"I was whipped down . . . as important anymore," Durham Morning Herald,* 10.7.86; *"Yes, we have heard . . . will be continued,"* Duke University Athletics Press Release, September 1950; on Dethman and death: United States military personnel files; interviews with Fred Dethman and Gerry Dethman; interview with Bob Dethman Jr.; OSC student file; *The Oregon Journal,* 8.16.47; *The Oregonian,* 8.30.57; correspondence from Donald Durdan to Alfred and Mattie Dethman, 9.3.57; State of Oregon Certificate of Death, September 1957.

CHAPTER 17: On Wade Sr.: interview with Al Buehler; *Wallace Wade: Championship Years at Alabama and Duke,* Bowling; interview with Lewis Bowling; interview with Diane Withrow; interview with Kerley; *The Durham Sun,* 8.25.80; *". . . you always are aiming toward the future in looking for calves,"* The Associated Press, 1971; *"You are, of course, aware . . . given in his honor,"* correspondence from Arthur Vann to Douglas Knight, 4.19.67; *"I have had a lot of pleasant experiences . . . thankful for everything tonight,"* remarks by Wallace Wade Sr., *The Durham Sun,* 9.30.67; *"When Wallace Wade talked . . . he expected of us," Durham Morning Herald,* 10.9.86; "Ode to Wade" created by Dr. Hersey Spence, 1967, published in *The Durham Sun,* 10.30.67; on Haynes's later life: *"An objective to the Army . . . and still be alive,"* journal entry from Haynes, University of North Carolina Archives, undated; interviews with Charles Haynes III, John Haynes (via e-mail), and Wendy Haynes Connor; on Parker's late life: interview with Terry Parker and Heidi Parker Morris; State of Alaska employment application; *"If you have something to say to me, say it to me,"* interview with Terry Parker; *"My head . . . need to go home,"* interview with Terry Parker and Frank Parker Jr.; *"That feels like her . . . this was not the plan,"* interview with Terry Parker and Frank Parker, Jr.; *"I spent my whole life on the water; I don't want to be buried under it,"* interview with Terry Parker; *"This is the commencement . . . are for your pain," PBS NewsHour* 7.29.08.

EPILOGUE: *"Coach Wade is not here tonight . . . thank you for that coffee," USA Today,* 12.18.01.

RESOURCES

There were several challenges in researching this book, not least of which was the fact that most of the participants are long gone, and, not unexpectedly of their generation, they rarely passed on stories of college and war to the next generation. Piecing together their personal journeys in college, the military, and life was difficult, and I have attempted to be accurate and remain true to the men I did not know. If there are any errors or inaccuracies, my apologies to all.

In researching and writing this story, I relied on many different sources of information, including interview subjects, published books, unpublished research papers, newspapers and magazines, videos, diaries, journals, military reports and personnel files, and thousands of other documents too voluminous to list individually but including yearbooks, game programs, radio scripts, reunion lists, itineraries, pictures, cards, menus, and telegrams.

The personal correspondences from many of the players and coaches were found deep in the libraries and archives of Duke and Oregon State or provided by family members. The letters from and to Wallace Wade Jr. and Sr., Eddie Cameron, Bob Nanni, Frank Parker, Charles Haynes Jr., Martin Chaves, and James Busch—among others—were excellent sources, as were the few diary entries from Wade Sr. and Haynes. The diary of a member of the 349th, Donald Duane Johnson, also proved valuable.

BOOKS

Alexander, Joseph H. *Closing In: Marines in the Seizure of Iwo Jima*. National Park Service, 2013.

Atkinson, Rick. *The Guns at Last Light: The War in Western Europe, 1944–1945*. Picador, 2013.

Baron, Richard, Abe Baum, and Richard Goldhurst. *Raid! The Untold Story of Patton's Secret Mission*. Putnam, 1981.

Beevor, Antony. *The Second World War*. Little, Brown & Company, 2012.

Bowling, Lewis. *Wallace Wade: Championship Years at Alabama and Duke*. Carolina Academic Press, 2006.

Bradley, James and Ron Powers. *Flags of Our Fathers*. Bantam Dell, 2000.

Burton, Jeffery. *Confinement and Ethnicity: An Overview of World War II Japanese American Relocation Sites*. University of Washington Press, 2002.

Caddick-Adams, Peter. *Snow and Steel: The Battle of the Bulge, 1944–45*. Oxford University Press, 2015.

Camp, Dick. *Last Man Standing: The 1st Marine Regiment on Peleliu, September 15–21, 1944*. Zenith Press, 2009.

Carlson, Kip. *Oregon State Football*. Arcadia Publishing, 2006.

Conrat, Maisie and Richard Conrat. *Executive Order 9066: The Internment of 110,000 Japanese Americans*. California Historical Society, 1972.

Costello, John. *The Pacific War: 1941–1945*. Harper Perennial, 2009.

Delaney, John P. *The Blue Devils in Italy: A History of the 88th Infantry Division in World War II*. Infantry Journal Press, 1947.

Duke University and the War. Duke Alumni Office, 1943.

Eggers, Kerry. *The Civil War Rivalry: Oregon vs. Oregon State*. History Press, 2014.

Hewlett, Richard and Oscar Anderson. *The New World: 1939–1946*. Penn State University Press, 1962.

History of the 349th Infantry Regiment. 88th Infantry Division Association, Kensington, 1973.

Hough, Frank O. *The Assault on Peleliu*. The Battery Press, 1950.

Inada, Lawson Fusao, Akemi Kikumura, Eiichiro Azuma, and Mary Worthington. *In This Great Land of Freedom: The Japanese Pioneers of Oregon*. Japanese American National Museum, 1993.

Inada, Lawson Fusao. *Only What We Could Carry: The Japanese American Internment Experience.* Heyday, 2000.

Kelly, C. J. *Red Legs of the Bulge: Artillerymen in the Battle of the Bulge.* Merriam Press, 2014.

Kershaw, Alex. *The Longest Winter: The Battle of the Bulge and the Epic Story of World War II's Most Decorated Platoon.* Da Capo Press, 2004.

Krussow, J. Patricia. *Pine Grove Memories in the Hood River Valley,* 1989.

MacDonald, John. *Great Battles of World War II.* Chartwell Books, 2014.

Mann, Ted. *A Story of Glory: Duke University Football.* Doorway Publishers, 1985.

Michelson, Herb and Dave Newhouse. *Rose Bowl Football since 1902.* Stein & Day Co., 1977.

Miller, Landon. *Lt. "Rose Bowl" Miller: The U.S. Navy's One Man Army.* CreateSpace Publishing, 2011.

Moran, Malcolm. *Rose Bowl: The History of the Granddaddy of Them All.* Whitman Publishing, 2013.

Nakata, Deena Kei. *The Gift: The Oregon Nikkei Story Retold,* 1995.

Norman, Michael and Elizabeth M. Norman. *Tears in the Darkness: The Story of the Bataan Death March and Its Aftermath.* Picador, 2010.

O'Donnell, Patrick K. *Into the Rising Sun: In Their Own Words, World War II's Pacific Veterans Reveal the Heart of Combat.* Free Press, 2002.

Overy, Richard. *The Bombers and the Bombed: Allied Air War Over Europe, 1940–1945.* Viking, 2014.

Reeves, Richard. *Infamy: The Shocking Story of the Japanese American Internment in World War II.* Henry Holt, 2015.

Robar, Keith. *Intelligence, Internment and Relocation.* Kikar Publications, 2000.

Roberts, Andrew. *The Storm of War: A New History of the Second World War.* Harper Perennial, 2011.

Rolf, David. *The Bloody Road to Tunis: Destruction of the Axis Forces in North Africa, November 1942–May 1943.* Greenhill Books, 2001.

Roscoe, Theodore. *United States Destroyer Operations in World War II.* Naval Institute Press, 1953.

Sandler, Stanley. *World War II in the Pacific: An Encyclopedia.* Routledge, 2000.

Skates, John Ray and Wayne Dzwonchyk. *A Brief History of the U.S. Army in World War II.* US Army Center of Military History, 2011.

Spence, Hersey. *I Remember: Recollections and Reminiscences of Alma Mater.* Seeman Printery, 1954.

NEWSPAPERS / WIRE SERVICES

Albany Democrat-Herald, The Associated Press, *The Charlotte Observer*, *The Chicago Sun*, *Columbia Daily Tribune*, *Corvallis Gazette-Times*, *The Dalles Chronicle*, The *Durham Herald Sun*, *Durham Morning Herald*, Duke *Chronicle*, *The Durham Sun*, *The Fayetteville Observer*, *Hood River News*, *Lincoln Journal Star*, *Los Angeles Examiner*, *Los Angeles Times*, *Milwaukee Journal*, *The New York Times*, *New York World-Telegram*, *The News & Observer*, *Omaha World Herald*, *The Oregon Journal*, *Oregon State Barometer*, *Oregon State College News Bureau*, *The Oregonian*, *The Pasadena Post*, *Pasadena Star-News*, *The Pilot*, *The Pittsburgh Press*, *The Register-Guard*, *The Roanoke Times*, *Santa Rosa Press Democrat*, *The Statesman Journal*, *USA Today*

PERIODICALS

Architecture Magazine, *Blue Devil Weekly*, *Carolina Comments*, *The Christian Science Monitor*, *Duke Alumni Register*, *Duke Dialogue*, *Duke Magazine*, *Ford Times*, *Marine Corps Chevron*, *Oregon State Magazine*, *Oregon State Yank*, *Oregon Stater*, *Our State*, *Time*

MULTIMEDIA

www.d3football.com, www.duke.edu, www.energy.gov, www.espn.com, www.goduke.com, www.history.com, www.militaryhistoryonline.com, www.offbeatoregon.com, www.oregonstate.edu, www.osubeavers.com, www.uchicago.edu, www.willamette.edu

DVD: *Pearl Harbor: Legacy of Attack*, National Geographic Ultimate World War II Collection.

PBS *NewsHour* 7.29.08.

Unaired interview footage of Charles Haynes and Frank Parker, October 1991. ESPN Networks.

RESEARCH PAPERS

Football at Duke (A. A. Wilkinson); *The Woman's College as I Remember It* (Alice Mary Baldwin); *Temporary Transplant* (Add Penfield); *Oregon Staters and the War in Europe* (George Edmonston Jr.); *Bond Drives, Blood Donors and Bean Pickers* (Lawrence Landis); *Last Saturday's Heroes* (John Eggers); *The 1942 Rose Bowl: A Story of War Adjustment and Southern Pride* (Michael Jacobs); *A Rose Bowl Transplanted* (Patricia Evert); *Early Jet Aircraft Mechanic* (Richard W. Kamm);

My Greatest Sports Thrill (Lathrop K. Leishman); and *War and Roses* (Michael Penn).

UNITED STATES MILITARY FILES

U.S. military personnel records, including service history, medical history, and personnel files, were located and reviewed for:

Robert Barnett, Glenn Byington, Martin Chaves, George Davis, Joseph Day, Robert Dethman, Donald Durdan, Ralph Felty, Roy Gray, Walter Griffith, Reginald Gustafson, Charles Haynes Jr., Aaron Hoover, Steven Lach, Robert Nanni, Theo Ossowski, Frank Parker, Norman Peters, James Prothro, Clyde Redding, Winston Siegfried, Everett Smith, Lloyd Wickett, George Zellick, Orville Zielaskowski

The following military reports were reviewed:

Unit History, 1st Battalion, 1st Marines, 1st Marine Division, November 1944

Unit Report, 4th Battalion, 12th Marines, 3rd Marine Division, November 1943

After-Action Report, 1st Battalion, 26th Marines, 5th Marine Division, April 1945

Unit Journal, 1st Battalion, 26th Marines, 5th Marine Division, February–March 1945

Unit Journal, 8th Marines, 2d Marine Division, October 1942–February 1943

After-Action Report, 1st Battalion, 9th Marines, 3rd Marine Division, April 1945

Unit History, 349th Infantry Regiment, 88th Infantry Division, June 1944

Unit History, 349th Infantry Regiment, 88th Infantry Division, July 1944

Unit History, 349th Infantry Regiment, 88th Infantry Division, August 1944

Unit History, 349th Infantry Regiment, 88th Infantry Division, September 1944

Unit History, 349th Infantry Regiment, 88th Infantry Division, October 1944

Unit History, 349th Infantry Regiment, 88th Infantry Division, November 1944

Unit History, 349th Infantry Regiment, 88th Infantry Division, December 1944

After-Action Report, 32nd Field Artillery Battalion, March 1944

After-Action Report, 32nd Field Artillery Battalion, April 1944

After-Action Report, 32nd Field Artillery Battalion, May 1944–February 1945

Unit History, 60th Field Artillery, 9th Infantry Division, 1943

Unit History, 60th Field Artillery, 9th Infantry Division, 1944

After-Action Reports, 60th Field Artillery, 9th Infantry Division, July 1944–September 1944

Unit History, 272nd Field Artillery Battalion, September 1944–January 1945

Unit History, 272nd Field Artillery Battalion, 1944

After-Action Report, 272nd Field Artillery Battalion, August 1944

After-Action Report, 272nd Field Artillery Battalion, December 1944

Field Artillery Guide. United States Field Artillery Association, 1942

The Final Campaign Across Northwest Italy 14 April–2 May 1945. Headquarters IV Corps, United States Army

INTERVIEWS

Richard Anderson, Patsy Ashby, Connie Felty Ashley, David Barnett, Robert Barnett Jr., Lewis Bowling, Werner Brown, Al Buehler, Valerie Calvert, Tom Childers, Wendy Haynes Connor, Shirley Costley, Bob Dethman Jr., Fred Dethman, Gerry Dethman, John Dethman, Andrew Dunavant, Steve Durdan, Steve Flanagan, Brad Halverson, Charles Haynes III, David Haynes, John Haynes (via e-mail), Fay Henry, Betty Stiner Ingram, Lynn Yoshihara Kanaya, Chris Kelly, Betsy Wade Kerley, Steve Lach Jr., Andy Landforce, Deborah Czech Lorenzen, Bill Markman, Jim Markman, Marlea Chaves Merikel, Karen Gray Mickel, Heidi Parker Morris, Frank Parker Jr., Terry Parker, Ann Prothro, Shirley Prothro, Jim Smith, Gloria Chaves Solberg, Martha Uzzle, Lloyd Wickett, Ron Wickett, Diane Withrow, Dick Wolff, Jim Zellick, Louise Zielaskowski

INDEX